What SMART PEOPLE DO *When* DUMB THINGS HAPPEN *at* WORK

CHARLES E. WATSON, PH. D.

What SMART PEOPLE DO *When* DUMB THINGS HAPPEN *at* WORK

Tips for Solving Real-World Work Problems

BARNES & NOBLE BOOKS NEW YORK

This edition published by Barnes & Noble, Inc.,
by arrangement with Career Press.

2001 Barnes & Noble Books

ISBN 0-7607-2496-2

Printed and bound in the United States of America

01 02 03 04 MC 9 8 7 6 5 4 3 2 1

FG

Acknowledgments

This book benefited from the efforts of numerous people. Foremost among them is Michael Snell, literary agent and constant encourager, whose wisdom and suggestions shaped this work into what it is. Marilyn Throne, a friend and colleague at Miami University, read early chapters and gave me invaluable suggestions. My friend Gail Denise provided support as well as superb ideas and examples of situations where she observed people encountering difficulties in the workplace, and Kate Ronald helped me find just the right words to use when I got stuck.

Others who contributed to the collection of the many dilemmas examined in this book include Carrie Bowen, Charlotte Caples, Alan Carey, Kathy Hiltz, Phyllis Kiefer, Maggie Maloney, Frank Triantos, and my brother, Bill Watson.

Acknowledgments

Contents

Introduction

While driving on a busy city street one night a few years ago, I flinched as something from out of the sky crashed down on my windshield, striking it with a tremendous thud. The thing startled me and I heard the glass give under the object's force—but it didn't crack. I stopped, got out, and looked around. On the side of the road I spotted the menace—a section of tailpipe that apparently had been struck and thrown up into the air by a passing vehicle. The rusty metal object landed hard, leaving a few deep scratches on my windshield—the safety glass held up under the pounding.

In a like manner the workplace hurls problems, challenges and setbacks at each of us every day. How well we hold up under these blows without breaking is a fair measure of our mettle. This is a book about workplace difficulties and the methods smart people use to deal with them effectively when they strike.

To get a better idea of the many blunders, traps, glitches, and setbacks found in today's workplace, let's consider their usual sources. One source is other people—a crabby boss, a manipulative co-worker, or a testy customer. Another source of workplace difficulties are chance circumstances—a last-minute request, a glitch in signals, unanticipated breakdowns. And of course, the third source of problems are brought to the workplace by—you guessed it—ourselves. We cause many difficulties through our own shortcomings—our quick tempers, our fat egos, our self-centered actions.

Yes, dumb things do happen, but it grows worse. Many people respond to their problems ineffectively. So every day, thousands of bright, skillful, hardworking people tarnish their careers and limit their futures by mishandling ordinary workplace difficulties. These people might be wizards in their technical specialties, experienced in their professions, and well-schooled in management principles, but they lack understanding, self-discipline, and good judgment when it comes to tricky workplace traps and setbacks not mentioned in their schoolbooks.

Clearly, today's workers and professionals alike need practical answers and workable solutions to all the dumb situations that threaten success. This book is intended to help you understand the many dangers, snares, and obstacles found in the workplace so you can anticipate them, attack them, and solve them imaginatively so they stay solved.

The Buried Treasure

Digging gems of wisdom from the lives of smart people.

For the better part of the past 30 years now, I have studied the lives and methods used by highly successful business leaders, sports heroes, renowned scientists, artists, and actors, searching for the source of their greatness. I paid particular attention to how they handled their day-to-day challenges. My research delved into the careers of people of great accomplishment, particularly industrial giants past and present.

I met with more than a hundred people of prominence to learn what kinds of things led to their success. I probed to learn which values they lived by, what they did to reach the top, the priorities they used in making tough decisions, how they solved difficult problems, and the ways they treated others.

In the mid-80s I set out on a grand adventure, traveling across the United States and meeting with our country's most successful business leaders, CEOs of some of America's largest and most respected companies: Ford, Bristol-Myers Squibb, Goodyear, Hewlett-Packard, JCPenney, Hilton Hotels, Westinghouse, Whirlpool, Quaker Oats, Dow Chemical, Xerox, DuPont, and Colgate-Palmolive. In all, I interviewed more than 125 CEOs and heads of major corporations.

I asked these business leaders tough, direct, probing questions about themselves and how they became successful. And I got forthright, thoughtful, honest answers.

These leaders were rugged thinkers, excellent communicators, and, above all, highly believable. They had their flaws, their eccentricities, their excesses—they, too, were human. If need be, they could be tough and demanding, and some were clearly that. But they also had dignity, respect for greatness, and reverence for what civilization most honors.

What emerged from my inquiry was not so much a simple formula for success but a definite pattern of living guided by what I'll call "gems of wisdom." It's possible that each of the people I talked with did not abide by these gems all the time, but they showed evidence of living up to them far better than most people do.

Smart people maintain the right course by adhering to high standards at all times.

The supreme rule of navigation is this: Believe what your compass tells you and follow its guidance. In life, smart people do exactly the same thing—they discipline themselves at all times to follow what they know to be true. They adhere completely to their moral and ethical principles.

There's a word for this quality and it's called integrity. It comes from the Latin *integritas*, meaning whole or oneness. Integrity is defined as uncompromising adherence to moral and ethical principles, and being of sound moral character. It is the common thread running through great lives, those whom others admire and see as truly making a difference in the world.

I have no doubt about the effectiveness of this remarkable quality, because I have observed its amazing power and the positive difference it makes whenever applied.

A person of integrity lives up to high ideals, not because of raw force or social pressures, but because that person is genuinely committed to those high ideals. The person with integrity is not one to bend the rules when it is convenient or when temptations are strong—not even "just this once." This is a person who is incorruptible, and you can tell it. Better still, you can depend on it.

Gem 2

Smart people make good decisions because they think clearly and insightfully. They do not make self-serving choices.

Indeed, humans are thinking creatures and their success and influence hinge on their ability to think clearly and critically. The great French philosopher, mathematician, and physicist Blaise Pascal (1623-1662) once observed, "Man is obviously made for thinking. Therein lies all his dignity and his merit; and his whole duty is to think, as he ought."

Superior performers are no strangers to the realm of careful thinking. In deciding important matters, they obtain ample evidence and examine it thoroughly. They do their level best to remove their own prejudices and partialities as they observe and weigh the evidence before them. In doing this, they probe deeply, asking themselves and others many questions.

Another thing that makes highly successful people superb decision makers is their habit of looking far beyond their own self-interests. They fully understand the inclination most people, including themselves, have in dealing with situations largely in terms of, "What's in it for me?"

Gem 3

Smart people strive to achieve excellence not gain popularity.

Anyone who tries to raise his head above the crowd invites harsh judgment from all the envious. Cruel criticism is one of the heaviest burdens to bear. The mediocre abhor the superior and often attack it. Tender minds respond to the pressures of conformity by fitting in with the ordinary, which is easy and comfortable and very cheap.

The desire for approval is a powerful force and serves as an effective means of holding members of society together and maintaining harmony. But wanting to be popular, to get more approval than the next person, to care more for praise than what's praiseworthy, is a dangerous thing. It is also self-defeating because the pursuit of praise for its own sake achieves neither enough praise nor self-satisfaction. There are two reasons for this. First, appetites for praise grow insatiably. Whatever the amount of praise received is, the person receiving it always wants more. There is never enough to satisfy. Second, those who pursue praise single-mindedly quickly turn to doing only what they think will bring praise and not necessarily what's praiseworthy. When they do this, they negate the chance to experience the only form of lasting satisfaction known, the realization that they did the right thing freely for its own sake and without expectation of reward.

If a life is to grow strong and rich, if it is to count for much, then it needs to be dominated by the desire for usefulness. For without this lodestar to guide, people drift aimlessly. They try to fit in and please; they may get momentary approval but that's never enough to make them really happy.

Gem 4

Smart people gain sterling reputations by doing what's honorable.

What good judgment might have led us to avoid, we create for ourselves. A liberating idea worth understanding is this: By always doing what's right—by following the established rules civilization has, through centuries of trial and error, come to honor—we can escape much harm and pain. To do what one knows is plainly wrong is simply dumb. And, to try to justify these wrong actions through rationalization is not just deceitful but dumber still. And to believe that one can get away with acting wrongly, even though one may succeed for a while, is very foolish. No one mocks the lessons of human history and gets away with it. A reliable fortress we can all take refuge in is always doing the right thing. Although it cannot shield us from the disasters not of our own making that pervade our world, it will provide us safety from those that are—whenever we act in ways against which the lessons of human history advise.

Gem 5

Smart people stand up for those things worth standing up for.

Courage. It's the quality of mind that allows a person to encounter difficulties and danger with firmness, to act bravely. It involves doing what ought to be done when no one is looking or when there isn't something forcing one to act in the right way.

Ample evidence exists that doing the right thing is good for business. Acts of good citizenship help win community support, which comes in handy when a firm needs the cooperation of local leaders. A company that markets top-quality products and stands behind those that fail to perform as promised holds on to customers and attracts others. The fair treatment of suppliers brings a business loyal service and assures timely deliveries. Humane treatment of employees yields dedication, loyalty, and satisfaction—things that translate into better profits. But none of these reasons are based on courage. They are merely pragmatic justifications, a quid pro quo arrangement. Whenever pragmatism is given as the justification for acting morally, it is abundantly clear what remains uppermost in the person's heart. And, because of that, we can be fairly certain that the person will act in unacceptable ways if doing so provides greater immediate benefit. This isn't registered as courage, but rather as calculation.

The most effective achievers do not succeed because of self-serving actions, calculated to gain them the maximum return. They act out of authentic commitments to lofty ideals. And because they do, others respect them, want to be around them, and follow them willingly and enthusiastically.

Smart people attack difficulties immediately and act positively when adversity strikes.

In the face of adversity, in the midst of disaster, and with bleak prospect for an agreeable outcome, the human spirit has shown itself able, somehow, to rise to the challenges at hand. Buoyed by a faith that a venture will succeed, that an answer will be found, that mending can restore, that a brighter future exists, and that life tomorrow will be better, the human spirit triumphs. No matter how rough the road, how pessimistic the forecast, or how overwhelming the stream of setbacks is, life goes on. It must.

At one point or other some calamity or setback befalls every life. The person's abilities may be diminished. Sight, alertness, strength, stamina, health—these may be lessened or wiped away altogether. And still the person struggles bravely and goes on. A reservoir of inner strength makes up for the diminishment. How can we explain the will to continue on found in people like Robert Louis Stevenson who, although bedridden and nearly going blind and confined to a darkened room, wrote some of the greatest works of literature? What is there in a man like Beethoven who, while deaf, wrote the most moving compositions music has known? We may be limited in our scientific understanding of the work of Steven Hawking, the Englishman called the most remarkable scientist of our time who gave us theories of black holes, quasars, and quarks to explain the cosmos. But all people, learned and simple, are unbounded in admiration for his will to shrug off his paralysis and turn it from an infirmity into an advantage for long hours of concentration on questions and purposes he considers important. This is positive living: turning thoughts away from defeatism and refocusing them on conquering adversity.

And so, we see ordinary people acting in extraordinary ways because of their inner strength to act positively.

Smart people achieve high levels of performance because they act boldly, doing what they believe to be right.

Thousands of people jam the world's highways to success going nowhere, their engines stalled. These are the people who hesitate to act on what they believe. And so, they never voice good ideas, they never implement workable plans, they allow splendid opportunities to pass by, they fail to give full effort to doing what they know ought to be done because they fear what others might say or do.

Nothing gets accomplished in this world that does not upset, alter, or annoy something or someone else. That's the nature of progress and there's nothing anyone can do about it. While we need to be respectful of others—we should consider the implications of actions beyond our own selfish interests—we must also take action to ensure that the things we want to accomplish eventually happen.

We are at our best when we act on our convictions without reservation, when we are not tentative or overly concerned with our happiness or not offending others by doing what we believe is right. Our best efforts come whenever we act boldly, doing what we believe should be done. Boldness is the thoughtful commitment to a position and the gallant, steadfast will to see it through to completion—even in the face of adversity and open hostility. Boldness is the bridge from our visions to great victories. It is the great enabler.

Smart people achieve magnificently because they have a sense of proportion. They put the best ahead of the good, the first-rate ahead of the second-rate.

Without a good sense of proportion people will encounter all kinds of problems. They limit their achievements doing small things while big things go undone, they worry about trivial issues instead of significant ones, and they allow concern for the second-rate to crowd out concern for the first-rate. This phenomenon appears in every imaginable way: It is as if one were to wear a cheap suit while a more expensive, better one, unworn, hung in their closet collecting dust.

First-rate accomplishments never spring from second-rate aspirations. To do one's best one must put the best first, ahead of the good. The excitement, sense of accomplishment, and ultimate fulfillment that comes from achieving superbly all begin with putting things in the right order—first things first. The secret to developing a good sense of proportion lies in finding a great endeavor and disciplining oneself to tend to pursue it ahead of distracting activities. It's focusing on the main things to be accomplished and not the trifling details because they are easy or fun or provide greater enjoyment at the time. People perform best when they totally commit themselves to something that they can give their "all" to accomplish and when they keep their attention focused on it alone, because it is far bigger and more significant than what they happen to desire at the moment.

Smart people find a great cause and serve it unhesitatingly and without calculation, thereby achieving magnificently and deriving lasting satisfaction.

Those people who achieve the most in life, including the deep respect of others and lasting personal fulfillment, have discovered that the more forcefully they hurl their best efforts outward, the more they gain in return. By authentically caring more about adding positively to the world than getting something for themselves they gain far more, both financially and personally, than they ever dreamed possible. This powerful idea works for both individual contributors and entire organizations. Consider the following:

Superior performers focus their efforts outwardly, not inwardly. They place service to others or great causes first, pursuing self-interest secondarily. By living this way they achieve well beyond their goals, earn respect, and find lasting personal fulfillment. Whereas success in the past was seen as gaining wealth, today's employee thirsts for a new, larger concept of success, one that involves both financial reward and personal fulfillment. To achieve this objective, tomorrow's manager and employee will have to commit themselves to creating and delivering valuable products and services to valuable customers in ways they can feel good about themselves. This involves shifting from an inward focus (maximizing personal gain and ego-glorifying) to an outward focus (creating and delivering valuable products that benefit others).

Smart people dignify their existence through serving, not by being served. "Through experience," wrote J.C. Penney, "I learned that to be free, one must follow; to gain success, one must serve." In other words, living is most exciting, and ultimately most worthwhile, when your aims transcend your own self-interests, when you strive forward in the service of something far greater, toward goals that possess genuine merit.

Gem 10

Smart people go out of their way to create and maintain trust between themselves and others, and between themselves and their organizations.

Organization and individual effectiveness demand trust, and hence trustworthy people. Don Lennox, when he headed Navistar, once stated the matter this way: "We can tolerate a mistake. We can tolerate occasional use of bad judgment in making a decision. But I, personally, in no way, can tolerate a lack of trust. And my feeling is if I can't trust an individual, then I don't want to work with him."

Trust is achieved by many actions, both large and small. These include: a clear commitment to high standards, thorough and consistent honesty, above-the-board dealings, placing the interests of others ahead of self, consistency of actions, and steadiness in living up to and honoring commitments.

Gem 11

Smart people build and maintain amicable and productive relationships. They bring out the best in everyone with whom they interact and get superior results because of it.

Practically no one goes it alone in today's world of work. Those who achieve the best results do so largely because they have a knack with people. They understand them. They value and respect them. They get along with them. Smart achievers have people skills, and these skills start from a single source: sincere respect. When he headed Ford, Don Petersen told me, "It's striking to me how much more important ability to work with people openly is than any other element, in terms of being a successful manager."

Having a deep, genuine respect for others adds up to treating others as one would prefer to be treated. Where there is genuine respect, there's the sincere belief that everyone matters.

Respect for people involves far more than merely being nice to them. It means seeing them as a source of great potential as Reuben Mark who headed Colgate-Palmolive once told me, "We have 35,000 to 36,000 people around the world, and therein lies an incredible reservoir of talent and excitement and ability to make things happen. The job of management is to unlock that talent."

Respect for people also means developing their abilities, encouraging them, and recognizing and rewarding them for their accomplishments. Andy Sigler, who ran Champion Paper, put it this way: "I think my job is to create the atmosphere where people can enjoy what they do, where they treat each other with respect, under the umbrella that says if we are not productive and profitable, we're going to fail."

Gem 12

Smart people stride ahead because they don't get tripped up by their own egos.

Most of life's troubles are not caused by external forces but by internal ones. Many otherwise capable individuals stumble over their huge egos. As Mike Wright who ran Super Valu Foods once told me, "All of us in life, whether you're a teacher, or a businessman, or a priest, or anything else, should worry about whether our egos have gotten out of control. I think more problems result from an imbalance of the ego than a lot of other things. It can easily destroy companies and families and individuals."

Out-of-control egos can transform ordinarily nice people into painful fatheads and insufferable snobs, who no one can stand to be around or work alongside. Jack Sparks, who ran Whirlpool, once mentioned to me, "Always be yourself. Don't try to be something you're not, because people are going to spot you if you start to pretend to be something you're not." Smart people know this principle and work hard to live up to it. Jim Casey, the man who founded the United Parcel Service, advised: "Don't overrate yourself. Lean a little the other way. Be constructively dissatisfied and you'll go further."

One thing smart people do to prevent their egos from growing too large is to realize that success is partly a result of good fortune and the help they received along the way from others—family members, teachers, supervisors, co-workers, people who taught them important lessons and gave them opportunities. A sizable part of your success stems from being in the right place at the right time and having the help of other people.

Gem 13

Smart people continually improve their performance by learning from their experiences.

Mental rigidity, caused by unthinking habit and sustained by the unexamined belief that "what I do is good enough," is a great destroyer. It leads to obsolescence, missed opportunities and lasting, personal dissatisfaction. This is a human tragedy, a situation where the body lives but the mind hardens and dies prematurely.

There is a remedy to this, and it has to do with self-improvement combined with on-going learning. Minds and hearts stimulated by novelty and challenge do not die but grow richer and stronger. People who make ongoing learning a habit not only improve but they find great satisfaction and they grow intellectually, emotionally, and spiritually.

Only through using ideas do smart people come alive to work their effect. Smart people are action people, putting great ideas to practical use and making themselves successful because of them. Their lives grow stronger and richer and more satisfying because they use the gems of wisdom that might otherwise remain buried, and hence, useless.

In the chapters that follow, you will read about how smart people rise above the many workplace setbacks that befuddle most of us. These smart performers succeed magnificently by skillfully applying the 13 gems of wisdom discussed briefly in this introduction. Each chapter from here on is organized around one of these 13 gems, and will show you how smart people handle dumb things by applying that gem of wisdom effectively. Their experiences illustrate what each gem puts forth and will provide you with concrete methods of how to respond better to the many dumb things that you might encounter.

Smart people are action-oriented because they know that, like a clock, wisdom is meant to be used. Ergo, the more they use that wisdom the stronger their abilities to handle workplace difficulties grows and the richer and more satisfying their lives become. The same will happen to you when you start putting the 13 gems of wisdom to good use yourself.

How this book is organized

This book will show you how to avoid career-crippling mistakes by addressing tricky workplace dilemmas with imagination and integrity. It is intended to show you how to deal effectively with the many blunders, glitches, traps, and setbacks that can sabotage your road to success. I wrote it for busy people like yourself who do not have time to read through hundreds of pages before finding the advice they need.

To fully understand my intention, note that the book's chapters are titled according to keen problem areas. This will help you to go directly to the category of problem you face and within 10 or 15 minutes come away with a solid understanding of the nature of your difficulty and smart strategies for dealing with it effectively.

Each chapter contains specific dilemmas within its topic category, and each dilemma's statement is followed by a standard pattern of analysis, insight, and advice. First, I illustrate each dilemma with a life-like case example. Next, I provide an in-depth explanation of the central issues involved in the dilemma to help you better understand what you are up against. After that, I offer useful tips for attaching and solving the dilemma, which I learned from examining the experiences of exceptional achievers. And last, I distill the wisdom of smart people into tailored, imaginative "how-to" action steps that you can use.

I wrote this book to give people added wisdom and practical skills for dealing effectively with a range of workplace difficulties not discussed in schoolbooks. By understanding its many lessons and skillfully applying the principles contained in this volume, you will not only improve your performance but also derive lasting personal fulfillment from it. The advice I offer in the chapters that follow comes from the experiences of many, highly successful people. It is not abstract theory but proven, reliable guidance that works.

Many situations present people with dilemmas because they are unable to perceive the preferability of bringing lasting value to the world over obtaining instant gratification and personal advantages for themselves. As you read this book, pay particular attention to both the practical skills and their underlying principles. Let the anecdotes and advice help you develop your own way of better responding to workplace difficulties. See if you can develop guiding principles for yourself, and, most importantly, find the courage to apply those principles toward a profitable, rewarding future.

Chapter 1

The Broken Compass

Reaching your destination by sticking to the best course

Every day, in countless ways, good people get trapped or become hopelessly lost in the unpredictable and uncharted maze known as the workplace. They run head-long into troubles while others skillfully negotiate through everyday challenges to reach their destinations of success.

To keep on course and to avoid the snags and pits that can entrap or destroy anyone along the way, you need a reliable internal guidance system—a compass that works, pointing out the best path around workplace difficulties and toward success.

The sad truth is that too many people never reach their destinations, because they try to navigate with broken compasses. A broken compass could be a warped sense of right and wrong, or disgraceful values, or self-serving purposes, or ignorance of performance expectations, or a poor sense of proportion. The list is long.

This chapter contains valuable lessons about the kind of compass that smart people use to achieve lasting success. It shows how smart achievers chart reliable courses that keep them moving forward on firm ground, where they travel safely around danger, leading to their desired destinations.

Dilemma 1

You are torn between taking a high-paying job that doesn't fully interest you and work that you love but doesn't pay all that well.

Tina discovered her love for science when she was a small girl. In school she devoured every science lesson and went on to earn a chemistry degree in college. Her first job involved laboratory work, a realm in which she knew she belonged and a place where she thrived. Tina did whatever her boss asked her to do and more. She loved her work so much that she'd arrive early, stay past quitting time, and even work at her laboratory over weekends.

After a few years in her position, Tina grew restless, as the challenges of her job did not expand to keep pace with her knowledge. Unable to find challenges that suited her, Tina decided to return to college and pursue an advanced degree. While in graduate school Tina learned about a new technology. This emerging branch of science fascinated her and she wrote her master's thesis on a topic in the field. Her publications gave her national recognition and several firms quickly offered her promising employment opportunities when she graduated. She accepted a position with one firm that offered her a chance to pursue applied research believed to have commercial possibilities. Tina reveled in this position and she produced excellent results; her work provided her employer with highly profitable technological breakthroughs. In recognition of her excellent accomplishments, upper management decided to promote Tina to director of a laboratory—a highly paid position with considerable responsibility and prestige.

In her new role Tina was in charge of the work of other researchers. It was the first time she had administrative duties: preparing work schedules, conducting performance evaluations, handling supervision matters, planning, etc. She spent less time in the laboratory and more time in her office doing paperwork, talking on the telephone, interacting with other people. And, too, there were those tedious meetings—Tina hated meetings. She began to long for the days when she was where she felt most alive and challenged. The money and prestige didn't seem to be enough to compensate her for the lack of challenge she had enjoyed earlier in her career.

Unhappy and confused people stream in and out of the offices of psychologists and therapists every day, because they flatly refuse to accept the law of life that says we cannot always have everything we want. The well-worn expression "have your cake and eat it too" presents this truth vividly. Tina wants interesting and challenging work that she loves and she wants to advance in her organization and reap the benefits: better salary, prestige, power. She cannot have both.

All too often people make themselves miserable because they refuse to face the simple fact that they cannot have everything they desire. Day after day they create their own pain and misery because the pursuit of one desire makes the attainment of another desire impossible and they refuse to adjust themselves to that reality.

This is how Tina's compass is broken—it points toward mutually exclusive directions at the same time, thereby confusing her. Tina needs a compass that will point her toward just one direction, a direction that's worth moving toward.

Clarify what you seek. Decide the priority of your aims.

There was once a television commercial that showed a busy professional woman driving her young daughter home from school. She told her child, "I'll be away for the next few days on a business trip." The child acted disappointed because her mother would not be able to attend her school play.

The mother tried to console her daughter, saying, "You like all the things you have and our nice car and you want us to get a bigger house don't you?" The child thought a moment and answered, "Do we really need a bigger house?"

The child's question was anything but childish. It was childlike in its penetrating honesty and it was extremely mature in terms of honestly facing the stark reality of having to choose between two mutually exclusive wants. This is what smart people do—they honestly face the reality of mutual exclusivity and clarify which aims they want more than others.

Choose doing over having.

Thomas Monaghan became a multimillionaire through building the Domino's Pizza chain. One day in 1980 he went to see Ray Kroc, the man who made McDonald's into the world's largest chain of restaurants. Monaghan saw Kroc as an entrepreneurial genius and he tried to emulate him. While sitting in Mr. Kroc's office, Kroc said to Monaghan, "Tom, you've got it made now. So play it safe. Open a few stores every year, but don't make any deals that could get you into trouble."

Monaghan was shocked. He couldn't believe that the entrepreneur he so admired would say such a thing—it defied what he thought Kroc believed in. Unable to restrain himself, Monaghan blurted out, "But that wouldn't be any fun!"

A long, silent pause gripped the room. Then, a big grin appeared on Kroc's face as he jumped to his feet and walked around his desk to shake Monaghan's hand. "That's just what I hoped you'd say!"

Red Adair, the man who made a name for himself by putting out oil field blazes—his firm was called on to extinguish the fires in Kuwait after the Iraqi army was beaten back—was no stranger to this important truth. He put it this way: "Life isn't *having* it made; it's *getting* it made. Each necessary task requires an effort of will, and with each act something in you grows and is strengthened."

Smart Solution 1

Tina was fortunate that she received a taste of both laboratory work and supervisory responsibilities. She found out first-hand what kind of work each involved. She could make an informed choice, because the longer she remained confused as to which direction to take, the more frozen she could become, entrapped in the false hope that she could have both what she liked to do and the many extra "goodies" she wanted.

Hopefully, Tina didn't obligate herself to financial responsibilities or entangle herself in interpersonal relationships that would have prevented her return to the laboratory work she loved.

Dilemma 2

An opening for which you are well-qualified exists within your organization in another part of the country. The idea of advancement appeals to you, but the thought of moving away from familiar surroundings and friends bothers you.

Lyle studied mining engineering in college and immediately after graduation he found employment with a mining company that had its largest operation in his hometown. He accepted the offer. Lyle had what he believed was the perfect situation: a good job located in the same community where all his friends and family lived and worked. Lyle worked hard, did well, and advanced rapidly. His employer liked his work and upper management identified him as a high potential employee, an individual who they felt could accept major responsibilities.

After seven years in various positions, Lyle was presented with an enviable opportunity: the operations manager's position of a new mine in South America, the number two position there. Management wanted to groom Lyle for the top spot at this new mine; they would give him that assignment within three to five years. As Lyle considered his opportunity, he thought about the challenge, the prospect of living abroad, and the fact he'd be far away from his friends and familiar surroundings. His friends and family wanted him to stay and they made their wishes known.

Do you follow the path of adventure into the unknown or stay where it's safe and familiar? Lyle will have to go in one direction or another—there's no way of going both directions. The smart thing to do is to make the decision himself, not have others make it for him.

All too often, people wanting two conflicting things allow others or other forces to make these different choices for them. Whenever this happens, the person diminishes himself or herself by not fully taking charge of his or her life. This is Lyle's challenge: to be an adult and decide for himself which option he will follow.

Lyle's compass was broken because it pointed him toward the security of a comfort zone which could eventually relegate him to the wasteland of "also-rans" and "could-have-beens." Lyle needed a compass that could point him toward his own self-determined goals, not somebody else's.

Know what's in your heart and follow it.

Milton was a wealthy man before he reached the age of 45. His candies were such a huge success that he was able to sell his caramel business for more than $1 million in 1901. Yes, Milton, you might say, had what practically everyone would liked to have had—his health, enormous wealth, and a young, beautiful wife. So, Milton thought he'd cash in and try retirement.

Milton wasn't content to sit back and enjoy his riches in the comfort of an easy chair. That wasn't his idea of enjoyment at all. He was a builder and he had something big in mind that needed building. It was then that Hershey decided to enter the chocolate business on a grand scale. "Not for the money that might be in it," said Milton Hershey, "but for the satisfaction of doing something that was worthwhile." It was the satisfaction of doing something big, something that made a difference that accounted for Milton's countless other business success stories.

Smart Solution 2

In Lyle's situation, what was called for was simple: honesty. That's the quality he needed to dwell on. He would do well to ask himself which option was the right one to take. Lyle would thrive if he acted like an adult, approaching his situation with the following considerations: This is my choice, my life which I have to live; I will choose for myself. I'll opt for challenges in which I can make my mark over the security of the familiar and the safety of the fireside.

Dilemma 3

It is time for you to decide whether you should pursue your dream of being self-employed or remain loyal to your organization for the security it offers.

Dawn discovered her ability to sell when she was quite young. She won the prize for selling the most boxes of Girl Scout cookies when she was 12. Dawn studied sales management and marketing in school. After that she worked in various sales and marketing positions while in her 20s and early 30s. For the past seven years, Dawn sold medical test equipment for a high-technology corporation. Her employer pays her a base salary and commissions. She also receives medical insurance and retirement benefits. It is a good job with good benefits and security. But Dawn wants more.

Dawn thinks she'd like to be her own boss and try out her own ideas of how to reach customers with new products. The medical test equipment industry sees a never-ending stream of new entrants hoping to market their breakthrough products. They need people like Dawn who have medical equipment sales experience. Dawn thinks that the time is ripe for her to go out on her own and begin a marketing organization to sell the equipment.

We all have dreams, and if we're lucky we dream about the right things—right for us, that is. We cannot state for certain that Dawn's compass is broken, because we do not know whether it points her toward destinations that are well-suited to her talents. Many a person follows a broken compass that point them in a direction which they are ill-suited to travel. In Dawn's case we should hope that her dreams are consistent with her abilities and temperament. This is a matter she has to address: Is there a good match between her dream and her abilities?

Open your eyes to the challenges of new endeavors.

Only a fool would strike out on a sailing venture across open seas alone without good navigation equipment and plenty of experience. Many misty-eyed idealists have encountered disappointment and defeat because the realities of what they contemplated turned out to be far different than what they imagined them to be.

The realities of an undertaking are generally not as glamorous or as easy as one might see from a superficial glance. Concert pianists practice passages for upcoming performances over and over, month after month—it's mostly drudgery. Shopkeepers have their own business; they are their own boss. But they do not have weekends to themselves, time for Christmas shopping, long vacations away from their places of business. Restauranteurs must be on duty watching every little detail every day; and they frequently have to pick up dishes, seat customers, and clean up dirty kitchens when their help calls in sick or quits at the last minute. These are the stark realities that a person with eyes open sees and fully understands.

Smart Solution 3

There's no substitute for first-hand information. Dawn would do well to get a taste of what owning and operating a business of her own would be like. She could talk to others who have successful businesses, learning how they spend their time and exactly what they do, finding out about the difficulties and unpleasant realities they face, discovering what makes their work life hectic and frustrating, and gaining a good understanding of the many rewards they receive and enjoy. She might even try spending several days with these people as they carry out their daily chores.

Taking stock of your skills, abilities, and temperament are some of the more difficult things Dawn needed to do. Additionally, Dawn could talk to others who know her to get their input. You have to be careful to not become blinded by the excitement of what only appears thrilling. Many young boys dream of becoming NBA players, but only one in a million have the talent that's required.

Dilemma 4

The fast-track career path you are on prevents you from being the kind of spouse and parent you want to be. There isn't enough time for both your work and family roles.

Robert studied finance in college and landed a top-paying job with a bank located in a major metropolitan area. His work with the bank involved buying and selling financial instruments. After a few years, another job opportunity came along, also involving buying and selling financial instruments such as commercial paper, notes, loans, and the like. Living in an apartment located near his downtown office was convenient. Robert enjoyed his free time, going to swank clubs and restaurants. He filled his bachelor days with work and girlfriends.

Robert performed his work duties well and advanced in his organization. He also met a young woman, fell in love, and married. They moved to a suburb many miles away from Robert's office, and started a family.

After several years, Robert and his wife had three small children. They needed full-time care and Robert's wife decided that she'd prefer to stay at home. This worked out all right, because Robert earned a handsome income. He also had more responsibilities, which grew each year along with advancement in his organization. By the time he turned 40, Robert earned a six-figure income and was in line for a vice presidency. He had to travel quite a bit of the time, because his growing responsibilities involved overseeing expanding operations throughout the United States, Canada, Mexico, and parts of Latin America.

What began to bother Robert was that he missed being part of the lives of his children. Robert realized that every day he wasn't with his family was lost forever—he'd never get that day back.

Robert's compass is working well in that he's already aware of the tradeoff he's making in giving up precious time with his family to meet the demands of his work. Some people never realize what Robert is beginning to realize, because their compass points them away from family matters entirely.

Another way in which Robert's compass needed to function was in directing him to live up to his family responsibilities day to day. To do this well, Robert would have to organize himself, scheduling hours for family and work according to their importance—and children and spouses are unquestionably important. Robert also needs the strength to spend his time doing what he believes to be important; he needs to be able to say no to demands that will carry him away from his family obligations. Discipline is required to maintain his solid work ethic while finding the necessary leisure time as well.

Smart Solution 4

Robert would succeed and his children would be the better for it if he heeded his heart. He knew that his family needed his personal attention, his time. He could schedule time for them if he put personal career desires secondary to his family's needs.

Many executives from the largest and most successful firms do the right thing for their children. They come home at a reasonable hour for sit-down family meals and are available to talk to their families. This is what Robert needs to do.

Dilemma 5

It bothers you to think of how much pay you get compared to all the work you do and how much more others are making for comparatively less effort.

Frances worked herself into a tizzy every time she thought about how much more Arlene made than she did. It upset Frances to know that her younger, less-experienced colleague took home a bigger paycheck than she did. And the more she dwelled on the matter, the angrier she got—it grated on her day and night.

Frances and Arlene sold prescription drugs for the world's largest pharmaceutical firm. Frances sold 12 lines of drugs, which included medications for conditions such as depression, asthma, and migraines. Arlene handled oncology drugs. Both reps earned a salary and received bonuses according to the dollar volume of what they sold. Frances had 12 years experience with the firm, and made a higher salary than Arlene did, who had been employed for 5 years.

Greed and envy. These are the two culprits that lead to the frustration that torments Frances. The more Frances thinks about the pay differential, the more it eats away at her. So, what's the solution? It begins with a solid understanding of the forces acting on Frances and her proclivity to allow them to eat their way into her thoughts and destroy her peace of mind and happiness.

Frances makes herself miserable because her broken compass points her toward envy and greed instead of thankfulness for what she does have. Her pain signals are a powerful indication that Frances is off course.

Understand the destructive power of greed.

Greed has a way of tricking us into thinking we can't get along unless we get what we want—all that we want, more than we want. It also fools us into thinking that we can get whatever we want, even if the getting isn't right.

I read a newspaper story about two people whose better judgment was twisted by greed—hardly a new phenomenon. According to the newspaper account, a man and his sister stopped for drinks at a McDonald's in Norwalk, California. McDonald's had a sales promotion going on at the time called Monopoly. It was a contest where customers received game tickets—much like instant winner lottery tickets—with their purchases.

The man looked at his ticket, and discovered it was the one that promised $1,000 a week for life. There was just one problem; the man was an assistant manager at a McDonald's, making him, according to contest rules, "ineligible to win prizes."

But the man had a scheme. He gave the winning ticket to his girlfriend. Their arrangement was that they'd share the prize. This went on for more than six years—to the tune of $330,409. But conflict between the two exposed their scheme. McDonald's, which had already become suspicious, found out about it and stopped the monthly payments.

Greed is a trap, and it has gotten the better of lots of people. I recall an ancient Roman proverb: "Greed is like sea water. The more you drink, the thirstier you become."

Smart Solution 5

An old Vaudeville routine involved a scene in which a man went to see a doctor. "Doctor," the man said as he raised and twisted his arm in an unusual position. "I have a pain. It hurts every time I do this." The doctor replied, "Well then, don't do that!"

The silly joke makes a deeper point: If something hurts, then stop doing it. This is the best advice for Frances: "Suck it up. There's nothing you can do about the fact oncology drugs have a higher markup and give Arlene a bigger bonus. That's life. Get over it."

Another thing Frances would do well to consider is developing a greater sense of gratitude for all that she has.

Dilemma 6

You work very hard and feel that you are knowledgeable and do excellent work, but your boss tends to treat you as though you are incompetent.

Heather felt confident about her knowledge of business. She held a degree in accounting from a good university and worked for a large firm. Her job was to find and negotiate lease agreements for her rapidly expanding company—it needed building space for warehousing and operating activities. After several weeks of research and negotiations, Heather not only secured an option to lease building space in a building, but got the owner to lower his asking price by several thousand dollars.

Shortly before his noon flight, the vice president of operations went to see Heather. "Tell me what we got?" he said.

"It's really a very good deal," Heather answered. "I got the owner to reduce his asking price by $5,000."

"That doesn't answer my question," her boss replied. "What will we be paying for the space?"

Heather grew nervous, wondering what the vice president wanted. She answered by stating the monthly rate she negotiated and then assured her boss that she felt good about the fact that the owner took less than his asking price. "Well then," the vice president continued, "how much space would we be getting in this building?" Heather answered, "It's three full floors. And, I think I negotiated a really good deal."

But this response did not satisfy her boss. The vice president asked her to find the exact square footage of useable floor space and to calculate the monthly rate per square foot. He also told Heather to get on the phone to find competitive rates for building space in the area. The vice president left her office peeved at Heather for not having the answers he wanted. She felt angry and confused.

Know what your boss wants done and do it.

Many young people create bad impressions of themselves at work because they fail to understand what their bosses want them to do. Bosses do not hire inexperienced newcomers to make major decisions and change the direction of the organization. They hire subordinates to do what they want done. If Heather is to make a better impression of herself in her boss's eyes, she'll have to start doing what he wants her to do. She has to focus on getting the information her boss needs in order to make an important decision and forget about trying to convince him of her negotiating skills.

The same kind of thinking that orients a business to please its customers serves employees effectively as they work for their superiors. A business that offers buyers what it can produce will not last long if customers do not want it. Give customers what they want. The same thing goes for employers. Employees need to give their bosses what their *bosses* want, not whatever it is they personally require themselves.

Smart Solution 6

Heather needed to forget about how great she thought she was, and pay more attention to what her boss expected of her. The first thing she should do is to orient her thinking more along the lines of business—revenues, expenses, profits—and forget about her skills as a clever negotiator.

Her self image was blinding her to the business realities her boss knew were critical to the profitable future of the company. She has to begin thinking along these lines instead of trying to project an image that's irrelevant to the well-being of the organization.

The second thing she could do is mend the bad image she created by sitting down with her boss and asking what kinds of things she should pay attention to. Her boss would more than likely give her several useful lessons that she could apply at once. Just imagine how pleased he would be the next time he asked Heather for the appropriate information and she would be able to supply it.

Dilemma 7

Your boss asks you tackle an assignment but you do not fully understand what you are supposed to do and you fear that if you ask for clarification and direction, your boss will become angry and think you are incompetent.

Karl was a newly hired data entry operator. His job wasto input information to update his company's inventory records. Karl wanted to present himself in a confident manner to impress his boss and coworkers. His supervisor showed Karl how to enter the code numbers and quantities received of incoming inventory. Karl acted as though he fully understood his instructions.

Unfortunately, in his act to appear fully knowledgeable and confident, Karl missed a step. As he entered the inventory codes of incoming inventory, he deleted the codes of existing inventory. This meant that the company's computerized records indicated a level of inventory that reflected only the amount of newly arrived items.

Too many people make the mistake of trying to look good when they are not in a position to perform good work. They falsely conclude that they will be able to get by without being found out. When we trace this difficulty back to its source, we come to something called the ego. Karl's compass was broken because his fear of appearing ignorant lead him to make dumb and costly mistakes.

A good boss explains how to do things before the fact.

Peter Drucker, perhaps the most widely acclaimed authority on management, once wrote that the most important role managers perform is to develop employees, giving them the vision and skills they need to perform effectively.

Managers are, first and foremost, developers of their employees. Their number one job is to teach employees what they want and equip them with the skills and abilities needed.

Smart Solution 7

Karl would be better off if he forgot about his desire to appear knowledgeable. For starters, he could begin asking questions, lots of questions. He was better off appearing ignorant than acting stupidly. A reputation for asking questions is not the same thing as a reputation for making dumb mistakes. Don't be afraid to ask questions, under any circumstances.

Dilemma 8

You anger a person whose high regard and cooperation you need. This person verbally attacks you in an ugly confrontation. You feel like saying "Back off, you big jerk!"

Maryanne was a sales representative for one of the world's premier pharmaceutical firms. Her work took her to the offices and hospitals of physicians, some of whom were leading authorities in their respective fields. Her company had recently developed a superior drug for people suffering from heart disease.

With high sales potential, Maryanne enthusiastically contacted heart specialists to get them to prescribe the new drug for their patients. She called both the world's foremost researchers and head of the cardiac cauterization unit of a distinguished medical school. Getting the doctor's endorsement of the new drug could boost her chances of selling the drug to other physicians.

But Maryanne's sales call turned out not to be what she expected or wanted. The distinguished doctor used the time to lecture Maryanne on the negative aspects of her firm's new heart medication and to extol the virtues of competing drugs. Maryanne listened patiently, but she did not make the sale.

Set back somewhat, but undaunted in her determination, Maryanne called on other members of the cardiac cauterization unit and sold her product to them. While calling on physicians, she encountered the distinguished doctor who had lectured to her but didn't buy her product. He was furious, and scolded Maryanne for "going around him" and selling the new drug to other doctors in his unit. This made her angry, and she wanted to speak her mind.

How Maryanne reacted to this tense situation reveals whether or not her compass is working correctly. She's come under fire by an angry, potential customer who is out of control with rage; it's an ugly encounter. When anyone comes under a verbal barrage, the natural tendency is to either duck for cover, escape, or fight back. Maryanne wants to go on the attack. What's the smart thing to do?

Project a favorable image of your organization by acting in ways that honor its name.

Parents of teenagers worry about the behavior of their children as they go out into the community. They want them to be safe and act responsibly. They want them to act in ways that will enhance, not tarnish, the family name. They know full well that how their children act reflects on them. So, parents tell their sons and daughters to have high moral standards, to walk away when there are bad things going on, to not engage in acts that are wrong, even if it isn't popular. Doing right and acting courageously bring honor. The same advice applies to employees as they interact with others, particularly the public, especially since they represent their organization.

Goodyear has a slogan: "Protect our good name," which executives sometimes twist slightly with a word change: "*Project* our good name."

Smart Solution 8

Maryanne was smart. She kept her mind on the goal her company wanted her to follow: sell drugs. She knew better than to fight back with the ill-mannered doctor who verbally attacked her. She followed her compass through the fog of the heated exchange, maintaining a cordial and professional demeanor. By holding her course, she regained the doctor's respect and earned his business.

Chapter 2

The Unbalanced Scale

Weighing options accurately to find the best decision

Making good decisions consistently is not the easiest thing in the world to do because they come at us so rapidly and unexpectedly and from so many different directions. Under these pressures, it's easy to slip up by deciding too hastily, or choosing before considering the possibilities adequately, or weighing the expected outcomes accurately.

One thing that leads people into deciding too quickly is the belief that "any decision is better than no decision at all." A snap decision is a dangerous thing; making one is like diving head-first into an unfamiliar body of water. You expose yourself to whatever dangers lurk in the dark unknown, while sending irretrievable ripples outward to work their effects on others. Indeed, it could be said that there is a crooked wisdom in choosing what to do too quickly in order to economize time and appear decisive.

A deliberate approach to decision making is better than a speedy one, but carefulness alone is never enough to guarantee success. The popular superstition that you can gain what you want without paying a price is the chief source of imbalance in most people's scales of judgment. All choices carry both desirable and undesirable consequences, and smart people see and face these realities squarely. This chapter will show you how to arrive at better choices by weighing all options carefully and seeing the full range of consequences.

Dilemma 9

You face a tough decision and turn to your key lieutenants for their advice but they are divided on what to do. Now what?

Henry ran a mid-sized firm that manufactured equipment used by the dairy industry. It was a steady business, but the company had not experienced technological breakthroughs in their products or manufacturing processes until recently. With the advent of computer software packages and computer-monitored controls, Henry's firm faced stiff competition, making it necessary to improve and modernize their product lines in order to remain a strong competitor.

Fortunately, Henry's firm had sufficient capital resources to invest in new technology. Money wasn't a problem. What made the situation difficult was the fundamental choice between two entirely different technologies. One option was to move to a newly evolving product technology. This route was costly and somewhat risky, because there was so little experience behind it, which meant Henry's company would have to let many employees go in order to hire new ones who understood the more advanced processes. The favorable aspect of this choice was that it promised to catapult Henry's firm far ahead of its competitors.

The other option was less costly and wouldn't require drastic changes in personnel. The downside was that it wouldn't provide Henry's firm with a strong advantage over its competitors. Personnel in the manufacturing, distribution, and human resources departments favored this option because it wouldn't disrupt existing processes or pain loyal, experienced employees. Henry had to look deeper and see the underlying reasons each side advocated.

Know the reasons for differing preferences, then decide on the basis of what's best overall.

Several years ago, I was in Peoria, Illinois visiting George Schaefer, who headed up the Caterpillar Tractor Company at the time. George, who is about as down to earth and decent as anyone I've ever met, told me about an experience he once had as the plant manager of a tractor factory.

One Monday morning, George found himself in the middle of a controversy. It all began when a plant employee had driven up to the plant's gate in his pickup truck over the weekend. The truck was loaded with Caterpillar parts and tools which the employee had pilfered over many years. However, his misdeeds had begun to bother him; the man's conscience couldn't take it any longer. So, he decided to return what he'd stolen and make a full confession. What should be done with him?

George faced a decision. The labor relations people and the head of the accounting department said, "He's reformed, he has a good record. Scold him and give him a mild punishment, but don't fire him." The head of manufacturing and the quality control and engineering people advised the opposite. "Wrong is wrong," they argued. "The company has rules. He stole from us and should be terminated."

George listened to all sides, weighing the matter from every conceivable angle. What would be best for both the company and the man? He had stolen from the company, but had come forward and confessed. George thought through the possible implications of each option: If we punished this man, what's that going to say to other employees? What will the union say in this matter?

Questions and concerns such as these circled through George's mind as he pondered what to do. He studied every scrap of pertinent information he could get and listened to his key lieutenants as they expressed their opinions. George wanted to make a fully-informed and reasoned decision. He ultimately chose what he felt was the best option: The employee was sent back to work with a stern warning that if he ever stole again, it would cost him his job.

Consider all the pros and cons, and then decide what to do on the basis of solid, guiding principles.

One of the best ways to ensure well-thought out decisions is to acknowledge all of the realities in the situation, both good and bad. Consider all the costs and benefits, all the pros and cons, all the positive and negative implications of each option. The idea is to lay everything out in full view, including figuring your own feelings into the equation.

How can this best be accomplished? It helps to be realistic, to acknowledge that we live in an imperfect world. Most of the choices we make harbor some unpleasant options. Everything we do has at least some unwanted or unsavory element to it, every choice its share of flaws. This is part of the human condition. While we might not be able to avoid doing some amount of wrong, we can at least try to recognize it. We can be honest about what we do.

Smart Solution 9

Henry had two options. He listened to his subordinates and saw that they differed over which choice the firm should follow. Henry needed to examine the reasons underlying both viewpoints, asking himself, "What did each side stand to gain or lose? What values did each side favor?" Once he grasped both viewpoints, Henry decided on the basis of which choice best served the interests of his organization, his customers, and his company's owners. He was not swayed entirely by any one group without knowing why they favored what they did, or did he become frozen in indecision due to a lack of 'trouble-free' options.

Dilemma 10

In your highly competitive industry, all is not "kinder and gentler"; sometimes, you have to resort to tough and unkind actions to get ahead.

Benjamin was General Manager of the Cosmetics and Fragrances Division of a pharmaceutical company. Most agreed that Benjamin was extremely bright and competitive. Several times, he didn't hesitate to step on toes to get what he wanted. He was shrewd when it came to knowing how to slash costs and squeeze profits out of marginal operations. And, politically, he knew how to work the system to his benefit and advantage.

Benjamin was astute when it came to reading the mood of the times. Sometimes this worked to his advantage—he was known to pick up on a politically sensitive issue quickly and run in the appropriate direction. Benjamin once realized the weight of public opinion in the matter of animal testing. He immediately called a temporary halt to it and began using the change of policy in consumer product advertising—he wanted the public to view his division's products as "animal friendly," yet he fully intended to resume the practice when the public outcries ended. Sales jumped as a result of his publicity.

His decisions to move rapidly were not without peril. Under his leadership, a major new product was rapidly moved from laboratory testing to production to meet an emerging need and fend off competitors from capturing substantial market share. Some felt the division's cash flow problems overrode the normally cautious testing standards—a costly mistake. Subsequently, several lawsuits had been filed against the corporation. Benjamin looked out for his own interests and worked the system to get what he wanted. In one instance, after an important sales conference in the Bahamas, he took out the corporate jet on an extended weekend trip. When skepticism arose about the propriety of this, Benjamin dismissed it as inconsequential.

Benjamin's actions depict what might be popularly held beliefs on how to achieve success in the brutish world of business. He doesn't hesitate to step on others to get what he wants. He's guided by power considerations, not principles. Should we accept Benjamin's beliefs and values and choose to live by them just because Benjamin appears to be successful?

Gray areas usually become the justification for what you should not be doing.

Several years ago I spent the day with Bill Huessong, who was vice president of manufacturing of Shopsmith in Dayton, Ohio. Bill told me something very important about Shopsmith's president, John Folkerth: "With John, there isn't any room for gray in matters of right and wrong. To him, it's either black or white, right or wrong."

Now, this is not to say that he thought any choice or action was either all right or all wrong. But what was significant was that he saw the existence of right and wrong. As a consequence, everyone who worked for John knew that certain things would not be tolerated. It served to give everyone at Shopsmith a clear understanding of what the boundaries of acceptable behavior were.

Smart Solution 10

Labeling right and wrong "a matter of opinion," is a fool's gesture. For one thing, it affords us a handy excuse to do anything we might feel like doing. For another, it blinds us to making an honest assessment of the issues we consider as we contemplate options.

Dilemma 11

You encounter a situation in which the rules don't make good sense.

When Segrid arrived in the United States from her native Sweden, she had high hopes for a bright future. Her training in accounting and her fluency in English made her highly desirable. After considering several opportunities, she decided to take a job with an office furniture company, where she could apply her accounting knowledge.

The firm's accounting department was in terrible shape. Transactions and tallies were backlogged. Much tedious work needed to be done. Segrid spent her evenings and portions of her weekends getting accounts updated and in order. Unfamiliar with U.S. employment law, Segrid did not understand the implications of her exempt status—it meant that she would not be paid overtime because she was considered a part of management. Ignorant of this, she kept track of her extra hours, expecting that she'd receive either extra pay or compensatory time off when she wanted it.

After six months of dedicated effort, Segrid eliminated the backlog. With things at work in order, Segrid thought it was a good time to take her vacation; however, she needed more time to see friends and relatives in Sweden than her two-week vacation allowed. The company wanted to grant Segrid extra time off, but its legal advisor suggested sticking to the rules, because skirting them would create legal problems between the company and its other employees.

Decide what's "best" overall and live by the spirit of the law.

There are some situations in which the law makes no sense. This occurred in regard to Segrid's situation, as the rules seemed made to inhibit a just act from taking place. Deciding solely on the basis of the letter of the law can be a source of unbalance in one's scales of judgment. It is preferable to look to the spirit of the law when making reasonable decisions.

A large American chemical company found itself in a tough spot at its Mexico facility. With a broken pump and no replacements available within the country, the plant was forced to shut down. The operating requirements demanded a special type of pump that, unfortunately, needed to be imported.

This plant was vitally important to the economics of the area and employed over five hundred people. What's more, Mexico needed the agricultural product the plant produced—it was the country's only source for the product. Employees would be unable to work until the breakdown was corrected.

Under ordinary circumstances, this breakdown posed little in the way of technical difficulties. The new parts could be air-freighted to the location immediately and installed within a couple of days after that. The plant might be closed down for a few days, but employees could be put to work with other tasks. The product from the plant would continue to be available for the Mexican market. So, the new parts were shipped right away.

Unfortunately, once arriving in Mexico, the speedy movement of replacement parts stopped until they cleared customs. There were two ways to accomplish this. There was the slow way, which involved paperwork and could take two to four months. Also, Mexican customs agents usually demanded a little something for their trouble.

The second method involved what's known as a facilitating payment, something that motivates customs agents to act. In this case, the agents felt that $500 was an appropriate amount for their trouble. Once paid, the parts would pass through customs and be sent on their way immediately. The entire process would take only a few minutes.

Of course, it's unlawful for U.S. companies to pay bribes. On the other hand, if the company chose not to make the facilitating payment, the plant would close down for two to four months, maybe longer. All the while, the employees and the local economy would suffer. And, too, there was the loss of product; it would not be available to the thousands of Mexican farmers who depended on it.

Smart Solution 11

After contemplating the matter for some time, her boss decided that Segrid was due a bonus. They arranged for five extra days off with pay. The resolution satisfied the company's attorney and Segrid enjoyed her visit with family and friends in Sweden.

Dilemma 12

You find it unfair that your company frequently makes demands on your time. You remind yourself of this whenever you begin to have feelings of guilt for doing personal business on company time or using company resources for your personal benefit.

Dennis was an engineer who worked for the climate control design group of a major automaker. His unit did the engineering work on the heating, ventilation, and air conditioning systems for their firm's line of automobiles. Design projects involved trying to improve HVAC performance qualities in new vehicles. The design group also tried to reduce costs.

The workload tired Dennis out. His five day work week sometimes extended into Saturdays and Sundays. Work days usually began well before 8 a.m. and ran past 6 p.m. Added to this was Dennis' daily commute, which took him over an hour each way. Because he worked so hard and without compensation for his extra hours, Dennis felt justified in using company resources for his personal use.

Dennis could make a bad decision if self-pity unbalances his scales of judgment. Most people tend to feel they should be compensated something extra for their inconvenience. As a consequence, these people do not abide by the rules and, in the process, set bad examples for others to follow.

Live by the rules at all times—especially if no one is watching.

Amos Alonzo Stagg was respected and admired, producing many winning teams during the 42 years he coached football and baseball at the University of Chicago. To the game of football he brought the concepts of the huddle, the "man in motion," and the end-around play.

Coach Stagg was also known for his integrity and uncompromising honesty, qualities he put ahead of winning.

Once when Stagg's baseball team was defending its college title, a batter singled, and as he raced home with the winning run, Stagg shouted at him, "Get back to third base. You cut it by a yard." "But the umpire didn't see it," the player protested. "That doesn't make any difference," roared Stagg. "Get back!" It cost Chicago the game but the player had learned a valuable lesson about character.

Set a good example.

Israel Cohen, who began a grocery business in Washington, D.C., knew the importance of setting a good example, particularly with his employees. Partly because of this, his Giant Food grocery stores grew to be among the largest chains in the country.

Cohen would frequently go to the dairy section in his store, pick up several fresh eggs and conspicuously pay for his purchase at the check out lane just like his customers did. A young lad who worked for Cohen would sometimes join him at the luncheonette where he usually ate. The young boy was puzzled by Cohen's purchases. "Mr. Cohen, why did you buy those eggs? They're yours."

Cohen answered, "That's exactly why I bought them. Everyone should see that everything that goes out of this store is paid for."

Smart Solution 12

If Dennis began taking company resources to compensate for what he perceived to be inconvenience, he ran several risks. He might have become so overly concerned about his daily 'reward' that it diminished his willingness to produce a fair day's work. He might also get caught for stealing from the company and punished, even possibly terminated because of it. Finally, he set a poor standard for others who might be tempted to follow his bad example. Dennis would be far happier and more productive if he focused his energies on making his finest effort rather than concentrating on self-inflicted burdens.

Dilemma 13

You must decide whether to break a promise to a friend or to remain silent and expose your employer to a huge risk.

Byron was a purchasing agent for a floor covering manufacturer. His job was to purchase items used in the manufacturing process. Byron's fishing buddy, Greg, also worked in purchasing for the company. They often took turns car-pooling to and from work. One morning, Greg bragged to Byron about the great deal he got on some hardening agent used to make floor tiles. The agent he had on hand came from the same supplier but was getting old, months past its expiration date. The supplier's sales agent convinced Greg that there wasn't anything to worry about; the worst that could happen would be that the tiles might shrink over time, but that would take years, and by then they would probably have been sold and installed.

Byron had to decide between being loyal to his friend or to his company and its customers. Placing the interests of those you know ahead of the interests of strangers unbalances your scales of judgment. It's really a very selfish way of looking at things when you stop to think about it.

Be loyal to the idea of loyalty.

Be loyal to loyalty. It might sound like convoluted thinking, but it isn't. In fact, the idea came from one of our country's most distinguished and respected philosophers, Josiah Royce, who taught at Harvard University. Recognizing that people can serve one cause so single-mindedly their actions cause harm to the causes of others, Professor Royce introduced the concept of "loyalty to loyalty" in his book, *The Philosophy of Loyalty*. This concept says that we should not be loyal to causes that are divisive of other's loyalties. This requires us to not do things in the easiest possible fashion if they prevent other good causes from being advanced.

Smart Solution 13

Byron remaining loyal to his friend might prevent his company from being loyal to its customers. The smartest thing for Byron to do would be to ask Greg to go to top management and admit his error in judgment. He would have been smart to tell Greg, "I'm going to management and tell them what I know, and I suggest that you get to them before I do." Byron owed a certain amount of loyalty to his company and its reputation. He also owed loyalty to all the strangers who purchased his company's products with the belief they would receive fair value for their money.

Dilemma 14

You and two other people worked on a project that turned out quite well, and your boss was pleased with the results. You contributed the bulk of the effort and do not think it's fair that the other two share the rewards and recognition you think should go to you.

Major Thomas worked in a staff role for the Army Medical Corps. His responsibility was to train professionals and implement quality assurance programs and procedures in Army hospital and treatment centers. Major Thomas determined that an Army hospital in Virginia needed to implement a quality assurance program. He quickly earned the endorsement of the hospital's chief of nursing, who directed that the Q-A program be implemented in all departments.

However, soon thereafter, Major Thomas ran into trouble. Professional staff lower in the organization resisted the program because it involved a lot of work on their part. They were busy running the 500-bed hospital and asking them to implement a Q-A program in six months was, in their words, "out of the question."

Major Thomas pressed ahead delicately. He presented the quality assurance model to the hospital's two head nurses, who resisted at first. After hearing the Major's proposal, they liked it conceptually, but saw the enormous amount of work it would require. They had the time to implement it themselves. Major Thomas assisted the nurses as they laid the necessary groundwork for getting the program accepted and adopted throughout the hospital.

Once accepted, the effort went forward. The Major conducted training sessions. He taught hospital staff about the concepts they would be using to improve quality. He showed them how to go about getting personnel at lower level positions to boost the quality of hospital services. He explained how to handle the many problems they would surely encounter in implementing the plan.

Gradually, the two head nurses understood the techniques and began implementing them. The program took root. In time, the seeds Major Thomas planted and had so skillfully cultivated came to fruition. Hospital services improved noticeably. The nurses who had resisted earlier, but later spearheaded the effort internally, won recognition. Major Thomas faded into the background while the kudos went to others.

Major Thomas needed to decide whether he would try to get what he saw as his fair share of the credit for a successful project. It's the kind of decision most of us make practically every week. We perform a piece of work alone or alongside others and the credit goes elsewhere. But should we try to set things right?

An inordinate desire to look good can throw anyone's scale of judgment out of balance. Major Thomas should remember that while he might get the credit he wanted by asking for it, he might additionally get something else: a reputation for being self-serving.

Remove yourself from the center of your concerns.

Getting yourself off center stage is never easy. Perhaps it's impossible for us to do completely. Every great personality I have known or read about who has the capacity to remove themselves from their own concerns has been committed to serving something far greater than themselves, something far more important and enduring. These people are reverent to something they believe is supreme and sacred, and they serve it faithfully.

There is one additional point to make in connection with this process. It doesn't do any good to disregard your self. Think of it this way: We are emotional vessels who must be constantly filled. We cannot be left empty because something will always arrive to fill our minds and hearts. To consciously remove the self from the center of your concern and replacing it with "nothing" inevitably re-introduces a new version of the self back into the center. This re-introduced version cannot help but be self-sacrificing, nobler, and far better than anyone else.

How can you prevent this? The answer rests in replacing concern for self with a greater concern for something else. It is much like what happens when parents give up their own welfare or safety for the good of the child they deeply love, a child they care about more than themselves. We can primarily love ourselves, or we can commit that love to something far greater.

Smart Solution 14

Major Thomas should've taken a long, hard look at himself and studied his desires and motivations. He could've asked himself these questions: Why is getting more credit for my work so important to me? Why do I need it? Why am I upset when higher ups leave me out or when they fail to give me all the credit I think I deserve? Do I demand more credit than I should rightfully receive? Just how miserable am I making myself by worrying about not getting all the credit I want? Is this a good thing to worry about?

The second thing that would help Major Thomas is contemplating what else he might get that he doesn't want. He should know that perceptive bosses recognize a "whistle-blower" when they see one, and they generally discount them when they're considering filling an important position within the company. If he was interested in such a position, Major Thomas should resist his self-serving tendencies and instead choose to remain reticent.

Dilemma 15

A person at work took advantage of you and you are angry about it. You want to even the score, but that might cause divisions within your organization.

Geri was a financial manager for an international paper company. Her boss assigned her to work with the president's secretary to coordinate her company's relocation of headquarters personnel to new offices in another town. Geri was a conscientious, hard-working employee who would sometimes act bossy because she was tightly focused. Dee, the president's secretary, felt she worked just as diligently, but as Geri saw it, Dee spent too much time putting on make-up, or socializing out in the hallway. Geri asked Dee about some information she was to have gathered and Dee didn't have it ready. Geri told Dee that she wasn't any help and that she wasn't keeping up with her part of the workload.

Dee responded, "You have no idea how many things I have to do. You don't understand what my workload is." Dee then went to her boss, the president, and complained that Geri "makes snide comments about me every chance she gets." Geri wondered whether she should try to get back at Dee for what was said, go to the president and defend herself against Dee's charges, or to just let it all pass and do nothing.

You can feel wronged and become angry trying to decide what, if anything, to do about a similar situation. However, prudence always suggests that making any decision under anger is an unwise thing to do. Anger unbalances even the best scales of judgment; it leads one to do dumb things. It would have held Geri in better stead to recognize this simple fact, which she knew well but did not fully respect when the time came.

Develop a reputation for cool-headedness by acting calmly and rationally, especially when you come under fire.

Hotheads are regarded as a menace in organizations, because no one knows in which direction their anger will take them. It's better to suffer a wrong than to create a bad reputation for yourself by acting impulsively. You can heal from wrongs inflicted by others, but a reputation for being a hothead is rarely overlooked. Every action you take does two important things. One, it moves you in a particular direction, presumably a step closer to what you want to achieve. Two, it shapes the perceptions others have of you. The smart choice is to do only those things that advance you toward meaningful goals while simultaneously reflecting positively on your reputation.

Smart Solution 15

The smartest thing Geri could have done was to forget about Dee's childish actions. If Geri had stuck to business and said nothing, she'd have been a calming influence to those in her organization. Her energies then might have contributed to something worthwhile, and strengthened her reputation as someone who exhibits grace under pressure. Had she taken a more constructive course, perhaps she'd have been recognized as an asset to her company rather than a nasty nuisance.

Chapter 3

The Applause Meter

Pursuing high purposes rather than seeking popularity

Human beings are social creatures. They want to feel loved, needed, and respected. They want to enjoy close and lasting bonds with others. Much of what human beings do, therefore, is motivated by their desire to fulfill these wants. It isn't surprising that most people are deeply concerned about their worth in the eyes of others and that much of what they do is intended to win popularity for themselves. This presents us with enormous obstacles, because what's popular isn't always the same thing as what's smart. Every day in hundreds of ways, we face decisions about whether to pay more attention to our applause meters or our consciences.

Consider the situation that John M. Griffin, Director of Engineering for the B-2 Stealth Bomber, faced. Hundreds of people had been working around the clock preparing for the B-2's initial test flight. Everything had been tested and re-tested and "all looked good." As dawn broke on the morning of the flight, the press, congressmen, the military, and the presidents of the companies contracted to build the new bomber eagerly awaited its take off. As the plane's powerful engines began to rev up, a glitch struck. The plane's computer sensed a malfunction, switching the main fuel feed to the back-up system.

John had to make a decision: please the eager audience and let the pilot fly—the back-up system was perfectly safe—or scrub the test. John immediately halted the much-anticipated flight because he was unwilling to relinquish his principles in order to win approval from the audience.

Whenever a need for approval and the desire to be popular becomes obsessive, it can destroy your integrity and peace of mind. When observing great people in action you'll see something important: They concern themselves more with pursuing high purposes than winning the approval of others. That's the way they build admirable reputations for themselves as they pursue worthwhile accomplishments. These people concern themselves not with praise but with what's praiseworthy.

This chapter shows the methods successful people use to rise above the limiting effects of their applause meters. It will help you avoid the pitfalls you might encounter by prizing acquisition and unilateral acceptance above all else.

Dilemma 16

You have an idea for improving the way things are done where you work, but your idea conflicts with established thinking and popular, long-held beliefs.

Many years ago, a group of industrial engineers thought they'd try an untested idea. It was one of the first moves toward employee empowerment in American industry, and it took place in the painting area of a wooden toy factory. The wooden toys, carried by an endless chain of hooks, passed by eight female employees. Each sat in a ventilated booth where they would take a toy from a nearby tray and position it in a jig inside the painting cubicle, spray on the correct color, and then hang the finished toy on a passing hook. It was all very monotonous.

The women complained about their working conditions: the hooks moved too fast; the bonus incentive rates were set too high; the room was too hot. They felt they couldn't keep up with the rigorous machine-paced assembly line. However, the foreman presented an idea to install a variable speed dial that controlled the pace of the hooks. The women could then manage their own routine and set their own pace.

The women were delighted. They spent their lunch hours and breaks deciding how the speed should be varied throughout the day, and as a result, production skyrocketed. Within three weeks, the women were operating at 30 to 50 percent above their previous capacity, their earnings correspondingly increased, and their morale was equally high.

From all this, you'd think management would have been pleased enough to implement this concept throughout various other departments of the factory. But that didn't happen. The superintendent didn't agree with the idea of employees deciding their own regimen. He believed that was a decision for management, and not for the workers on the line, to make. He ordered the painting operation to return to its original status. Production dropped and within a few weeks all but two of the women had quit. The foreman stayed on for several months but he eventually left as well.

Be obedient to standards, not popular opinions.

The belief that the accepted wisdom of the day is forever valid frequently hinders progress. This kind of thinking categorically dismisses anything other than current methods as being unworkable, forbids their questioning, and discourages further experimentation. Acquiescence to those who insist on maintaining established procedures because of their popularity is an enemy of change.

The position that "what's popular is best" is untenable. What pleases people or makes them feel comfortable isn't necessarily the most effective course; thoughtful individuals can see the difference between what is popular and what is effective. Smart people, people who free the feet of progress, place correctiveness ahead of popularity.

A wise person neglects the changing and conflicting opinions of others and faithfully follows the standards that are worthy of obedience. Benjamin Franklin, whose advice shaped many minds when our nation was young, knew this. In a letter to his sister he said, "True happiness depends more upon one's own judgment of one's own self in acting properly, and with the right motivations, than upon the applause of the unthinking, undiscerning multitude, who are apt to praise him one day and condemn him the next." Do what you believe is the right thing to do, neither to earn praise nor avoid blame, but because you believe in what you are about to do.

Don't calculate the odds of winning praise.

The next time you contemplate an important action, don't ask yourself, "Will it be praised?" Instead ask, "*Should* it be praised?" No amount of favorable responses to the former can justify a negative answer to the latter. Ideally, you should be unconcerned with winning the praises of others and impervious to their criticism. This brings to mind a passage in Socrates' *The Apology*: "A man who is good for anything ought not to calculate the chance of living or dying; he ought only to consider whether in doing anything he is doing right or wrong—acting the part of a good man or of a bad."

The greatness of Abraham Lincoln is revealed by his steadfast adherence, despite the bitter attacks of the press, to what he believed to be right *and* good for the nation. When asked why he chose not to defend his actions, Lincoln said that history would be a far better judge of him than contemporary critics, and that if he were to respond to every attack, it would not be possible for him to attend to the things that really required his attention.

Smart Solution 16

The tragedy of the toy making factory is in management's unwillingness to change their methods of employee leadership. They almost got it right—productivity and morale were high—but because employee empowerment collided with previously-held notions, top management scrapped what might have become a competitive advantage. It's hard to believe that top management chose to return to old, less productive, and less satisfying methods because of their intractable beliefs. Unfortunately, the same kind of thing occurs in thousands of other workplaces whenever popular opinion refuses to bend to evidence gained from experience.

Uncompromising honesty and being impervious to such opinions give human beings the best chance to progress. Without these qualities, it's impossible to fully learn from the examples of history and further improvements.

Dilemma 17

A member of your organizational unit made comments that go against the group's values. It's caused some individuals in your unit to look for "dirt" on this person, with the hope they will receive the appropriate verbal discipline or even termination.

Rose was a 53-year-old office manager who worked for a non-profit social agency that represented abused and neglected children in court. The agency, which was funded by private donations, had a staff of eight white women. Its director reported to the agency's board chairperson, a successful, middle-aged black woman.

Rose, a high school graduate, was employed by the agency for more than 20 years, which was longer than anyone else. She had a good work record and was a skilled communicator across multiracial lines, which was significant because 80 percent of the children the agency represented were black.

Lonnie, a 20-year-old college intern, did not get along with Rose, who expected Lonnie to treat her with deference and respect. She was bossy to Lonnie, telling her what to do and exactly how to do it. Lonnie, who was dominated by an independent streak, resisted Rose's authority and avoided her as much as possible.

Once, Rose returned from lunch and a trip to the nearby post office in an angry mood, having become annoyed from waiting in long lines. Back in her office, Rose said, "Now I know why black people don't sweat. They move too slow." Lonnie, who was white and dated a black man, heard what Rose said and responded, "I guess I move too slow, too."

The other six members of the agency staff were bothered by Rose's comment and perplexed as to what should be done about it. They spent quite a bit of time gossiping among themselves, recounting the episode and taking sides in the ongoing rift between Rose and Lonnie. The agency's director brought the matter to her board's chairwoman.

Few things are as simple as they appear at first glance. Rose's emotions took the upper hand over her judgment and she lashed out with words she came to regret saying. She had good relationships with her black co-workers, but her inappropriate comment might have jeopardized those relationships for the future.

The demon of popularity drives Rose far more insidiously than the demon of stupidity; inevitably, she creates an illusion of "purity" in an effort to gain that popularity.

Every day, people try to purchase the applause of others by pointing their fingers and condemning others for their bad behavior. They use the tragic situation of someone's wrong deed to elevate themselves in the eyes of others. The louder and more viciously they exhibit their outrage, the louder and more perfect they claim to be themselves. They condemn Rose permanently, thereby making themselves feel superior alongside those doing the same.

Solve problems before they grow bigger and more troublesome.

The time to handle messy situations is before they grow and divide people into hostile camps, before their own momentum enlarges them out of proportion. Left unchecked, even minor frictions can fan themselves into unquenchable infernos.

There is a higher purpose than merely being on the "right" side of an issue. The goal of this purpose is to be a peacemaker, a healer who repairs broken relationships and makes them productive. Many people spend too much time and energy "policing" the actions of others. They look for behaviors that violate accepted standards and point out these infractions immediately.

All too often these "policemen" are motivated largely by a desire to win approval for themselves, rather than functioning as peacemakers seeking a more harmonious situation.

Smart Solution 17

The director needs for Rose to apologize for her remark and ask forgiveness from those she hurt. Rose needs to express remorse and vow not to repeat her mistake.

But this is only half of the solution. The other aspect involves stopping those who were offended by Rose's remarks from acting to further ostracize her. By failing to forgive Rose, they engage in unending rounds of retaliation that will only serve to further undermine employee morale and poison the organization's environment.

Dilemma 18

You learn that one of your subordinates may have violated company policy, and from the information you have about the matter, it appears to be true. This gives you an opportunity to impress your new boss by demonstrating you "run a tight ship."

Late one night a bicyclist inadvertently rode into the path of a city bus as it carried passengers through the countryside. Luckily Mike, the driver, spotted the cyclist in time and swerved to avoid hitting him directly. The bus grazed the cyclist, sending him skidding along the side of the highway and crashing into a low stone wall. The cyclist was badly skinned and bleeding, but conscious. Mike saw that the bus wasn't drivable.

Moments earlier, Mike had been talking to his dispatcher by portable telephone, but dropped the receiver during the excitement. Without a means to communicate, a busload of dismayed riders, and an injured cyclist on the side of the highway, Mike decided to walk to the nearest public telephone and report the accident. He believed that another bus could be dispatched to pick up his stranded passengers. Mike also reported the accident to his union steward.

En route back to his bus, Mike encountered a small child crying. The tike was lost, having wandered into a seedy part of town, where, weeks earlier, two kidnappings had occurred. Mike helped the child find his way home a half mile away—something that further delayed his return to the damaged bus.

By the time Mike got back to the accident scene, the bus and its stranded passengers were gone. There was nothing for him to do then but to return to the terminal on foot—a 45-minute walk. His shift had ended at midnight, some 30 minutes before he neared the terminal, so Mike decided to stop at a local tavern to have a quick beer, relax, and cool off.

Jennifer, the transportation director for the City Transit Authority (CTA), learned of the accident later that afternoon. She spent the following week piecing together the recommendations for her report to her newly hired superior, Arnold. Jennifer's report stated that although Mike had been an above-average driver for eight years, his performance had fallen off recently. He was suspected of drinking on the job, and, furthermore, someone had spotted him having a drink at a tavern near the CTA terminal on the afternoon of the accident. The terminal dispatcher had also reported smelling alcohol on Mike's breath later the same day. Jennifer concluded her report, citing the two relevant sections of the CTA Transportation Agreement, the violation of either resulting in automatic dismissal. Jennifer recommended that Mike be terminated immediately.

With Jennifer's report in hand and wanting to establish firm control over the CTA, Arnold called Mike into his office, read her charges and then terminated him, citing the relevant sections of the agreement.

Ask yourself this question: Am I trying to "look good" or "do good"?

A useful guideline for us to follow as we move through life is to search our souls for underlying motives. We all want to have a good reputation, do the right thing, and act with courage. However, it is deceptively easy to pursue these aims at the expense of others whose flaws and shortcomings can be exploited to our advantage.

Truth is, there are plenty of flawed people who unintentionally and unthinkingly slip up in what they say and do. These otherwise well-meaning people frequently become the targets of anyone who wants to promote their popularity. Each of us is vulnerable, because each of us is flawed in one way or another.

The desire to look good blinds accusers to interpretations regarding someone else's "bad" behavior. Those who heed the gossip travelling through the organizational grapevine join the condemnations, becoming swept up in the unproductive and divisive conflict. The only way to stop this is to prevent it from happening in the first place, and for that you need to inspect your heart and weed out motives that place "looking good" ahead of "doing good."

Smart Solution 18

This problem might have been handled better had both Jennifer and Arnold approached the situation differently. Jennifer should have worried more about the well-being of the community and the company's employees rather than her own standing in the eyes of her boss. Arnold should have suspected that, as his 'underling,' Jennifer sought to achieve his approval at the expense of others.

Dilemma 19

You observe a person in your unit performing in ways you think are inappropriate and wonder whether you should report it.

Adrienne prided herself on her work habits and positive attitude toward her employer. She always arrived early, did everything asked of her, and displayed initiative. At meetings, Adrienne supported everything her boss said, and sided with her company whenever co-workers complained about their duties. Adrienne couldn't understand why others didn't share her opinions about how employees should behave; she secretly thought the world would be a better place if there were more ethical people like herself in it.

One day, Adrienne noticed that April came to work 20 minutes late and that both April and Phyllis took an extended lunch break. While walking past their workstations, Adrienne observed that April and Phyllis were not following the prescribed work procedures. Combined with what she observed the day before, Adrienne went to her boss to complain about April and Phyllis. She told him about their tardiness, their extended lunch break, and their "incorrect" work methods.

Don't listen to tattletales.

Once tattletales get going, it's hard to stop them. However, the problem lies with those who give them credibility, who encourage them to maintain such behavior. The truly misguided person is the one who rewards tattletales and feeds their need for applause by listening to what they say and acting on the information.

Merely relaying stories is bad enough, but something else happens that's even uglier. Proficient tattletales know how to embellish their stories. They make those they talk about sound worse than they really are. Meanwhile, they portray themselves as innocent victims who are correct in carrying important information to those willing to listen. In so doing, tattletales destroy. In so doing, tattletales ruin relationships and turn people against each other.

Smart Solution 19

There is an old saying: "When a stray cat shows up outside your door, don't feed it. Maybe it will just go away." This same idea can be applied to Adrienne. Don't listen; don't feed your need to feel superior by gaining your boss's approval. Adrienne, unfortunately, isn't the slightest bit interested in self change, but the person who ignores similarly empty office banter can go a long way to halting the flow of misinformation and hurtful gossip.

Dilemma 20

One of your subordinates voiced an opinion in a meeting that contradicts the practices you've insisted on for many years. This person appears to have relevant facts and a reasonably credible argument but is not well accepted by others.

Kent was a loner who didn't engage in office watercooler talk or company politics, preferring to stay in his office working on his assignments. Kent also looked at things differently than others around him, and this bothered many. He ideas were well-conceived and informed with sound logic; however, he sometimes irritated others who disagreed with him when he pointed out their own fallacies. He won arguments but lost friends. Still, management rightfully accepted Kent and held on to him because he was a useful employee with a good record.

In the morning meeting, Kent proposed a radical way of handling a customer service problem. His suggestion sprung from a set of assumptions different from the unquestioned parameters held by his firm's management.

When Kent proposed his ideas, most thought he had suddenly become a dry-humored comic. However, Kent was serious, and the more he spoke, the more those present became uncomfortable, since Kent's propositions exposed potential weakness in management. More troubling was that their arguments rebutting Kent continued to paint management in an unflattering light.

Most people don't like to acknowledge their own flaws, because it leads them to become defensive and hostile. This is what those present at Kent's meeting were tended to do. Rather than pursuing a direction of honesty by facing up to their shortcomings, they want to turn against the unpopular Kent, making him into the "bad guy."

Listen. You might hear something useful.

Many managers never get the benefit of an opinion other than their own, and when they do, often they move to hush it up. There is a strong tendency to resist that which reveals how incorrect we are. In organizational settings, popular opinions, the accepted patterns of thought, are rarely questioned or challenged. When they are, the person risks being labeled as disloyal, perhaps even a troublemaker. What is the best manner with which to gauge opposing, differing ideas? Encourage the presenters of those ideas—and listen.

Entertain diverse points of view.

You have to be of mature, tolerable character to accept disagreement while simultaneously entertaining diverse points of view. Tex Thornton, the driving force who pieced together the "Whiz Kids" for the Ford Motor Company and later built Litton Industries into a large-scale enterprise, was one person who insisted on honest thinking. He encouraged dissent from his inner circle of trusted associates.

Thornton didn't allow "committee thinking." He demanded that everyone form and express their own opinions. He once said, "I had a boss who made a wrong decision, and I decided to tell him so. He said he judged the loyalty of subordinates by how well they carried out his wrong decisions. I judge their loyalty by how well they tell me I'm wrong."

Thomas J. Watson, Jr., former chief executive of IBM, understood the importance of hearing the ideas of others. "I never hesitated to promote someone I didn't like," he explained. "The comfortable assistant, the guy you like to go on fishing trips with, is a great pitfall. Instead, I looked for those sharp, scratchy, harsh, almost unpleasant guys who see and tell you about things as they really are. If you can get enough of them around you and have the patience enough to hear them out, there is no limit to where you can go."

Learn from what others have to say.

I came across an account of a highly successful entrepreneur named Jo-Anne Dressendofer who headed up a 30-person marketing firm, Imedia, in Morristown, New Jersey. She didn't allow her ego to shut off a source of useful ideas, but instead, listened to what her employees told her, and it proved beneficial.

When you are in a position of power, it's natural to want to hold on to that power, but this brings on conflict. Fighting for complete control gobbles up valuable energy that could be applied more productively elsewhere. Jo-Anne thought she ran a non-hierarchical company.

The truth was that Imedia suffered from an inordinate CEO supremacy. Jo-Anne called all the shots, though she didn't fully realize it. Then she met the unexpected. Fed up with her autocracy, seven employees, hungry for autonomy, confronted Jo-Anne in her office with an ultimatum: either loosen the reins or they would quit. It was a rude awakening and difficult to bear, yet, Jo-Anne listened.

But the benefits gained from altering her methods overshadowed her slightly bruised ego. Over the months that followed, groups met and discussed how they could better run the company. The idea was to keep the organizational hierarchy intact, but not allow status and authority to stifle creative ideas or stop their momentum. Groups of employees would be responsible for most operational matters, and Jo-Anne found it unnecessary to approve every decision personally. A year into the change, business increased by $1 million.

Smart Solution 20

Management should have listened with an open mind to what Kent proposed. They should have nurtured an atmosphere where diverse views are not merely acceptable but highly desirable. They should guard against allowing popular opinion to rule over an honest search for internal resolutions. This is yet one more situation where integrity of leadership becomes the differentiating ingredient between mediocrity and excellence.

Dilemma 21

You went out on a limb to help a friend who later let you down. You are angry about it and wonder what you should do to regain your credibility.

There was an opening for a position at Joyce's employer that paid more than the position her friend Cindy held. Cindy asked Joyce if she could help her get the job. Joyce said she would and proceeded to speak to the supervisor of the relevant department, telling her how reliable Cindy was. The supervisor agreed to interview Cindy.

Based on Joyce's recommendation, Cindy got the job, but after only a week decided she didn't like it and quit. Due to this, Joyce felt her coworkers lost respect for her, and that her credibility was shot with management as well. She wondered if she should apologize to her supervisor for recommending Cindy.

Sticking your neck out to help others can be risky, and Joyce found this out when she tried to do a favor for her friend. Understandably, Joyce wants to hold on to two things in this situation: her friendship with Cindy and her reputation with co-workers and management alike. Many people will badly handle situations like these by vowing never to help a friend or associate again because of the requisite risks.

Listen to both sides of a dispute before deciding what to do.

Nothing is ever as simple as it might first appear. By simply observing someone's facial expression, we might draw a (possibly hasty) conclusion about what's going on inside that person's head. Or we hear a story that portrays someone in a bad light and we are inclined to immediately accept it as truth without making an attempt to investigate the facts without obtaining information from both sides. Arriving at a misinformed conclusion is nearly always a big mistake. Whenever someone tells a disparaging story about someone else, it's a reasonable thing to assume that the narrator is putting his or her own spin to the story, distorting the facts. Certainly, prudence suggests it's ill-advised to make hasty judgements and seek a course of action based solely on a single, unsubstantiated opinion.

Help others, but don't be used by them.

We are here to make life better not only for ourselves but also for friends, neighbors, and strangers alike. However, helping an individual for the express purpose of "purchasing" their friendship demonstrates a contemptuous intent on their part. Their actions could be authentic, arising from altruistic motives, from the sheer desire to give, but motivations for such actions could arise from unhealthy sources as well.

Smart Solution 21

Joyce should go to Cindy and find out why she quit. Making assumptions about the nature of Cindy's reasoning could only prove to be a mistake on Joyce's part. It could well be that Cindy was mistreated or that the duties of the position itself were miscommunicated to her upon her initial interview.

Regardless of the reasons for Cindy's sudden departure, the issue at stake for Joyce was that a perfectly legitimate reason might have existed to force Cindy's decision, and the particulars of this information were beneficial for Joyce.

Nevertheless, despite the awkwardness of her position in relation to Cindy, it remains important that Joyce still "square things" with her supervisor. If Cindy was irresponsible, apologies from Joyce would go a long way to reasserting her professionalism and assuaging her supervisor's concern that her judgement in personnel is poor.

Joyce is better off aligning herself with high standards and a solid ethical foundation than with questionable "friend" who might have placed her in an awkward position. If Cindy quit for substantial reasons, Joyce will earn respect for her actions if her supervisor is explained the reasons behind her choice of Cindy.

Joyce also needs to make it clear to Cindy that her sudden departure was both irresponsible and terribly unprofessional. Even though Cindy might have felt she had good reason to quit, her quitting jeopardizes Joyce's reputation with her supervisor. Putting aside the temporary discomfort arising from the situation, Joyce's confronting Cindy helps to repair her relationship with her friend, search out the facts, and armed with those facts, prevent her from succumbing to similar traps in the future.

Chapter 4

The Fool's Gold

Earning yourself a 24-karat reputation

Many years ago, B.C. Forbes, who started *Forbes* magazine, interviewed John D. Rockefeller, the most remarkable man the world of business has ever produced. Rockefeller told Forbes, "The most important thing for a young man starting life to do is to establish a credit, a reputation, character. He must inspire the complete confidence of others."

Do you want to have the full confidence of everyone you deal with? Do you want others to consider your word to be as good as gold? Do you want to live above the trouble and pettiness that enter into people's lives, eating up their time and energy? Of course you do. Everyone does. These are the kinds of things a priceless reputation brings.

Every waking hour, and in countless ways, you are earning a reputation by your actions. You can earn a cheap one as worthless as a wooden nickel or one highly-valued. A good reputation is not just a desirable aspiration, it's a real possibility.

The most effective way to earn a priceless reputation is to observe the guardrails civilization erected from the combined experiences of human beings throughout recorded history. This chapter will show you how you can handle difficult situations intelligently enough to earn you a 24-karat reputation that will last forever.

Dilemma 22

You were overpaid for a job because of a billing mistake to a client.

Robin supported herself and her three small children. Her former husband had abandoned the family and since then, Robin found employment with a temporary agency. Every penny she earned went out as fast as it came in. One of her children needed glasses, so Robin charged them on her credit card. She had no choice at the time and wondered how she'd ever be able to pay the bill. Then, a "windfall" came to Robin. She noticed an extra $78 in her biweekly paycheck that she suspected was a mistake. She checked her pay stub and found it showed more hours worked than the client should have been billed for.

Robin faced the temptation of doing what she knows is wrong to get something she desperately wanted. Anyone who has lived long in the thick of life has faced this kind of situation. You know the full range of conflicting thoughts that race through your mind as you try to decide what to do—the wrong thing or the honorable thing. Inevitably, rationalizations come to rule the day: The more you dwell on what you want, the more your want becomes a desire, then ultimately something you need as a means to offset all the terrible things that have befallen you.

If she's seriously tempted to hold the money, Robin's rationale might be, "Who will ever know that I kept this money? If nobody ever finds out, what's the harm?" Hopefully, her better side will reason that her decision to keep the money and capitalize on the company's error could result in various, negative repercussions.

Weather temptations by anchoring yourself to high standards.

Off the coast of Labrador float huge icebergs towering 300 to 400 feet into the air. Sailors have reported them moving south directly into strong headwinds—some gales were up to 50 knots—yet, the icebergs sail on. The secret lies in the fact that 7/8 of an iceberg is submerged.

The great Labrador current flows strongly toward the south, gripping the frozen behemoths and carrying them onward no matter how the surface winds blow. So it is with human beings. Lives disciplined in the art of establishing standards and maintaining them are unaffected by tempting winds. J.C. Penney put it this way: "Second-rate standards never make a first-rate person."

The truth always come out. Do the right thing.

The media had learned of a major scandal involving a company that had gotten itself into serious trouble. The authorities caught the firm selling products composed of synthetic ingredients instead of the natural apple juice concentrate their buyers expected. This sordid affair began after the Beech-Nut Nutrition Corporation found itself stripped of its best money-making products. Squibb, the parent company, sold off the most profitable divisions to raise cash, leaving the baby food division the sole remaining department. This division almost never earned a profit, while arch-rival Gerber enjoyed a 70 percent market share. With only a 15 percent share of the market, Beech-Nut could not match Gerber's advertising outlays. Finally, Squibb sold the baby food division to an investment group.

The new owners borrowed heavily to purchase the company. This huge debt placed added importance on profitability. As costs were cut to increase profits, management searched for areas to trim. They discovered that 30 percent of the company's sales came from products containing apple concentrate. The new owners looked for a low-cost supplier and found the: Interjuice Trading Corporation, whose prices for apple concentrate were 20 percent below market value. Profit pressures became too great for the owners to purchase the concentrate anywhere else, so they bought from Interjuice.

The research and development people at Beech-Nut were suspicious when they learned of the bargain prices. Voicing concern, their director wrote to the investment firm's top management. Senior officials ignored the memo. Years later, however, the truth came out. What was supposed to have been pure apple juice concentrate was a synthetic blend, a chemical cocktail blended with real juice. Several Beech-Nut executives pleaded guilty to 215 felony counts; they had violated food and drug laws by selling adulterated apple products. People who choose to ignore the right path invite trouble.

Smart Solution 22

The smart thing for Robin to do was to report the error immediately and return the check. Her boss and fellow employees will value her as a person to be trusted. Upper management will in turn value her choice of action, respecting the fact she examined her difficulty with honesty and resolved the problem with clean hands and composure.

Dilemma 23

Profit pressures in your line of work are enormous, as management continually pushes for tougher bottom-line targets. You feel caught between doing what's demanded or losing out to others who are eager to move ahead.

An eager young stockbroker named Caleb Warren spent many of his spare moments at work charting companies' performances, looking for good investment opportunities for his clients. One day while he pored over his pads of notes, a manager walked by, noticed what Caleb was doing, grabbed the pencil from his hand, and broke it. "That's for our research department," the manager snapped. "Your job is to sell!"

Caleb was momentarily taken aback by the manager's reaction. He was certain of one thing: The practice of "pushing" his firm's in-house products to earn handsome commissions didn't set well with him. In the years that followed, he went to work for two other brokerage houses, but their marketing practices were little different: Brokers were to produce commissions, even though the products didn't benefit customers. The compensation systems at these brokerage firms were all geared along the same lines. Sales contests that paid higher commissions led brokers to sell customers unsuitable products. The net result was that brokerage houses were increasingly manned by sales-oriented brokers who were out not to increase the value of their clients' portfolios but to make money for themselves.

Too often, business fails to get the best out of its bright, capable young employees because too much pressure is placed on them to produce benefits for themselves instead of their customers. Everyone likes to earn a good living, but not everyone is willing to do it at the expense of fairness. Businesses can destroy this sense of employee fairness if they are careless. Enlightened companies structure work and rewards so that employees are not made selfish. They arrange conditions so their employees can work for their own self-interest and create value for customers simultaneously. Firms pay employees for providing customers with genuine value, and employees feel good about the value they've passed on.

Never mislead others into ways that are harmful to themselves.

A number of years ago, *Days of Wine and Roses*, a popular motion picture starring Jack Lemmon and Lee Remick, illustrated the idea of how harmful it is for a person to lead another into self-destruction. The film was about two young people and the tragedies they experienced. Each person was attractive and talented, and great possibilities laid ahead for both. Joe, played by Jack Lemmon, had one flaw: He wanted too much to have a good time. Added to this, he had an overpowering capacity to convince and his charm was irresistible. At first, he enjoyed having just a few social drinks, but after a while, those drinks became a few too many. Lee Remick's Kirsten had not grown up with alcohol; hers was a well-ordered life of sobriety and respectability. But all that changed after Joe and Kirsten were married. Joe, and then Kirsten, turned from social drinker, to lush, to alcoholic.

Unchecked, each character moved down the path towards hopelessness. But something deep within Joe awoke to the problem he had brought upon himself. He realized he needed help and turned to friends who helped him overcome his illness, and slowly he regained his self-respect, his dignity, and his life. But this was not to be with Kirsten. She was unable to commit to sobriety. As the film ended, viewers knew that her life would forever be destroyed by alcoholism, a disease from which she had not the will to escape.

It is one thing to harm another person; it is quite another thing to lead another person into harming themselves. An individual can always choose to change, but no one has the power to make another person choose to change. That choice comes from within and can only arise if the wayward individual freely chooses it. This is why some organizations, and those responsible for their policies, should take great care not to mislead employees into areas that are harmful to themselves.

Establish high standards and make following these standards the most important thing you ask your employees to do.

Tom Phillips, who headed up Raytheon as its CEO, told me of an instance when high standards saved a man in his company from almost certain ruin. During meetings at which plans were being devised to win contracts abroad, Phillips felt a strange sensation overtake him. He thought there just might be too much pressure on his people to make profits for the company. Something said to him that maybe he ought to temper the company's competitive tone with words of caution.

So, he told the company officers present, "We don't want any *dirty* money at Raytheon of any description. And, if you ever get into a situation where you have to give or get *dirty* money in order to win some business, the only proper thing to do is not to win that business; it is to bow out completely. And, when you come back and tell your boss that's the reason you had to get out, that will be perfectly acceptable with Raytheon."

A few years later he learned that one Raytheon executive who was edging very close to getting into trouble heeded Tom's warning. This man made the right decision, which spared both his company and himself from scandal.

Smart Solution 23

After several years of pressure to produce bottom-line results, Caleb quit his job. He formed his own money-management firm. He didn't collect commissions any more from what he sold his clients, but instead collected a monthly fee based on the value of their portfolios. The more his clients earned, the more he made. It was a win-win arrangement for both, as Caleb's pay increased in proportion to the value he generated for his clients.

Dilemma 24

You discover some minor wrongdoing within your organization that should be stopped immediately, but doing so is a problem. Stopping it requires making the matter public, which could be highly embarrassing. But ignoring the problem and trying to cover it up could lead to a bigger difficulty—if the problem is discovered later, you'll be accused of being a party to it.

As field superintendent for a construction company, Scott's responsibilities encompassed everything that took place on job sites. Scott was a top-notch performer; his employees gave their best for him and he always completed projects on time and within budget. Scott also served on his organization's safety committee, an advisory panel made up of representatives throughout the company. This group had chosen Scott to serve as chairman of its safety committee, reviewing records and setting standards and policies for employees to follow.

Scott didn't always agree with the overly strict safety policies regarding the wearing of protective equipment such as hard hats, gloves, and safety glasses. Employees working on site generally abided by their employer's safety code anyway. They kept their hard hats on when they were in construction areas but they didn't always wear safety glasses when they were in restricted areas that were some distance from direct hazards.

One day, a freak event injured an employee. A truck traveling on a gravel road passed by an employee when one of the truck's tires kicked up a stone, hurling it into the employee's right eye. At the local hospital, doctors found the eye bruised and swollen, but otherwise alright. The supervisor sent the employee home without filing a report, fearing it would count against them in an on-going safety contest. Scott heard about the incident, but didn't give it much thought.

History is lavish with examples of people who unfortunately miscalculated by covering their tracks. Sooner or later, the truth comes out anyway. The smart thing to do whenever you consider covering something up is to move in the opposite direction, to reveal the truth. Open disclosure is the best way to avoid a guilty conscience. Openness removes doubts, suspicions, and the chance that false accusations might arise from those around you.

Step in and correct problem spots immediately.

Lockheed's former chairman and CEO, Roy Anderson, told me about a situation he faced. Lockheed was bidding on an overseas job, a major contract worth millions of dollars. A competitor called who was bothered by the fact that Lockheed, through a business consultant, had gotten hold of his company's original proposal for the contract. This was the first time Anderson heard of such a thing, and he agreed to look into the matter.

Anderson immediately called the division involved. "Was this true? Do you have a copy of our competitor's proposal?" They did. Then Anderson asked them, "Do you think that it's fair for you to be making a proposal?" Lockheed returned the competitor's original and withdrew from the bidding.

The foreign government that had invited competitive bids came back to Lockheed and said, "We want you to make a proposal." So Anderson called the competitor back., "They are after me to make a proposal. What do you want me to do?" The two talked for a while and agreed on a solution. Anderson went to the foreign government, and told them Lockheed would not make a proposal unless their competitor was likewise invited to submit a new one.

Get the truth out immediately.

"Tell them the truth," said Paul Galvin, founder of Motorola, who insisted on honesty and fair play. "First, because it's right, and second, they'll find out anyway if you don't. If they don't find it out from us, we'll be the ones to suffer." The truth always comes into view; therefore, it makes good sense to expose it, and the sooner done, the better.

David Kearns, who ran Xerox, told me, "Our experience has been that you're better off getting the truth out because in the long run it's best for the company. I also think it's right. From an overall relationship perspective, you're better off. If you are up front with things you can deal with them much better."

Don't rely on excuses. Fix problems immediately.

In 1987, a scathing story broke about Chrysler. It was something that could have erupted into a major scandal for the giant automaker, which was struggling to survive. It had been learned that up until October of 1986, managers at assembly plants had been driving new cars home to sample production quality. These cars had been sent to dealers and sold as new, who were unaware plant employees had driven them up to 400 miles. This was not all: Some of the cars had been damaged during testing. These vehicles were repaired, sent to dealer showrooms, and sold as new.

A cynical press was on hand when Chrysler chairman and CEO Lee Iacocca appeared at a news conference to discuss charges of hoodwinking customers. Iacocca didn't skirt the issue; he faced it head-on with candor and contriteness: "Did we screw up?" he asked, rhetorically. "You bet we did." He admitted Chrysler employees had disconnected odometers on over 60,000 test cars. This, Iacocca said, "went beyond dumb and reached way out to stupid." The chairman didn't stop there. The next morning, two-page ads appeared in major newspapers admitting the mistake: "Testing cars is a good idea. Disconnecting odometers is a lousy idea. That's a mistake we won't make again at Chrysler. Period."

To make things right with buyers who had purchased the suspect vehicles, Chrysler extended warranties to include brakes, suspension, air conditioning, electrical and steering. They also offered free inspections and to replace any vehicle that was damaged in testing with a new 1987 model of comparable value.

Smart Solution 24

Scott would have destroyed his credibility if he covered up the accident. Doing so would have also created a disregard for safety rules, the consequences of which might have been disastrous. The smart thing for Scott to do would have been to come clean and report everything as it happened. By doing that he'd have earned a better reputation and helped promote conscientious behavior on the part of his employees.

Dilemma 25

Your boss assigned you to perform an important task, and you botched the job because of a stupid mistake. You can try to escape responsibility by shifting blame to others and identifying conditions that led to the failure.

Frank owned and operated a small firm that made and installed imitation marble bathroom sinks and shower enclosures. He spent most of his workday in the field doing installations. He employed crew to make the sinks and enclosure materials and to label and pack his truck with the correct items to be installed. Frank depended on his people to take work orders and ensure that all the necessary materials needed were labeled and correctly loaded on time. This had to be done correctly because job sites were often located many miles from the business.

Dave, one of Frank's employees, misread an order and loaded the wrong color bathroom sink backsplash for a job. Frank discovered the mistake the following day and could not complete the job because of it. When he returned to his plant, Frank asked his employees who loaded the truck. Tom, who also works for Frank said, "I think Dave did." Frank asked Dave, who said it was Stan, who had just quit the day before. Frank walked away shaking his head.

You make a mistake your boss discovers, but he is unaware you are the culprit. Should you avoid taking the blame? This is the predicament Dave faced. He tried to push the blame off on Stan, a person who quit the day before. Frank can't do anything to Stan, who's gone, and he can't prove that Dave or Tom is to blame, either.

Most everyone engages in a process known as impression management. This involves people who try to make others view them favorably, often setting their sights on those higher up in the organization. When something turns out well, they reach for the lion's share of the recognition and rewards. When something turns bad, they produce excuses to minimize their responsibility. It sounds childish, but adults in the workplace do it every day and they do it very well. And, although it might provide instant gratification, impression management usually won't engender a good reputation for you in the long run.

Don't let clouds of doubt accumulate above you.

Your reputation is formed by more than just what you do. It's also formed by the troubles that surround you and by those with whom you associate. It's not enough to be blame free. A good reputation can be spoiled by honest doubt that arises because of unwanted troubles or from undesirable associates. The best way to prevent the formation of a cloud of doubt is to stay apart from undesirable types and be totally up front with others when you're to blame. By accepting responsibility, others will not suspect you are at the root of the problem, and they'll be quicker to forget about it when you are.

When you make a mistake, admit it immediately and fix it.

Everyone makes mistakes from time to time—the smart thing to do is, when one occurs, admit responsibility. Douglas Danforth, who ran Westinghouse Corporation for many years, told me he created a climate of trust between himself and those whom he answered to by being completely open. "When I make a mistake, I tell them I made a mistake. They love it, and they are more supportive of me than if I tried to hide it. I clearly think it's a much better policy. And you sleep better."

Jack Reichert, who headed up the Brunswick Corporation, was one of the most ethical and financially savvy businessmen I ever met. He did many things that demonstrated both a commitment to quality and the importance of meeting obligations to customers. Several years ago, Brunswick came out with a new, high performance bowling ball, which proved to be an instant success. Professionals used them to win tournaments. The country's best bowlers endorsed them with glowing praise. But success was short lived. The balls were susceptible to heat; left in the trunk of a car on a hot day, the cover would soften. Upon learning of the problem, Jack responded immediately. "Recall every ball." Managers scurried in with their calculations: it could cost Brunswick over a million dollars. Reichert insisted: "Recall them all with a full cash refund to customers." His words throughout the ordeal effectively were, "If our name means anything to a customer, it means that when we make a mistake, we've got to pay for it."

Smart Solution 25

What bothered Frank was not the mistake that was made, but the blatant denials of it by his employees. He lost respect for them because they tried to escape responsibility for their actions. He could tolerate a mistake, but he couldn't tolerate listless excuses and displacement of blame, something which casted doubt on a person's credibility.

Dave would have been better off if he simply admitted to the mistake. In so doing, he'd have removed a burden from his mind and given Frank reason to believe he could be trusted to not repeat the mistake again. Anyone in Frank's situation might consider this: Would you have continued trust and respect for a person who freely admits an error? Most would be wise to say yes.

Dilemma 26

Sales are slow because competition is intense and your product does not have the competitive edge it once enjoyed in the marketplace. You think you can draw customers away from your rival's products and gain much-needed sales by telling them about flaws in your competitor's products and services.

Springbank was a small, stable community located in the Midwest. Its population growth rate was scarcely 1 percent annually; the surrounding region doesn't grow any faster, either. Real estate sales are slow and agents have great difficulty making a living. Rusty worked for a national chain that had good name recognition. The firm pioneered the use of national advertising and data-based computer listings. It also developed close working relationships with lenders, which helped make financing easier for customers. But eventually, competing firms offered the same services. Because of this, agents tried anything to get listings and draw potential buyers to their firms. Rusty kept tabs on who had what listings and if a property listed by another agency didn't sell, he telephoned the owner a month before the agreement expired and tried to get the seller to switch to his agency. Rusty pointed out his competitor's shortcomings and promised immediate results if the seller listed his property with him.

It is deceptively easy to harm your reputation by the single-minded drive to get what you want. Everything you do or say adds to your reputation. You may get what you want by a particular action, but at what cost? By saying bad things about his competitor, Rusty might get a new listing, but at the expense of being seen as someone who poisons both another's reputation and his own.

Promote your products by praising their performance qualities, not by bad mouthing your competitor's wares.

A number of years ago, salespeople at Levi Strauss & Company came to their superiors with a problem. The sales force of a competitor was telling retailers untrue stories about Levi's, that the quality of Levi products was dropping and that the organization was not supporting its product or promises of delivery. The apparel industry being hotly competitive, a mere one percentage point shift in sales makes a huge difference in bottom-line results. The Levi organization had a long-held tradition of not "trashing" its competition. In fact, they had then (and still do now) a policy of not badmouthing their competitors or their competitors' products. Nevertheless, in the face of this competitor's tactics, Levi's sales were being harmed. What were Levi's salespeople to do—stand by and let it happen or retaliate in a similar manner?

We all have had this same sort of thing happen to us. Our natural reaction is to fight back, so we go on the attack. But Levi's chose a different philosophy—one grounded in the wisdom of not resorting to dirty tricks.

I recall an appropriate piece of advice that applies: It never pays to kick a skunk. Don't get down in the gutter and fight because you'll get dirty in the process. It is far better to compete in a realm that really matters—product quality and customer service. That's what Levi's top management decided. They decided, "Don't say anything negative about the competition. Let Levi quality and dependability reveal itself. Point out our product's quality to the retailers. Demonstrate to them through what we do that we are reliable. Let our product quality and our actions speak for themselves."

Attract customers by your positive actions.

Once while shopping at my local Ace Hardware store, where I've traded for 25 years, I overheard a woman looking for storeowner Jeff MacDonald. She wanted to purchase a plastic birdfeeder, but was bothered by the fact that it had been on a back shelf so long that the box was dusty and contained dead insects. She wanted to know if Jeff would reduce the price. Jeff looked at the box and readily agreed with her that, indeed, it was dirty and the dead insects were unpleasant to look at. He then checked his price book and told the woman he'd gladly knock off a few dollars. Jeff got the sale, turned the slow-to-sell item in his inventory, and made a potential cynic into a happy customer. It was better than advertising; for a few dollars, he earned the loyalty of a customer, one who will think about her wonderful bargain every time she drives past Oxford's Ace Hardware store.

Smart Solution 26

Rusty should work as hard at developing a good reputation as he did getting listings and selling properties. There's nothing wrong about aggressively promoting yourself, but it should never be done by badmouthing one's competitor. When this becomes the pattern of competition, two terrible results occur. Competition becomes more a matter of pointing out a rival's flaws than of providing superior quality products and services. And competitors are not inspired so much to improve as they are to find fault with their rivals. This is much like the feeling you get when going to the polls on election day to vote for the lesser of two evils.

Rusty should develop unique strategies that his rival cannot hope to duplicate, strategies he can then tout as he attempts to obtain new listings. By becoming a superior performer instead of a better "badmouther," Rusty could make himself more competitive and secure a superior reputation in the process.

Dilemma 27

Your realize that a job you promised will not be completed on time or within budget. It's supposed to be a team effort but there isn't any teamwork; people just don't get along. As a result, the assigned project is in deep trouble. You try to think of ways to keep yourself from looking bad by blaming people from other departments, whose full and careful cooperation you did not receive and whose help would have made the difference.

Jack was a plant manager for a sizable firm that contracted to manufacture parts and assemblies for equipment makers. His firm made many of the parts that went into the machines that assembled paper cartons and bottling equipment, as well as other machinery used in various manufacturing processes. Some of the parts Jack's plant produced were fairly standard; they churned them out by the hundreds. Customers began lodging complaints about problems they were experiencing with certain new parts. Jack dispatched his technical services team to identify the problem and found that it resulted from a design error. He promised to rectify the matter and have redesigned parts shipped within three months' time.

Jack realized that he was not going to meet his promised delivery date. He wanted to blame the corporate engineering staff for taking so long redesigning the part and preparing the drawings shop workers needed. He wanted to blame purchasing and procurement for telling engineering about parts that were unavailable, which inevitably caused further delays because engineering had to rework their initial designs. And Jack wanted to blame his own production planning and scheduling people for starting a long production run that would go well into a successive month.

Jack's situation exemplified an important aspect of the modern workplace—the dependency on others to see goals realized. Organizations are really complex networks of specialized contributors. The quality of overall performance is directly tied to how well the separate parts work together. Organization and coordination make the difference between ordinary and extraordinary performance. One of the biggest sources of coordination problems in organizations is the independent desires of each unit to both look good and make its work demands bearable. This can be seen when people, in response to customer pressures, promise more than their organization can deliver.

Promise only what you have control over, otherwise you'll create inter-unit conflict.

An organization might be able to fulfill promises they can't keep from time to time, but not from multiple directions at once. The more people in specialized units want to look good, the more they put pressure on all other parts of the organization. Whenever performance fails to live up to promises, blame is assigned and badmouthing commences, which sour the relationships needed for effective organizational performance. This diminishes one's reputation not just with customers, but also within. Interdepartmental feuding makes cooperation and teamwork harder to achieve.

Show concern for those who depend on you.

A dapper, fast-talking salesman called on a young grocer named Barney, trying to sell him canned corn. The salesman had a convincing routine; he was especially proud of the fancy label on the can. Customers wouldn't be able to resist it, he told Barney, who decided to give the salesman's product a chance. Barney had a small stove at the rear of his store where he brewed tea and tested products. As he walked to the back, he tore off the fancy label and deliberately threw it on the floor. "My customers don't eat labels," he told the salesman, just to make a point. "They eat what's inside." Barney opened the can—it was full of hulls! He sent the salesman on his way without an order. Word spread and Barney Kroger's—of the Kroger supermarket chain—business grew.

Smart Solution 27

Before Jack promised something to a customer, he should have approached the other departments to get their okay. He should never have promised things to others without first asking those whose help he needed. If he promised things that he needed others to help him with, and later found those others were unable or unwilling to help him, he certainly should not subsequently push any blame on them. This is a certain irritant to anyone involved, and could be a sure-fire way to ruin his reputation with his co-workers by cutting off their goodwill and losing their future cooperation.

Dilemma 28

You can probably get something you want by not revealing the entire truth about a situation.

Beth marketed medical diagnostic equipment for a Fortune 500 company. She called on clinics and hospitals to sell her products. Rival firms had similar products, making competition for sales intense. Beth was on commission—her pay depended entirely on her performance, as selling sophisticated equipment required patience and discipline. She also knew a typical representative spent considerable time cultivating customers. Plus, the selling cycle was slow, often taking several months, sometimes a year. You had to educate the buyer about the product and what it could do. This salesline was not for people who were unable to work hard or couldn't wait forever for sales to develop.

Beth worked hard, making numerous time-consuming calls and hoping to sell to a major hospital the largest and most expensive piece of equipment her firm had. A few days before the hospital told Beth that they decided to go ahead with the purchase, Beth learned that her firm was having difficulties with the unit. She learned that reports coming from other locations told of problems users were experiencing with the equipment she hoped to sell. When Beth entered the conference room where the procurement personnel were signing the final papers, she wondered whether she should say anything.

Beth brought a customer to the brink of buying her firm's equipment, and then she found a huge glitch that put the sale on hold or destroyed its chances altogether. She wanted the fat commission the sale would bring, and she wondered whether she should spill the beans and risk not losing it. In her mind, it was a matter of getting what she wanted versus telling the hospital's purchasing people the full truth and losing a sale she worked hard to get.

At one time or another, we all face situations similar to the one Beth faced. To look at such things in an immediate time frame is a huge mistake. Getting a much-wanted result immediately would diminish or even eliminate the possibilities of getting results in the years ahead. Beth's commission was not the only thing hanging in the balance as she entered the conference room; she could be signing away her reputation not with just the hospital but with many other potential customers the hospital purchasing people deal with. Those who get raw deals often tell many others about them, and in very angry ways.

Earn respect by being completely open. It will give you a good reputation and save you from unwanted suspicion in the future.

The Caterpillar Tractor Company was accused by one of its competitors of "dumping" in the French and Spanish markets. "Dumping" in this context meant selling products in foreign markets for less than what it cost to make them. By producing large volumes of product, average costs are lowered because fixed costs are spread over a larger number of products. This allows firms to capture a higher gross margin on products sold at home, which more than offsets the small loss incurred from those "dumped" abroad.

The French equivalent of the IRS received the charges against Caterpillar and decided to investigate the matter. The French government's auditors went to Caterpillar's European manager in France, where the machinery was being produced. They told Caterpillar, "We can ask for the invoices of your French dealer and the invoices the product manufactured for the Spanish dealer, but we can't ask for their customer invoices or the invoices to your selling agent in Geneva. If we could get the invoices all the way down the chain, then we could have the whole story, but we can't legally ask for that."

Caterpillar's European manager dealt with their request with openness, telling the auditors, "You can have anything you want. I will give you the serial number of any machine that's been manufactured here which we have sold to our merchandising company in Geneva, which in turn has sold it to our dealers in France or Spain. And then, if you want, I'll give you the dealer/customer invoice."

The French officials asked, "Can you get that kind of control from your dealer?" The European manager said, "They'll respond if we request it, because we review the dealer's transactions. We want to be sure that everything is going as it should be." The French officials got the information they needed and decided that the charges had no merit. They dismissed the complaints. The officials resolved in a matter of days what could have dragged on in the courts for years and, in the process, sullied many otherwise fine reputations.

Smart Solution 28

The smartest move Beth could have made was to be completely candid. She should have told the hospital purchasing personnel what she knew. She also should have asked them to put the sale on hold until her company assured her the equipment was trouble-free.

Beth's concern for her customers' satisfaction would have determined her long-term success in selling equipment to them, earned her a good reputation, and won their confidence to purchase from her in the future because of the goodwill she generated.

Dilemma 29

Your group is behind schedule on a major assignment. Everyone will have to pitch in and work extra hours to complete the project on time. But this will interfere with other plans you have for the weekend.

Diana was a member of her company's customer service improvement team. The group's purpose was to identify failure points and then recommend solutions on how to fix them. The first phase involved surveying customers by means of questionnaire and telephone interviews to identify and learn the nature of trouble spots. Once collected, the data needed to be examined and discussed to more fully understand the nature and possible problems.

The examination time involved lengthy meetings, which frequently extended beyond normal working hours. Because the committee needed to finish the first phase of its work in a week's time, its members had to spend most of the upcoming weekend completing their discussions for the interim report. Diana had a ski trip planned for that time and felt backing out of it now would be a big imposition on her friends. She felt the committee could do its work without her help.

Were this a case of merely having to choose between duty and leisure, the answer would be straightforward. But this situation involves a choice between performing your duty and backing out on a social commitment made to others. Since Diana cannot be in two places at the same time, she must either let down her colleagues at work or place an imposition on her friends. She has to choose which obligation to honor, which reputation to soil.

Create a pattern of honesty; don't make an exception for your own convenience.

A little stupidity can crumble a mountain of respect. Trust forms through a consistent chain of honest events, not from just one, isolated situation. Like a weak link, one falsehood could destroy a chain of trustworthy actions.

Gerald Mitchell, who once ran Dana Corporation, put the matter this way: "Every time you break your word or are proven to be dishonest, the hurt is magnified a million times. So you must never let it happen."

Smart Solution 29

We cannot be all things to all people—we have to decide which is most important and choose accordingly. But once we do choose, we must be prepared to accept all the consequences. Diana had to decide which activity was the most important and which aspect of her reputation she most wanted to maintain.

Dilemma 30

You made a mistake that could cause problems for others in the future. You'll look bad if you bring this out into the open; If you keep your mouth shut, no one will ever know that the problems caused were your fault.

Jason represented his production planning and scheduling department on a special team charged with the responsibility of improving delivery adherence. Delivery adherence meant getting product shipments to their correct destinations when promised. Adhering to promised schedules was critical to the firm's overall success in the current competitive environment.

Unfortunately, the committee couldn't seem to get its priorities in the right order; its members tended to point fingers at other units for poor records instead of making the entire organization's performance its main concern. The first meeting deteriorated into a round of name calling and bitter feelings between those present intensified.

The second meeting got off to a good start, as members realized that they needed to get along and work together. At this meeting, the group discussed causes of the poor delivery performance and decided to collect information and examine past performance records in select areas of the organization.

Time pressures between meetings prevented Jason from doing a complete and careful job of assuring the accuracy of the information he was to gather. Wanting to appear prepared, Jason made the best guesses he could to fill in gaps where necessary data was not readily available.

At the next meeting, Jason presented his findings along with overly optimistic performance projections and promises of what his unit could do, because he did not want his unit to appear to be the source of the problem. Using the information presented by Jason and the other members of the committee, the group prepared its delivery adherence improvement plan.

Cooperation depends on confidence, teamwork on trustworthiness. Just as Jason's team appeared to be coming together to do what was best for the organization as a whole, Jason acted to save himself from the embarrassment of making a mistake. It's a natural impulse we all have, an impulse which, whenever followed, inevitably leads others to mistrust us. If Jason failed to reveal his misinformation, the team would not perform as well as it might have otherwise. Jason had a choice to make: save face and let the team's performance turn sour, or look bad for being unprepared.

Put doing the right thing ahead of escaping blame.

Openness and up-front actions earn one the confidence and respect from others. Here's a personal example of this principle in action. Late one day after work, I got into my car to go home. I was deep in thought as I backed out of the parking space. Not paying attention to how far I had backed up, I turned my steering wheel too soon. This caused the front of my car to strike the left rear panel of the car parked to the right of me. I immediately realized what I had just done.

I wanted to drive off as if nothing had happened, to escape free and clear, undetected. Fortunately, we have this thing called a conscience, that little voice in our head that tells us when we do something wrong. If we let it do its job, it will cause us to suppress negative urges and protect us from bigger problems later on.

I stopped, got out of my car, and wrote a note to the owner of the damaged vehicle, then called campus security and waited for an officer to make a report. As the officer and I spoke, the car's owner arrived. I told him what I'd done and we handled the matter from there. That evening I felt bad about my carelessness but also at ease knowing I had set matters square with the owner of the car.

Smart Solution 30

If Jason admitted to his error and put the good of the organization ahead of saving face, he might have encouraged others to do the same. Surely Jason was not the only one with time pressures. A short delay in the process might actually do his organization more good than harm because others could come clean about their shortcomings.

Chapter 5

The Shrinking Violet

Finding the courage to do the right thing

You never know when your courage to stand up for the right thing will be tested. How you react in such a difficult situation will make or break you. It all depends on how you choose to respond, whether you decide to fight ferociously like a lion, or become a shrinking violet and helplessly bend inward, closing yourself off from challenges.

One of the most appealing and inspiring behaviors to behold is someone who stands up for those things they are most proud to honor. This is right versus wrong in action, a human quality that's inspired and stirred us to greatness and all manners of triumph since the dawn of civilization.

Good is inherently attractive, and we all want it to triumph over evil, but few have the courage needed to win the battle. Like a shrinking violet, most people lose their resolve; they fail to pursue what's right.

This chapter will show you how to become someone who others will honor and want to associate with. It demonstrates how smart people take courageous stands to do the right thing.

Dilemma 31

Your organization expects you to accomplish something that requires unsavory actions. Other people seem to do these things everyday and it doesn't bother them, which leads you to question your own reluctance.

As an experienced model, Francie knew exactly how difficult getting professional assignments could be. Being attractive was only a small part of what was required. You had to know how to walk, speak, and carry yourself to model clothing in a pleasing, convincing manner. Most models were made, not born; they had to learn modeling skills, and the earlier, the better.

Eager to help their youngsters enter modeling, many parents enrolled their daughters in special schools, which generally consisted of three hours of instruction each week for thirty weeks. These parents paid substantial sums for their child's training, believing the experience would be something that helped build self esteem, provide a healthy outlet of expression, and cultivate good manners and social graces.

As a sales person and instructor at a downtown modeling school, Francie talked to parents about the benefits of sending their daughters to her modeling school. The school's owner insisted that all salespersons do whatever it took to set the "right" price and say the "right" things in order to enroll as many students as possible, and this bothered Francie.

One of the sales techniques the owner expected her to use was to "size up" what the parents might be willing to pay. If, for instance, in the course of conversation, she learned that the parents had a healthy level of income, Francie was supposed to explain the cost for schooling was $1,800. If the parent balked, she indicated that the school was having a weekly special, which dropped the price down to $1,500.

There were several versions of this sales spiel, but the basic idea behind each was to attract customers and charge them whatever the salesperson thought was possible, anything between $1,200 and $1,800. To entice parents to enroll their child in the school, the salesperson might say, "We're offering a $1,500 special that ends today. You have to sign up now." If the parent remained dubious, the sales person suggested, "Oh, look at your daughter. She's a beautiful girl. I just know we can get jobs for her." This caused many parents to believe the schooling would pay practical dividends in the future; it led them to think of the enrollment fees as an investment, not an unrecoverable expenditure. But of course, the promised modeling jobs never materialize.

"Everybody else is doing it. I suppose I can, too." These words typify the shrinking violet's reasoning processes, which is not reasoning at all but a convenient rationalization for doing whatever it takes to get what's wanted. This is the problem that Francie faced. Will she choose to be a shrinking violet, going along with the actions of those who will do whatever it takes to get what they want or will she act courageously by thinking through the implications of what's expected, and then choose to do the right thing?

Make yourself into an extraordinary person by living up to extraordinary standards.

I'd like to tell you about an incident that I observed. It conveyed a very high standard of business conducted in no uncertain terms, and the way it came across was both dramatic and convincing. This situation unfolded during a panel discussion that I once led on ethics in business. It was part of the activities surrounding the dedication of the Miami University school of business administration. Richard T. Farmer, whose endowment gift led to the naming of our business school in his honor, was one of the panelists.

Toward the end of the hour, one of the students raised a frequently asked question about "facilitating payments." "Isn't it alright for companies doing business abroad to pay small bribes?" Mr. Farmer said that he personally didn't like the idea but hadn't any experience in that area—his company, Cintas, Inc., only did business in the United States. A few of the professors in the audience, and some of the students present, voiced the frequently heard, "When in Rome, do as the Romans do." The implication of this was clear—go ahead and pay what's asked for. "What's so bad about that? It's only a small amount," they said. I was reasonably sure that someone would take a stand against this shady practice but no one did—at least not immediately.

Just as I was about to speak my piece, something unforgettable happened: A man dressed in a dark brown suit stood up. Everyone there knew who he was: John Smale, recently retired chairman and

CEO of Cincinnati-based Procter & Gamble. Stories were circulating that ailing General Motors would soon announce that Mr. Smale was to be their new chairman of the board. And, a few hours later, GM did just that. But, at the seminar, Smale had something important he wanted to offer regarding the opinions expressed about embracing bribery as a business tactic. He didn't want there to be any mistake about what he had said or any confusion over how strong he felt about it.

In a steady, convincing tone, he said, "You don't have to pay bribes to do business abroad. We [Procter & Gamble] do business all over the world and we don't pay bribes. You just don't do it!" With that, he sat down. Silence overcame those present for a moment as each of us reflected on what had just been spoken. And there wasn't the slightest bit of doubt in anyone's mind that he meant every word of it. I learned in that moment one of the key reasons why he was such an effective leader.

By acting with integrity—by doing what is clearly right when circumstances call for taking a stand—a leader makes it clear what he believes to be acceptable. By standing up for high standards, you stand tall in the minds of others.

Just say no and walk away.

Many years ago, the managing director of Caterpillar's European operations in Granoble, France, searched desperately for a suitable apartment. The housing there for Americans was very hard to come by. The city was bulging, and decent accommodations were not to be found.

The director persisted to look for an apartment to buy. One was finally located—a brand new, seven room suite on the sixth floor of the Park Hotel. When they got down to negotiating the final price, one which was already agreed to and determined, the negotiator for the seller said, "Well, of course there's an accommodating payment needed to give you first priority over anyone else who might want to obtain the apartment."

This was the first time the issue of such a "payment" cropped up within the negotiation. At that, Wally, the managing director, merely got up and said, "The meeting's adjourned. I don't want your apartment." And he walked out. That particular example permeated the whole community. Everyone knew from then on that whenever they dealt with Caterpillar or the managing director in particular, all cards would be laid on the table.

Smart Solution 31

Francie must decide if she should engage in the shady sales practices her company expected her to follow. She preferred not to use them, but her employer tells her to act otherwise. Many people in similar circumstances unthinkingly look for excuses so they can feel okay about doing what their hearts advise against. They try to make an exception for themselves, as if rationalizing their decision will make it 'all right' to do. In doing this, they evoke the phrase "even though" into their thinking so as to make the distasteful appear tasteful. Francie might be tempted to think, "I should refuse to engage in these tricky sales tactics *even though* I will probably lose my job because of it." With the possibility of losing her job in mind, Francie will say to herself, "I shouldn't have to give up my job. I'm only doing what I have to do." Thus, she arrives at the reason she needs to excuse herself from doing what her heart says is wrong. Is it courageous? Is it admirable? Or is it acting the part of the shrinking violet that collapses?

One of the best protections we can apply when facing tough decisions like Francie's is raising the question of "should I." Too many people think in terms of "can I?" and run headlong into trouble, which could be avoided by asking "should I" instead. There isn't an "even though" reason large enough or important enough to warrant going ahead with something that begs the answer to "should I."

Dilemma 32

You have to solve a nagging problem that is impeding your unit's effectiveness, but careful study of the problem poses difficulties. It will be time consuming, and it may reveal that your actions are to blame for the problem.

Shannon led a work crew consisting of three other employees and herself. Her unit planned, scheduled, and coordinated the installation of wall coverings, draperies, and accent pieces for large interior decorating jobs for industrial clients. Timing and coordination was critical. Shannon's unit had to be ready to move in and complete its work when the company's newly constructed buildings were ready. But Shannon's unit rarely completed its jobs without some major catastrophe, which required a lot of added, last-minute overtime work. Socially, Shannon's three subordinates got along with each other just fine, but when working together to meet important deadlines, they invariably had terrible squabbles over who was supposed to do what and when. They accused Shannon of being incompetent and saw her as the main reason for their less-than-acceptable performance.

Everyone runs into snags on the job. We work our way out of them or forget they ever happened, believing each to be a solitary occurrence. Perhaps some of them are, but many difficulties persist, and we never get around to clearly identifying their causes and eliminating them altogether.

This is what Shannon faced in her work. She needed to give the time necessary, time which could be above and beyond her normal working hours, to determine the cause of her unit's poor performance and face up to what an honest investigation might reveal.

Have courage to find the truth.

Whenever things go wrong, the natural impulse is to blame others or additional external conditions for the error. No one wants to accept blame for mistakes and screw ups. We want to think well of ourselves and have others think highly of us, too. While these very human reactions are at the heart of many behaviors, they also stand amongst our greatest obstacles to improvement.

Perhaps the most formidable foe anyone faces is not some objectionable other person, but one's self, a self with terrific defense mechanisms that only real courage is capable of tearing down. Anyone can fight another, defend and argue for self, concoct excuses and find extenuating circumstances to excuse his or her own behaviors.

These types of behaviors are commonplace and they have little value other than to protect something that should not be saved: personal flaws and shortcomings. These self-protective defenses may leave you feeling better but still frozen in attitudes and practices that could cause problems for yourself, and others, later on.

Have the courage to change practices that may have worked well at one time, but which no longer produce desirable results.

It's always much easier to do nothing and live with a problem than to face it head-on and affect remedial changes. From a simple annoyance like having to clean a junk-filled garage, to more complex interpersonal entanglements like an out-of-control teenage child, most people pursue the path of least resistance. They just don't want to deal with the difficult. We grow comfortable within our ruts and choose, unthinkingly, to live in them without objection. We even get used to their rough edges, as calluses grow around our senses and make us believe the annoyance really isn't "all that bad."

Some of our tried-and-true practices work okay. They get us by, if only barely. We find them safe and comfortable. They produce marginal results, and for many that's good enough. But we do far better when we face difficulties—particularly weaknesses that produce mediocre results—head on, and discipline ourselves to implement them. Self change begins with the courage to see yourself honestly and then to affect the necessary corrections.

Smart Solution 32

Shannon would win respect and cooperation from her subordinates if she searched out how she mismanaged things and proceeded to correct her mistakes and shortcomings. Overly concerned with saving face, living the belief that problems will not re-occur, and giving in to laziness all work to Shannon's disadvantage. They permit ineffective practices to continue, which eat away at her credibility and reduce the overall quality of her unit's performance. She could have conducted post mortems on her unit's slip ups. She should have gotten employees involved in identifying failure points and their causes.

With the above problems identified, Shannon could have created workable solutions, especially if they involved herself. After all, she does have control over that part of the problem, and she could succeed so long as her courage permitted it.

Dilemma 33

Your boss asked you to do something that's not only wrong but against company policy. You stuck with company policy and now your boss is angry with you.

Upon joining an investment company, Valerie attended a month-long training session, which covered company policies, organization and investment analysis methods. She learned how to evaluate investment proposals and the standards her firm used to gauge risks. From the training, Valerie clearly understood that her organization purposely avoided high-risk ventures. Occasionally, Valerie's firm would gamble on ventures that her company deemed "questionable," provided senior level people had good reason to believe the propositions were acceptably sound. After having worked at her job for about a year, Valerie's boss called her aside. He explained that he'd be away on vacation for the next three weeks and that a personal friend of his would be submitting a proposal. "I want you to go over this proposal very carefully," he said. "And I want you to take good care of this person." Valerie agreed.

When the proposal came in, Valerie read it carefully, applied her firm's criteria, and determined it to be a high risk/high reward proposition. She marked it acceptable, but noted her reservations on the cover. When the loan committee met, it examined the proposal and decided to turn it down.

When Valerie's boss returned, he found an angry voice mail message on his answering machine from the person who submitted the loan request. Upon hearing the telephone message, he became angry and called Valerie into his office, whereupon he scolded her for not approving the loan, and threatened her. "This sort of thing had better not happen again, or else."

Someone at work asks you to do something that's not right. What should you do? Present this vague question to others and notice how many of them ask you for clarification. Is what's asked really wrong? Who asked you to do it, your boss or someone else? Can you get away with it? How much harm could come from it? Who stands to get hurt, you or someone else? The motives underlying these questions are fairly plain: to figure out ways to escape detection from doing something illicit and to find "legitimate" excuses if caught.

Valerie did not act the part of a shrinking violet by meekly going along with her boss's request. She did not worry about finding clever ways to go against her company's procedures or look for ways to cover herself if she got caught violating its policies. Instead, she followed her company's rules and procedures as she was instructed. As far as her company was concerned, Valerie is in a good position. She followed company guidelines as instructed. But she's in a bad position with her boss. What Valerie does the next time her boss asks her to violate company policy will reveal what Valerie honors more: good relations with her conscience or good relations with her boss.

Build a reputation of playing by the rules, and trouble should stay away.

A firm that lives by high ideals attracts good people. Its reputation seems to speak out in subtle ways, saying, "If you aren't decent and honorable we won't have anything to do with you."

The James River Corporation was founded by two men, Brenton S. Halsey and Robert C. Williams, who from the start, saw the need to establish certain values and beliefs to guide the growth and direction of their expanding firm. They sought an honorable identity for the growing company they were building. The co-founders realized they had a unique opportunity: to establish a new identity for their new company.

They wrote down on paper what values and beliefs they wanted their company to operate by. The first and most important one they identified was ethics. The co-founders were competitive, but like any other game, they believed you "won" by playing by the rules. They believed that there was no real reward or justification in winning by any other way than the rules.

It wasn't long before their commitment to ethical business dealings was tested. Filter papers for the automobile industry was one of the first product lines that James River entered, and it was the cornerstone of their move to profitability. James River, as was true with many firms starting out, experienced losses during its early days. There were high expectations for success in the higher profit margin line of papers.

One day, a buyer demanded something extra, under the table, if his company was going to purchase from James River. The co-founders were dumbfounded by the buyer's blatant demand. They didn't like it one bit—it flew in the face of what they had committed themselves to. The new owners told him in no uncertain terms, "If that is what's required, we'll find some other way to sell our products." While it was difficult for them to turn down good business, it was not difficult for them to stand tall by standing up for their principles.

By choosing to do business on a highly ethical plane, they moved further ahead with their plan to compete by making products of extraordinary quality and implementing superior customer service. Their products and services would be so good, and entice customers so much, that asking for kickbacks became even more morally reprehensible. Their papers were of exceptionally good quality, so competing with "real" value proved to be the best competitive edge their growing company could have. Had they tried getting sales through kickbacks, it's doubtful whether they'd still be a profitable business.

Do what's right because it's the right thing to do and not because it will earn you something you want.

If you justify ethical behavior simply because it pays, you are, in reality, little more than a crude materialist. You can bet that sooner or later some unethical scheme that boasts a large payoff will present itself to that you. When that occurs, how do you choose your course of action? Will you do what's right for the sake of ethical reasons or will you choose to do what pays?

Here's a useful suggestion that can guide you whenever such a choice needs to be made. Ask yourself, "Am I choosing what I'd be proud of doing, or am I choosing something because it will profit me?" It all comes down to what you want to be: principled or profit-oriented.

Smart Solution 33

Valerie didn't need advice about following company policies and doing the right thing; she needs help handling her boss. On the one hand, she didn't want to be disloyal and uncooperative. On the other hand, she wanted to follow company policy. Her boss might wish to learn what

Valerie will and won't do. And Valerie would be smart to make this known publicly, to protect herself against requests such as the one made of her by her boss.

When Valerie had a better idea of what her boss was like, she'd be smart to ask for clarification whenever she suspected a request was dishonorable or against company policy. When her boss requested, "Take good care of this person," Valerie should have said say, "Do you want me to handle the loan request immediately and apply all the company's decision criteria carefully?" Unlike a shrinking violet, she could clarify what her boss was asking her to do. She should clarify his commands by notating them in his presence. By doing this, Valerie would send a powerful message to her boss that she has documentation in her possession describing in detail his requests and commands. In so doing, Valerie indicated that she would not be pushed around or intimidated into doing something that was morally or ethically questionable.

Dilemma 

You observe what you believe to be wrongdoing on someone else's part. This person could make life difficult for you if were you to make an issue of what you saw.

As administrative assistant to the superintendent of schools in a rapidly expanding rural community, Camille's responsibilities entailed everything her boss needed her to do. These duties ranged from organizing meetings and analyzing budgets, to arranging social functions. Camille, a 24-year-old college graduate, took the job primarily to learn practical aspects of education administration. The position provided Camille the opportunity to observe the school administration first-hand, and, in the process, she gathered data and prepared reports. One of her tasks was to solicit, receive and analyze proposals from qualified consulting firms for a massive study of the school district's future building needs.

Camille pored over the solicited proposals. One had yet to come in, even though the deadline for submission was days earlier. Based on Camille's analysis, three of the proposals studied were sure to be rejected by the board. Harry, the assistant superintendent and person likely to succeed the superintendent when he retired, called Camille into his office and asked for the strongest proposal received. Camille saw him make a copy of it and place it in a manila envelope. Later, she noticed Harry leaving the office carrying what looked like the envelope in which he had placed the proposal. She asked Harry's secretary if she knew who Harry had been talking to earlier. "Oh, it was Mr. Matthews from some company I don't recall the name of." This made Camille suspicious; the company that had yet to submit its proposal was owned by a man named Matthews.

Camille's predicament was not unlike those faced by all of us at one time or another. We see what appears to be wrongdoing and wonder what, if anything, we should do about it.

Two aspects of this situation deserve our special attention. First, should we get involved or should we do nothing? The answer is, of course we must get involved. We are already involved because we witnessed the occurrence. By not acting, you become, in effect, a party to the wrongdoing. This is why shrinking violets are not innocent bystanders but, by their silence, accessories after the fact.

Second, it is easy to misinterpret what we see. What appears to be one thing can often be something else. There may well be another explanation for what was observed than the one we first drew up. It should be noted that false accusations should never be made until you hear the other side of the issue, before you gain proper perspective. Be careful not to believe those who act too quickly in a situation; there are some excellent liars out there who can concoct very convincing explanations for their despicable acts.

When you observe wrongdoing, confront the person immediately, but privately.

A wonderful story that J.C. Penney told about concerned his selling of watermelons. At 17, an age when most boys enter their senior year of high school, Penney had already developed an entrepreneurial flare. His summer's crop of watermelons was bountiful and prices were good. An average melon went for a nickel and the largest ones brought a dime. Young Jim Penney felt he was going to do quite well with what he had brought to market. He rented a horse and wagon, and began driving throughout the town, peddling his crop.

Then he got an idea. The county fair was opening, and there would be lots of people eager to enjoy a slice of refreshing watermelon. He drove his wagon as close to the main entrance as he could and began selling melons.

His plan was short lived, however. Feeling a hand on his shoulder young Penney heard his father's voice say, "Better go home, son. Now."

Bewildered and embarrassed, Penney obeyed. Arriving home, the senior Penney found Jim in front of their house sitting in the wagon, his head slumped down.

"Do you know why I told you to go home?" his father asked him.

"No sir." Jim said.

"Did it mean anything to you that the fair was supported by concessions?"

Again, Jim answered, "No."

His father explained that everyone inside the fair grounds had paid a concession fee.

"But I wasn't selling inside the grounds," young Jim argued.

"That's just it," his father said. "Without paying anything toward the support of the fair, you were taking advantage of those who did. Everyone is entitled to earn a living, you and everyone else, but never by taking advantage of others."

Don't jump to conclusions.

Everyone is prone to jump to conclusions. A person observes someone doing something, and immediately draws conclusions about which things are based more on assumptions rather than actual behaviors. Too many innocent actions get mistaken for sinister deeds; too many perfectly understandable behaviors are mistakenly perceived to spring from despicable motives that observers ascribe to those they observe. The smart thing to do is to exercise caution. Say to yourself, "There may be a perfectly logical explanation for what I observe."

Smart Solution 34

Camille should've confronted the assistant superintendent with what she saw, but she must not falsely accuse him of things that may not be true. She also has to avoid being fooled if he tries to convince her of something untrue. Her first step should've been to talk with Harry directly, telling him what she observed. She shouldn't accuse him of anything, because differing explanations might exist. Additionally, Camille needs to indicate to Harry that she will report her observations to those higher up in the organization. Bringing light to bear on your actions might well work wonders.

Dilemma 35

You encounter a potential conflict situation with people in another part of your organization. You can either passively go along with them, which you believe to be the wrong thing to do, or you can stick your neck out for what you believe to be right by making an issue out of your differences, even though you don't stand to gain anything personally by doing so.

George headed the human resources division for his company, which had operations located throughout the world. His responsibilities included manpower planning, training and development, and the selection and placement of personnel. Rapid international expansion of his firm through acquisitions made George's job complex. He faced the many difficulties associated with integrating acquired foreign businesses into his firm's corporate structure. Different cultures had different values, and the operating personnel within these business entities had their own peculiar styles and established methods.

One of the overseas businesses George's firm acquired needed to be turned around. Although its products enjoyed growing demand, its performance lagged behind that of its competitors, due to the fact that local management failed to understand the ramifications of the newly emerging technology.

Headquarters' top management wanted to replace key personnel with technically competent people in order to affect a much-needed turnaround. George suggested and top management selected two highly competent and experienced individuals from the U.S. to be given the assignments. These individuals traveled abroad to talk with the local management running the foreign operation. Before the two candidates returned from their trip abroad, George received a telephone call from the head of the acquired business, who said that women and minorities were out of the question and that the two people sent were unacceptable because they "would not fit in."

What is important to remember about courage is that it involves doing the "right thing," not what's convenient or what immediately returns the greatest benefits. Courage means standing tall and doing what should be done because higher concerns call for it. We pay a terrific price whenever we give up principles to gain just a little more peace or prosperity.

Have the courage to do what's right. Don't settle for something just because it's easy or convenient.

Many people have demonstrated the capacity to act courageously in various ways. The leaders of Levi Strauss & Company, which have long exhibited a genuine commitment to human dignity and fairness, are a good example of this.

Top management there worked very hard throughout its history to make the work environment one that ennobled its employees. Levi Strauss & Company bought out a plant in Blackstone, Virginia, where all the employees were white; there were no blacks. After a time, the plant's manager, Paul Glasgow, came to Walter Haas, Jr., who ran Levi's at the time, and said, "I think the time is right to integrate." Walter responded, "Good. We're with you." Glasgow went to the town's leaders to make his intentions known, where he learned that they wanted to divide the plant into "black" and "white" sections. Levi's management said, "No, we're not going to do that."

The town's leaders then asked that a dividing line be painted to keep blacks on one side and whites on the other. Again, the company refused.

Next, separate drinking fountains and toilet facilities were requested. And again, Levi's said no. The people at Blackstone didn't like Levi's stand—it violated their long-standing customs. An attempt was made to pressure the company. The local employment service stopped sending applicants to the plant for available jobs.

Paul Glasgow asked headquarters in San Francisco what to do. Walter Haas, Jr. replied, "Close the plant."

The plant didn't close. Seeing that Levi's was that serious about their commitment to equal opportunity, the town's leaders backed down. It was a great victory for equality. Today, the plant operates efficiently and on Levi's terms of equal opportunity. Because of this courageous stand, the employment practices throughout the entire community were altered.

Smart Solution 35

George should pursue principles, not struggle to make his work-life peaceful. He would be better off to think more about the future of his organization than the current-day standards of a single unit. If George wanted to be able to attract the best people available, and have his organization reap the benefits of their talents, he should insist that those he selected fill the vacancies abroad over the objections of the local managers. If need be, George should force the matter by getting support from his superiors. Doing anything less would produce neither peace nor progress.

Dilemma 36

You witness an unpleasant scene at work that upsets you deeply. You'd like to say something to the person who caused it, but fear what might happen if you voice your concerns and feelings.

Audrey was a clerical worker at the corporate headquarters of a large insurance company, an hourly employee with 28 years of service. Her organization had transferred a new manager to take over responsibilities of a unit that had office space next to Audrey's. One afternoon, the new manager became terribly upset with one of his assistants for badly mishandling a routine matter. The assistant tried to make up excuses, which intensified the boss's anger. It led to shouting. Audrey overheard the heated discussion, which took place not more than 30 feet from her workstation. She tried to ignore it, but found it impossible to do when the manager's words grew louder and uglier. He suddenly lost control, slamming his fist on the assistant's desk several times and used the worst kind of profanity.

Although not directly involved, Audrey began to tremble as the shouting intensified. She abhorred violence and foul language. A quiet and gentle person, Audrey could not get the incident out of her mind and the more she dwelt on what she witnessed, the more upset she became. Audrey wanted to tell the new manager what she felt about his unprofessional and ungentlemanly behavior, but feared that he'd retaliate in the same, foul manner.

Audrey found herself in a situation not of her own doing. She witnessed something that upset her, something she had no control over, and the more she thought about the incident, the more upset she became. Were she able to forget what happened, Audrey might be able to function unhampered. But the image of what she observed tormented her. This was simply the pattern of Audrey's personality, and little could happen that would change it.

So what are her options? One option was to do nothing, to not say anything to the person who upset her. But taking that course left Audrey even more emotionally distraught. Her other option was to confront the person whose conduct so upset her. She could tell the new manager how his behavior created a most unpleasant atmosphere. He could get upset with Audrey, but she doesn't know for sure that he would actually do that.

When someone offends, you go to that person immediately and discuss it with them, privately.

One of the most useful guides in human relations is this: When another person harms you, immediately let that person know how you feel, but hold your discussion in a private setting. Many people have great difficulty accepting this wisdom and fewer still have the courage to apply it because they fear retribution. As a consequence, most people pay a terrific price by ignoring this idea, and the situation usually grows worse. One offense unchecked leads to other offenses, some more severe than the initial offense.

Although following this advice will not always produce the most desirable outcome, it does not follow that it will always produce the most negative outcome either. Most people are not antisocial. They are concerned with how others might perceive them and they do not want to be nuisances. Most people would prefer to be liked and accepted than disliked and rejected; they really do not intentionally choose to harm or offend others. Most harmful and offensive acts arise unthinkingly and unintentionally. When told how their actions offended another person, how their actions demeaned or harmed or caused pain, most people feel ashamed and tend to refrain from repeating their objectionable actions.

Smart Solution 36

Audrey did exactly what the ancient wisdom advised—she went to the new manager and voiced her feelings. This course of action proved beneficial. He could see how intensely upset and troubled she was over the incident, prompting an apology to Audrey. Furthermore, because Audrey spoke up and courageously drew the line, the manager approached the individual he injured directly, and apologized as well. Although his unkind behavior had harmed his professional standing and diminished the respect others had for him, his acceptance of his mistake and his apology afterward helped restore a bit of what he had earlier destroyed.

Chapter 6

The Strangling Vine

Nipping difficulties in the bud

The world is full of vicious creatures and sharp edges. We try to avoid its snags and bites as we make our way through, but without exception, a difficulty strikes each of us—and it hurts. You may have encountered one recently: A boss might have mistreated you, or perhaps you were the victim of a grave injustice, or maybe you've learned that you have a serious health problem. Now what?

Many people handle such situations badly. They do dumb things, things that worsen matters and enfeeble their ability to handle it effectively. An important idea to keep in mind is this: Human beings are always growing emotionally. What direction that growth takes depends on what you choose. You may choose unwisely: Resign yourself to your difficulty, deny it, try to escape, pity yourself, take revenge, or continue to follow tired-out approaches. Or, you may face your difficulty head-on and work imaginatively and productively to overcome it. Turn your difficulty into a challenge and work to rise above it. If you do, you will grow wiser, stronger, and happier.

As our world moves faster and faster, and troubles flow with it, the ability to defeat your difficulties becomes increasingly useful. This chapter describes five difficulties many people face, and illustrates how otherwise intelligent people tend to respond to them, how they choose unwisely, and fail as a consequence. It offers practical advice in the form of effective solutions that anyone can apply when each difficulty arises.

Dilemma 37

Others see you as mediocre—they might be right. You are discouraged by the realization that there are so many things you cannot do well, or do at all.

Gary grew up happy and contented, perhaps too contented with himself for his own good. He barely got by in school. His teachers said he did what was expected—nothing more, nothing less. Actually, they seemed to not notice Gary too much; he was just one among many. They described his abilities and performance as "adequate." As a youngster, Gary never got into trouble, but he never did anything worthwhile, either. Throughout his life, everyone accepted him; he fit in with the crowd. Perhaps it was because he went unnoticed that Gary was never challenged, and because he was never challenged and his passions were never ignited, he slipped into a rut of ordinariness.

Gary took piano lessons for a while as a child, but gave them up when he turned nine. He read few books on his own. For entertainment, he listened to popular music and sometimes attended current movies and sporting events. He never developed a hobby.

Gary's boss looked upon him as an adequate performer. Looking over Gary's past, it was clear he never excelled at anything, and eventually, he began to believe in his own inabilities. As Gary saw it, all he needed was a good break, but one never seemed to come his way. Instead, only bumps and setbacks visited him. What's more, little evidence appeared to offer much in the way of a turnaround. Gary was now fairly deep into his career. His major aim was to just get by. Gary bought lottery tickets nearly every week, hoping that Lady Luck might arrive to carry him out of his colorless existence.

Gary is known as an "average person." Throughout his life, he practiced the art of being unnoticeable so well he has grew up neglecting his own possibilities. When he looked at himself, he saw more "can't do's" than "can do's." Holding this perspective, he shied away from challenges of any sort. Many people's experiences are similar to Gary's—and probably for good reason. They, too, live what can only be called an average life. Because they see more things they *cannot* do rather than things they believe they *can* do, they possess little inclination to accomplish anything that might propel them forward.

What do they do? They resign themselves to their situation. They accept the idea that they cannot accomplish anything noteworthy. In countless little ways, they hold themselves back from challenge. They accept the routine tasks at work; they only go to movies their friends say are good; they join the clubs their bosses tell them they should join; they marry acceptable spouses and are horrified when their children grow up talented and unpredictable. Day by day, they turn away from excellence in order to pursue a goal of mediocrity. They erect a mental barrier halting them from achieving success or finding personal fulfillment. They continue on with their work and life, doing what they have become good at doing—being average.

Find and use your "can do's" to their fullest.

It's easy to grow accustomed to being "the average Joe," and over time, to accept oneself as such. Imperceptibly, one's many, insignificant limitations and the tendency to "just get by today" can prevent you from doing anything particularly well or meaningful. You become a slave to a daily routine of mindless habit.

The trap of mediocrity is deceptively difficult to overcome because it arrives gradually and goes unnoticed for many years. Like a creeping grape vine, it slowly covers the "trees" (talents, opportunity, individualism) and smothers the "forest" that might have been. And its "fruit," the grapes, are small, sour, and hard.

Taking the right steps might be a solution to overcoming this problem. The key is to stop waiting for success to arrive and, instead, create a pattern of personal achievement that builds self confidence and encourages better performance. This involves overcoming two barriers: the habit of doing just enough to get by, and a self-deprecating image. The first barrier leads to the second and the second reinforces the first. How does one get out of this debilitating cycle?

Build yourself up.

First, make a list of what you love to do. What excites you about your work? Next, identify your talents and abilities, the things you are good at doing. Then, identify some improvement you can make that requires you to use one or more of your special talents, however small or ill-developed they may seem to be at the time. Set achievable targets for yourself and identify the steps needed to get you there. Finally, act to carry out your plan.

Vision and action—these are essential elements of success. It is indeed a fact that most work is performed better when people have goals and action plans to follow. Plans are logical. They are products of the mind. But there is something else equally, if not more, important to what defines success.

Just as one forms a logical plan for the work, one also needs to forge the right convictions to implement the plan in the face of any obstacles that may arise along the way. I am speaking here about two emotional dimensions: to hold an enthusiastic belief in a brighter future, and to have a determined will to persevere and accomplish the impossible when failure looms large. These are products of the heart, and they should be created alongside your plan before any undertaking begins. To produce your best, choose to approach what you do with the belief that you will succeed.

Form a "can do" approach to life.

You can see what you want to see in a mirror. If you want to see a nobody without hope for the future, you will. If you want to see a person on the road to success, you will see that person. It's all dependent on you and your self-image. Some people see only their warts and wrinkles; others see only their own eyes, bright and sparkling with imagination and optimism.

There is no doubt about the fact that what we see in ourselves affects our actions, and our actions transform us into who we are. Many people have demonstrated this fact in various ways. Two important events took place in the life of Itzhak Perlman when he was only four years old. Physically, he was struck down with polio. and emotionally, he was lifted when he heard a recording of Jascha Heifetz. One was a life-crippling blow; the other was an inspiring standard.

The first event would have subdued a less forceful child, but young Itzhak chose to transform his life heroically by focusing his special talents on the music he heard Heifetz play, music he understood in his mind and heart. Because he focused on the music and not his crippled legs, Itzhak Perlman became one of the world's greatest violinists and an inspiration to children everywhere.

Whenever you consider yourself, remember to consider the impact of what you choose to see and of what you choose to ignore. Jazz great Ray Charles captured this important idea when he said, "My eyes are my handicap, but my ears are my opportunity." Ray Charles is blind; but music is a talent of hearing. That's the secret: Focus on those things that build yourself. Subordinate your limitations to your abilities.

Getting out of the quagmire of one's "ordinariness" begins with saying yes to one's "can do's" and ignoring one's "can't do's." It might be difficult, but running away from challenges is a big mistake, one that may ruin you. Your mental outlook must be positive. Think about the times when you were successful at some undertaking and you'll discover that you went into these ventures believing you'd come out a winner. This is precisely the attitude you need to pursue. It is the bridge across the morass of the average to the high, firm ground of success.

Take charge of yourself and your situation.

Everyday life asks each of us a question: Will you be a hero or a coward? Becoming a hero allows you to do more and do it better than you would otherwise have imagined possible. Heroism contributes toward overcoming the habit of laziness that maintains your getting through just one more day without any meaningful progression.

If you want success and lasting fulfillment, let yourself continue to grow, make something good out of whatever happens to you. It's all a matter of having the right perspective and drawing on that perspective as a means of getting things accomplished. It means taking charge of your situation by focusing on what you can do and not paralyzing yourself by thinking only on trouble areas.

I recall a story about a British airliner that encountered a rough thunderstorm. Lightning flashed throughout the sky. Violent winds shook the aircraft fiercely. Suddenly, the engines went dead and the plane began to lose altitude. The passengers were terrified. They saw the lightning along the wings and felt the plane descend rapidly. The stewardesses, white-lipped yet businesslike, checked seat belts and food trays.

Then, when it seemed as if the last few seconds of everyone's lives were at hand, the engines restarted, the plane leveled off, and then began to climb back to its original, safe altitude. As the passengers cheered with relief, the pilot came on the plane's speaker, and, in a crisp, British accent, announced, "Ladies and gentlemen, you may have noticed we just experienced a spot of bother back there..."

What was seen as certain catastrophe to everyone else was just a "spot of bother," to the pilot. While the passengers stared fearfully at the stormclouds and lightning, the pilot and cockpit crew proceeded quickly, without panic, through the established emergency procedures. Nor did the pilot pause to congratulate himself when the engines restarted; he proceeded to the next step and pulled the airplane out of its dive and back to where it belonged.

Herein lies the difference between reacting positively to your circumstances, however bad they might be, and becoming a victim of them. Determined to remain master of his situation, the pilot concentrated and focused clearly on outsmarting the difficulty, demonstrating confidence and determination, qualities that spell the difference between the ordinary and the extraordinary.

The important lesson to keep in mind here is that we choose how to respond to what happens to us, and what we choose to do is usually far more important than the event which triggered the response. Where we arrive is not so much a result of the stormy blasts life hurls our way as it is how we respond to them.

The poet Edna Wheeler Wilcox perhaps expressed it best when she put to paper the following.

"One ship drives east and another drives west
with the self-same winds that blow;
'Tis the set of the sails and not the gales
that tells them the way to go."

Smart Solution 37

Gary needed to get out of his habit of just getting by and start accomplishing something beyond mediocrity. His opinion of himself was a product of his actions, not the other way around, so the solution lay primarily in instigating action, not thought. That first action should be the establishment and accomplishment of concrete goals. If this involved doing something he loved, his chances for success would be stronger.

Another thing that would help Gary out of his difficulty is the development of a "can-do," take-charge outlook. He could develop such an outlook by repeating to himself, "I choose to accomplish this goal." Then, as those initial goals were finally realized, his "can-do" confidence would expand accordingly, and his self image would become increasingly positive and confident.

Another useful technique might be to visualize successfully accomplishing his goals. This helps to build confidence. Of course, then comes the hard part: the doing. This is not a time for Gary to wimp out—he has to persevere until the desired result is attained. When it does, he'll feel that he can do larger things; plus, the more goals he reaches, the longer his "can-do" list becomes, and he'll escape from the traps he worked himself into.

Dilemma 38

You have suffered a personal setback. A promotion you thought was yours went to someone else, and you're at odds with yourself on how to handle the disappointment.

Brandon was passed over for a promotion that he was certain was his. He was with his company longer than any of the other sales associates, and was regularly at or near the top in sales commission levels. But the vacant district manager's position went to Helen, who the national sales manager said showed the most managerial ability.

After the decision was announced, Brandon refused to accept the thought that Helen edged him out of what he thought was a "sure thing." He conducted himself as though Helen was just temporarily filling in until corporate personnel reviewed the situation and made the final decision.

Denying an unpleasant event is a commonplace reaction when things go wrong. Perhaps this is because it's so easy to do. Denial involves pretending that the situation isn't happening. This is what Brandon was doing, but the decision had been made, and Brandon was in store for more pain and disappointment when he finally faced it. Dreamworlds can't be maintained indefinitely; eventually people wake up. Once they do, their adjustment to reality is often more difficult, and their responses afterward far less effective than they might have been.

Living in an imperfect world—one with disappointments, diseases, and mishaps—can be painfully difficult. Few things ever go as we intend for them to go. Failures, breaks, and snags of one form or another strike everyone, and are never spread around evenly. Some people are hit harder and more often by setbacks than others. Regardless, there are ways you can deal with difficulties which work to your ultimate improvement, ways which start working immediately and win you the admiration of others.

Face the difficulty head-on.

One theme permeates effective responses to difficulties: facing them squarely and taking definite, constructive steps forward to enable yourself to deal with them. Consider the story of Ana Fidelia Quirot, a world-class middle-distance runner. This brave, young Cuban woman nearly died in a 1993 house fire which left her badly scarred, with third degree burns covering more than a third of her body.

Doctors believed Ana's days of athletic competition were over. She refused to accept their grim prognosis, and, while still in the hospital, set about rehabilitating herself. At first, she could not close her hands nor lift her arms, but within two months the determined Ana began working out on an exercise bike and a rowing machine, and jogging up and down the hospital steps. Her rapid recovery astounded her doctors. In August 1995, Ana won the gold medal for the 800-meter race at Sweden's 5th World Track and Field Championship with the world's fastest time. She captured the silver at the Olympic Games in Atlanta.

Facing your difficulty head-on is the first positive step in the process of fixing it. Your promotion went to someone else—now what? Face it directly. There must be a reason why your boss selected the other person. Get your hurt and anger under control and go find out why you didn't get the promotion. Ask your boss what you need to do to improve yourself so you'll be considered more seriously next time. If you have just learned that you have a health problem, face it squarely and intelligently. What is the best treatment? Ask the top specialists for their advice. Follow the remedies they prescribe. If some project you are working hard to finish on time encounters severe problems, examine the difficulty as a scientist would. What caused the problem? What are the options? Try to discover the best ways of dealing with the realities you face, focus on what will be most beneficial, then act accordingly.

Focus attention on performance, not pain.

How we view a predicament can make it easier to deal with or impossible to handle. It all depends on where we place our attention. One night, during a performance of the ballet *Don Quixote* at the Sydney Opera House, Misha Baryshnikov made a grande jeté across the stage. He landed badly on his left foot and felt his ankle turn under. "I could hear the bones crushing," he later told *People* magazine. The pain was excruciating. Yet, incredibly, he danced through the injury right up to the final curtain.

Dancing through injuries is something professionals learn to do, lest a grimace of pain spoil the illusion they wish to create on stage. Misha invented a different series of moves to keep himself going. By reversing the direction of a series of pirouettes, he managed to shift his weight onto a right leg. When the curtain fell for the second time, Misha dropped to the floor in a dead faint.

This is the human predicament in microcosm—can you finish the performance after such a painful incident? It all depends on your pluck, your ability to rise above the pain, fighting with a scabbard after the sword is gone, and winning with what's left after defeat.

Demonstrate undaunted determination.

Human history is ample evidence of the fact that a seed of greatness exists within each of us. That seed may lie dormant, ready to be activated, but it is still there. In this seed of greatness lies the spirit to take positive steps, to fight back—it's the will to conquer. In the face of adversity and with bleak prospects for an agreeable outcome, you can allow this seed of greatness to help you overcome your obstacles. It can help you rise to the challenges you face by making you brave, resourceful, determined.

Think of a time in your past when you chose to activate this miraculous power. Do you remember how it buoyed your faith when you succeeded in the venture you planned, or that you found an answer to a vexing problem? This element of your inner self can help you surmount seemingly impossible obstacles when you call on it. It can help you defeat your difficulties if you release it to work on your behalf, but you have to do something to make that possible. You have to focus all your attention and energies on your performance and your goals, not your pain.

There is at least one common denominator among the great achievers of the world: they possess an unshakable enthusiasm for what they do. They produce magnificently because they live positively. They stick to business. Their secret for rising above adversity is found in the fact that they focus entirely on their performance.

The great heavyweight boxer, Muhammad Ali, fought on after suffering a broken jaw at the hands of Ken Norton in an early round of the 1973 championship fight in San Diego. Ali continued on, despite his pain, and finished the fight. Howard Cosell said of Ali, "This is the mark of a champion."

Hobbled by a sprained ligament in his right knee and a severely pulled hamstring in his left leg, Kirk Gibson sat and watched as the Oakland Athletics led the Los Angeles Dodgers in the opening game of the 1988 World Series. "He just can't do it; he just can't do it," lamented Dodger manager Tommy Lasorda, discussing the playability of his best hitter and team leader.

With the Dodgers trailing 4-3 in the ninth inning and two outs, the A's walked Mike Davis. Lasorda turned to his best hope: Gibson. In severe pain, Kirk limped to the plate to pinch hit for the Dodger's fourth reliever, Alejandro Peña. Fouling off two pitches, Gibson staggered noticeably on his right leg but worked the count to 3 balls and 2 strikes. Then, dramatically, he reached out across the plate and pulled a long drive to right field, where it carried into the seats for a two-run homer and an unlikely 5-4 Dodger victory. These are examples of performance at its finest in the midst of pain at its worst.

Smart Solution 38

Brandon should face his setback squarely and acknowledge it honestly. Going up to Helen and congratulating her is one way of facing disappointment directly. This gesture would have made Helen feel good, demonstrated that Brandon was big-hearted, and would have been an effective way to face reality while relieving his own disappointment.

Brandon needed to develop a realistic plan for achieving what he wanted: a promotion. Not being good enough initially didn't necessarily mean he couldn't develop himself well enough for consideration in the future. He needed to find out where he was lacking, set up a program of self development, and then stick to it. The best way for anyone to achieve a desired result is to concentrate fully on performance and ignore pain—stick to the business at hand and better results will follow.

Each of us is much like Brandon in that we work to make our hopes into realities. But events do not always go as we want them to go. Unexpected snags and bad breaks have a way of cropping up just as we think we're about to succeed. Disappointments can set us back or stop us altogether. When situations of a negative nature occur, denial is never a good response. Brandon thought he'd get the promotion but it went to Helen, who the boss believed was better qualified. Brandon needed to get away from the situation for a short while to enable his hurt feelings to diminish. He needed to get over his disappointment, to think rationally and realistically, and thus begin acting effectively again.

Dilemma 39

Your work situation is intolerable and you think it will not improve.

Brian was only 35 years old and already next in line for the job of technical operations chief at a rapidly expanding biotechnology firm.

Feeling that a promotion was right around the corner, Brian purchased what he had been eyeing for weeks: an expensive European luxury sedan. He had wanted to buy the car for months in order to demonstrate to the world that he had "arrived."

Then, in a short span of time, everything turned sour. Brian's boss informed him that their firm was being sold to a much larger organization. As a result, Brian's job was being eliminated. Brian left the laboratory without saying a thing, and drove directly to a favorite tavern where he drank heavily until closing time.

Escape behaviors work to save your conscious mind from facing unpleasant news. They can take several forms. Self-deception is an obvious one, but there are others: You may sleep more than usual, or behave aggressively toward others, or eat or smoke too much, or turn to alcohol or drugs. But escape is never a permanent solution. Before long, reality creeps through the leaky walls of protection that escape behaviors promise.

The tendency to escape springs from the inability to squarely face up to the hopelessness of a situation—to admit that some particular, hoped-for end result is now impossible. Compulsively, many people, unwilling to forget the door that closed, stand paralyzed outside of it, hoping it will reopen. As they wait, they distract themselves with diversions. After a while, their escape methods become their primary focus, and their crutch becomes a compulsion.

Look to the future and find its possibilities.

At the end of *Gone With the Wind*, Scarlet O'Hara spoke an important truth: "There's always tomorrow." Perhaps Scarlet was childish in her thinking, but this realization can be especially helpful to anyone who has just encountered a setback. Who wants to live in a world of misery and despair? Yet we find it all around us. What can you do? The healthy response is to move on, to find new opportunities, and to make something of them.

The best answer to "hopeless" situations lies in choosing the right perspective. How we look at things is largely because of two important beliefs: what we want, and what we believe we can make happen through our own efforts. Normal, healthy-minded people much prefer to encounter better days, and so they think of the future as possessing opportunities for good fortune rather than bad. They know that better days are a product of their own volition than what happens to them purely by chance.

Consider the life of Abraham Lincoln, whom many believe to be the greatest American. He never earned much money. He lost more elections than he won, the press ridiculed him viciously, he suffered from bouts of depression, had a nervous breakdown, and lost two sons. Yet Lincoln chose not to be stopped by his difficulties. Instead, he got himself elected to the country's highest office and then spent nearly all his energies holding a young nation together. Clearly, Lincoln endured many more failures than successes. But he pushed on, doing what he believed he was intended to do.

Look for another door, one that opens to new opportunities.

It seems to be a rule of life that no sooner does one door slam shut in our face than another one opens up. Have the good sense and courage to venture through the new door. Do it immediately and you'll regain the enthusiasm that makes living a joy.

During the years leading up to World War II, a young French Naval officer's search for adventure led him to enter the fleet aviation academy at Hourtin, an Atlantic coast town west of Bordeaux. The approach of the war notwithstanding, the years preceding were filled with excitement and adventure. The young officer's interests centered on airplane performance, cars, and women. Then one foggy night in 1936, his car's headlights failed as he drove down a mountain road. A hairpin curve lay just ahead. His car left the road and rolled several times.

When the young man regained consciousness hours later, he realized he was losing blood and would surely die. But help arrived, and he was taken to a nearby hospital. The accident had crushed several ribs and perforated his lungs. Broken bones in his left forearm stuck through his skin. Doctors thought amputation was the best course because of massive nerve damage to the arm and the likelihood of infection. The young officer flatly refused. He underwent therapy for eight months. Finally, after much painful struggle, he willed himself to move a finger. Many more months passed before he regained control of all his fingers. The young officer saw his ordeal as a test. Every morning, as he recalled years later, he considered how lucky he was to be alive. The car crash had possibly kept him from entering a war that eventually took the life of every other cadet in his flying class.

The Navy sent the 26-year-old officer to Toulon, on the Mediterranean coast, where he met Philippe Tailliez, a Navy lieutenant. Tailliez encouraged the young man to swim in the sea to strengthen his arm. One summer's day, Tailliez handed the young officer a pair of goggles, and using them for the first time, the young officer opened his eyes to the world beneath the surface of the sea.

It was then, swimming below the water's surface, that the young French Naval officer, Jacques Cousteau, witnessed a new world of undersea flora and fauna for the first time. It was the beginning of a career as the world's premier explorer of the ocean, and finally as the host of an acclaimed television series.

Don't be too sure you can tell whether something will ultimately be good or bad for you.

Things are not always what they seem to be. What we desire is as likely to bring us pain and trouble as it is to bring happiness and satisfaction. It's difficult to say for sure, therefore, whether something will ultimately be good or bad for us. We just cannot foretell what might spring from an unusual event.

An ancient Chinese fable illustrates this idea. There once was a wise old man who owned many wonderful horses. One was particularly strong and fast and beautiful. It was his favorite, and the wise old man's neighbors wished that they could own such a fine animal. One day, however, this horse escaped from his corral and ran away, far into the mountains. The wise old man's neighbors helped him look for the marvelous horse but it was nowhere to be found. They sympathized with him. "We are so sorry this terrible thing has happened." The wise old man said, "Things are not always as they seem. Who can tell if this is good or bad?"

The next day the horse returned leading a herd of more than 50 equally beautiful wild horses with him. The neighbors gathered to admire the many beautiful animals and said, "Such good fortune has come back to you. You are a very lucky man."

To this, the wise old man replied, "Things are not always as they seem. Who can tell if this is good or bad?" Shortly after he said this, his only son tried to ride one of the wild horses, fell off, and broke his leg.

The neighbors said, "What a tragedy; such misfortune you have suffered." Again the wise old man said, "Things are not always as they seem. Who can tell if this is good or bad?" The next day the Emperor's general of the Army came to draft the old man's son for a dangerous mission, but since the young man's leg was broken, he could not go. A neighbor's son was selected in his place. Again, his neighbors considered the wise old man's fortune. They said this turn of events was good. And again, the wise old man refused to say whether the events predicted good or evil.

This story goes on and on through many more twists and turns. What the man's neighbors thought was good fortune turned out to be bad and what they saw as bad fortune actually was good. The story illustrates that what comes in the end is not always what it might appear to be at first.

Growing up in Louisville, Muhammad Ali was as delighted as any 9 year old boy could be when his parents presented him with a bicycle. One day, he parked it outside of a gym. When he returned the bicycle was gone, stolen. Someone told him to go find a policeman. "I'll find the guy who stole my bike and beat him up," Ali told the officer. The policeman found that the boy didn't know how to fight and offered to teach him to box. He never found the bike.

Smart Solution 39

Many people have faced the same difficulty that Brian now faced: loss of job through corporate downsizing. There was far more to this problem than the mere loss of a job. Brian had lost a sense of security and emotional well-being, perhaps, the more important issues he needed to figure out how to effectively grapple with. Escape is a feeble attempt to relieve pain, and like a weak drug, its relief-giving power wears off eventually. It cannot provide security or emotional well being—only genuine hope accomplishes that. Genuine hope arises when you achieve positive results from the concentration of your efforts.

This is what Brian needed to do to regain his loss of well-being, to take definitive steps that showed promise for an agreeable outcome. Brian needed to uncover whatever opportunities existed. Action is the key. Doors of opportunity rarely open by themselves; Brian must act to find them and test what he finds to ensure whether they will open for him. This meant searching for opportunities actively and intelligently, not waiting around hoping to be rescued.

Go to a library or bookstore and select several volumes on how to find the right job for yourself. Read and follow whatever practical advice is suggested regarding self-assessment, job search processes, the preparation and formatting of resumes, search firms, networking, interviewing skills, and so on.

Dilemma 40

You were dealt a bad break while good fortune shines on others.

Janine had just completed a grueling and frustrating month, juggling an overload of work, nagging, demanding superiors, and a surly, irresponsible staff of office help. To top things off, her boss asked her to complete an important assignment by 10 a.m. the following Monday.

Being a Friday, Janine was tired and annoyed, resentful of the fact that she'll have to give up Saturday and most of her Sunday. Frustrated by her work situation, Janine treated herself to a lavish meal and spent the remainder of her Friday evening buying herself "rewards" at the nicest stores around town to make up for the unfairness she felt she endured at work.

Later that night she ran into an acquaintance and insisted they have a drink together. Janine had a load on her mind, and after the drinks were served, she began: "I'm always the one who has to pick up the slack while others get to play. My last boss treated me the same way. Maybe I should have stayed there; this job isn't any better. Actually, this job is a lot worse in many ways. My present boss is much more picky—everything has to be just right. And all the really difficult jobs get dumped on me. Does she ever work overtime? No. She says she has to be at home with her family on the weekends. I don't have a husband or children, so guess who gets the last minute rush jobs? I'll never have a social life working for her..."

Pity affords people an opportunity to express their hurt feelings, which they do over and over. Perhaps in the face of a setback, you may have said things like, "Why me? Life isn't fair. It's not my fault. I am the victim. My life is ruined now." That's pity. This is a very human response; we all engage in it. Nonetheless, it's still a dumb thing to do because it weakens our ability to work out a permanent solution.

At first, you may feel alone from the hurt of a setback, but in time, your self-pity might attract someone who has experienced a similar misfortune. Drawn together by the bond of their common experience, the "injured" form informal support networks, where they tell and retell their sad tales and give sympathy to each other. This process can fortify a growing belief that the world has many innocent victims, victims who have been stung by misfortune. When you engage in pity, you are unwittingly paralyzed by feeling sorry for yourself and not thinking productively. Does any of this sound familiar?

Work, do not worry. Busy yourself with action.

Time for a reality check. Consider your disappointment and what you are doing about it. Exactly where is your focus, on the pain or on doing something positive? Are you still complaining, telling others about the wrong you've suffered? Or are you "getting on" with your life, focusing on an undertaking worthy of your talents? Here's a helpful hint for dealing with your disappointment. Replace your worry with work. Let imagination fill your thoughts, not anger, pity, or sorrow.

Mary Kay Ash is among the brightest stars of American business, and her approach to making herself successful is worth telling. Hers was not a life of ease and comfort, but it was rich with accomplishments. Before she turned ten, Mary Kay was given the responsibility of cooking, cleaning, and taking care of her invalid father while her mother worked. Mary Kay accepted this responsibility and was very successful in school and in sports. Her mother's words to her were simple but effective: "You can do it." They made an indelible impression on young Mary Kay, helping to spur on her self confidence. This served her well during the Depression, when Mary Kay's husband of 11 years deserted her, leaving her to support three children all under the age of eight. She took a job selling Stanley Home Products, which she excelled at with great distinction. She went on to become the national training director of another company, World Gift.

Tragedy struck in 1962, when Mary Kay's life and career were threatened by a rare paralysis on one side of her face. But again, she rose above her adversity. Recovering from surgery, Mary Kay retired from World Gift. She was remarried by then—now, Mary Kay Ash—and living comfortably in Dallas, but she soon became bored. She decided to write a book on direct selling. As she wrote the book, it dawned on her that women had a terrible time in the business world. There were so many problems they faced working and keeping a family going.

So, Mary Kay made a list of what she saw was wrong with male-run companies, and how they could be fixed so that working mothers could reach their full potential in business. This gave her the idea and incentive to start her own company, employing the very women she wanted to help. Her organization would be structured differently than the others: flexible hours, few rules, autonomy, and no sales quotas.

Ten years earlier, Mary Kay had become acquainted with a woman who had tried unsuccessfully to market her own line of skin creams. In 1963, Mary Kay purchased the formulas for $500. In the years that followed, her marketing organization took form. She set up a nationwide network of independent sales representatives called beauty consultants. Mary Kay saw a need for cosmetics as a desire of American women to feel good about themselves by earning added income and achieving recognition. Mary Kay hit upon a method—a very good method—to meet their needs and it evolved into a thriving enterprise: her skin care cosmetics business.

Here's the fascinating thing about Mary Kay's business: it didn't consist of skin creams and beauty care products. Mary Kay Ash was in the business of selling small businesses women could run out of their homes. And this is what she did, for thousands of women all across America.

Mary Kay's philosophy for running her firm was to market skin care products in a way that provided sales representatives with recognition and a sense of independence. Mary Kay sold her creams and other beauty aids to these women who, in turn, sold them to customers in their towns and neighborhoods. Unquestionably, the real factor behind Mary Kay's business success was her genius for inspiring and recognizing the accomplishments of her beauty consultants. Her meetings and conventions featured motivational speeches, sales incentives, and prizes for the top performers, such as fur coats and pink Cadillacs. Mary Kay's "customers" were the independent businesswomen who sold Mary Kay Cosmetics. What Mary Kay Ash sold *them* was the chance to have a profitable business and to feel good about themselves though their effective performance.

Smart Solution 40

Janine's case was a special one, but it involved the same kind of remedy. Simply telling her to work harder—in the conventional sense of work—was not an effective solution. She was a hard worker, and will probably will remain one throughout her life. If something needed doing, Janine could be trusted to get it done. She possessed a highly developed work ethic, certainly a most admirable character trait.

Janine's difficulty lay in how she saw herself in the scheme of things. She loved being the one to get stuck with all the difficult assignments—she *wanted* to be "dumped on." This is because Janine took pride in the thought that she suffered more than others. She distinguished herself, in her mind, as being better than others because of how hard she had to work. However, Janine "suffers" by relying on her two greatest strengths: responsibility and hard work. Janine was saying, in effect, "Please don't ask me to work on the weekend and be responsible." But that's precisely what she wanted to feel for herself, and for others to sympathize with as well.

Janine could most help herself by not whining and start working at "getting a life." This would be a different kind of work for her, one that she doesn't appear to excel at. If she wanted friends, a husband, a well-adjusted family, in effect, a 'complete life,' then Janine needed to busy herself with those pursuits. She needed to work at developing herself in other ways, such as focusing on becoming a whole person, one who does more than just work. A first step might be to simply decline when asked to work a weekend, or perform some other duty she'd rather not do. She had to stop making herself the focus of attention, and stop complaining about how miserable her life was. She could cultivate better relationships with those around her by not involving them in her personal affairs.

For most people, hard work is the best antidote to their troubles. It shifts their focus off their worries and enables them to concentrate not only on their requisite business duties, but on those daily actions that led to productive ends.

Dilemma 41

You are the victim of an underhanded trick or unfairness.

Jolene had her heart set on a new position opening up in a different department. It matched her training and interests perfectly. She prepared her resume and gave it to the department head, who seemed very interested. But Kathy, one of Jolene's co-workers, wanted the job so much she badmouthed Jolene publicly. Jolene was certain that the department head got wind of this gossip because Kathy got the job. Jolene was tempted to start a rumor about Kathy.

James was in charge of a team that was responsible for the development of a new product. The team was extremely successful, but James' immediate supervisor did an extraordinarily good job of taking credit for James' work. His staff knew that James completed the work, not the supervisor. "How can you let him do that to you?" they asked. James thought about going over his supervisor's head and reporting the truth to his superiors.

"Don't get mad, get even." That seems to be the appropriate response when someone "does you wrong." It may sound worthwhile and appealing when you've been the victim of an underhanded trick, but ultimately it is self defeating. Follow such a maxim and you destroy yourself. It will destroy your reputation, your self respect, and your ability to think straight and act intelligently.

Get rid of your bitterness.

One of the most liberating concepts we can apply to our daily lives is that of ridding our hearts of bitterness. Perhaps you have become troubled by an unpleasant situation or by a mean-spirited person you have gotten into nasty encounters with. Of course, the most tempting thing to do is to fight back, to try to even the score. I have read numerous accounts of the corrosive effects bitterness has on the human mind and physical health. They all say the same thing: it's detrimental to your mind because it prevents you from thinking clearly. It's bad for your health because it makes your body work against itself; and it's bad for your relationships with others because your decent side becomes dominated 0by its bitter counterpart.

Focus your attention outwardly.

The ability to turn away from disappointment and direct your best efforts toward productive pursuits can bring astounding results.

Many years ago, a woman named Pat Gifford moved with her husband and two children to the town where I live. Her husband, Jack, began his teaching career in our university's department of marketing. Pat thought she'd like to teach too, and because she had an advanced degree in textiles, landed a position in Miami University's department of home economics. Pat's teaching was good, but her scholarly qualifications didn't meet her tenure committee's expectations, and she was subsequently let go.

Now, this sort of blow would have probably crippled the spirit of most people. Pat's feelings were hurt by it, but she wasn't the kind of person to be destroyed by disappointment. She certainly didn't fume and fret and allow herself to be consumed with bitterness. Instead, she moved on, looking for something else suitable to her abilities.

Shortly afterward, a job opened with a small department store chain in nearby Dayton. Pat applied and got the job—her role was to set up and conduct employee training. This work matched her interests and abilities, and she performed exceedingly well. She found she liked personnel work and studied for another advanced degree at Purdue University.

Her supervisors noticed something else, something quite rare, something they needed for their growing enterprise. a positive, friendly attitude. Everyone liked her and what she did. She was not one to hold bitterness in her heart, but instead, took setbacks in stride, ignoring the little things and marshalling her best towards realizing the big challenges.

Advancement after advancement followed. Today, Pat Gifford is vice president of human resources of Elder Beerman.

Smart Solution 41

The illustration of Jolene and Kathy, and the illustration of James and his boss were set side by side to make a point: there are times to stand up for yourself, and there are times when it's better to let others do it for you. Kathy, it appeared, had acted in a manner damaging to Jolene's reputation. This might permanently cripple her chances of doing well in her workplace. Confronting someone directly with a complaint works wonders for at least two reasons: The act sends a clear signal that the complainant will not tolerate the other person's actions, and it forces both parties to face the truth.

One approach Jolene might take would be to have a discussion her boss directly. "I understand that Kathy said these untrue things about me. I want you to know the truth and how I feel about having my good name damaged." Her boss might understand Jolene to be a very direct, down-to-earth individual with a good deal of personal integrity, qualities that were universally respected. Her intention must not be to harm Kathy but rather to bring out the truth about herself.

Chapter 7

The Stalled Engine

Jump-starting performance by acting boldly

Playwright Garson Kanin once asked Arthur Rubenstein, "Am I right in thinking that you're playing better now than ever before?"

"I think so," the great pianist answered.

"Is it experience, practice, or what?"

"No, no, no," said Rubenstein. "Being 80, I take chances I never took before. You see, the stakes are not so high. I can afford it. I used to be so much more careful—no wrong notes, no too bold ideas. Now, I let go and enjoy myself, and to hell with everything except the music!"

There can be little doubt that we are at our best when we act on our convictions without reservation—when we are not tentative or overly concerned with what others think. Our best efforts come when we boldly do what we believe should be done. Boldness involves thoughtful commitment to a position and steadfast effort to see it through, regardless of difficulties encountered along the way. Boldness is the bridge from our visions to great victories, the great enabler in all of us.

Too many men and women in the workplace clog the highways to success and accomplishment because of their misfiring and stalled engines. These people fail to do well because they are overly cautious, or consumed by self doubt and needless worry. They allow themselves to become preoccupied with the fear that they might slip up and fail to perform flawlessly, or live in fear of offending someone else with their novel ideas. Cautiously and timidly, they act, not with full force and confidence, but with hesitation. Being too tentative in taking steps forward, they fail to give their finest efforts and fail to advance their cause. They remain stuck where they are—their engines of progress stalled out.

This chapter tells you how to jump-start your engine with the spark of boldness so you can speed ahead toward your desired destination, with the full force needed to get there.

Dilemma 42

You think you have figured out a good solution for solving a difficulty at work; however, defining the problem and resolving it conflicts with the views of top management.

Tony's work combined his two loves: boating and interior design. As the new member on a design team for a major boat manufacturer, Tony's responsibilities included identifying customer wants and needs, and designing boat interior layouts that were both functional and pleasing. For 11 months, Tony traveled abroad to study European styles. He also spent considerable time talking to boaters about their likes and dislikes. He made notes, sketched some of the more unusual boats he saw, and doodled with several shapes and forms of his own creation.

Tony thought he had a fair idea why his company's boats—cruisers from 30 to 65 feet long—didn't stack up against their rivals' boats in the market. Tony knew it wouldn't be easy to get the others in his design team, all older and more experienced than he was, to go along with his ideas and concepts.

Tony's firm produced boats that had a reputation for roominess. Tony saw that customer preferences were moving towards boats with character in their interior, meaning interesting spaces rather than accomodating living quarters. European boat interiors reflected this change in customer desires, but the higher-ups in Tony's firm disliked the "new" look. They believed their boats should have the "traditional" look exemplified by the design schemes of fifty or more years ago. These managers thought sales were off not because the market was changing, but because dealers around the country were not pushing their products hard enough. They saw poor marketing as the reason for their company's slide in the market, not out-of-date designs.

Practically everyone wants to fit in and be well thought of by their peers, Tony included. This is a normal and healthy concern, but one that could be carried too far. Tony needed to be aware of this. Whatever the matter at hand is—a person, an object, an idea—there are always those who might prefer an alternative. Tony should've realized that he can either advocate what he believes to be true and gain self-approval, or he could go along with established mores and make himself agreeable with upper management. Tony's engine could stall out if he tried too hard to fit in by not introducing any worthwhile innovations.

"To thine own self be true," the King of Denmark advised his son, Hamlet. Boldly following one's own heart and mind—going ahead with one's own thoughts and ideas—and, thereby, pleasing one's self, can produce wonderful change and lasting improvements that can better the world. The person who does not "fit in with himself," who acts in ways to please others, may eventually fit in, but such a person becomes troubled, full of sharp edges in his personality that continually remind what little rewards a lack of boldness brings.

Follow what's inside your heart and mind.

Georgia O'Keeffe did what few women were able to do in the early part of the century. She established a reputation as a world-acclaimed artist in what was for a long time a man's world. She showed that a woman could equal any man in her chosen field, while leaving her mark on the history of American art. O'Keeffe was described as strong-willed, hardworking and whimsical—she painted as she wanted to paint, and America and the rest of the world loved it.

She achieved greatness because she boldly painted what images her imagination revealed: the skull of a horse with a pink Mexican artificial flower in its eye socket; animal skulls, horns, pelvises and leg bones that gleamed white against brilliant skies; New York skyscrapers, Canadian barns and crosses, and oversized flowers.

Painting as she pleased, O'Keeffe sold her works for very good prices. She was accorded entry into the inner circle of modern American artists, maintaining a step ahead of everyone all the time. This rugged individualist asserted herself because she chose to paint as she wanted to paint, even though it was out of step with the popular taste and accepted style of her time. This was a conscious decision, and Miss O'Keeffe made it deliberately. "One day," she said in her later years, "I found myself thinking, 'I can't live where I want to. I can't even say what I want to.' I decided I was a very stupid fool not at least to paint as I wanted to."

Smart Solution 42

Tony could himself miserable if he went along with what those in his organization thought about boat design. Winning their approval was of minor importance compared to what Tony had to offer. If his heart wasn't in his work, Tony would certainly not perform well. By following what his heart and mind told him to do, Tony could rest easy at night knowing that his actions were consistent with his beliefs, which might force some movement of value to occur in his company. At least his ideas stood a fair chance of helping his company compete effectively. Years from now, the owners might thank him for revitalizing their firm's sales through his daring boat design concepts.

Dilemma 43

You face a difficult situation at work and see three ways of handling it. Each approach offers advantages and disadvantages, which you fully understand. You find it impossible to select a course of action, because none promises to deliver all you want without any of the drawbacks you hope to avoid.

Margaret supervised production work at a die-casting company and had to decide who of the five people on the day shift should be moved to the night shift. She asked their supervisor for input, but he didn't add anything to what she already knew. Margaret made a list of the five individuals and wrote down what she knew about each one, and how they might react to a change in their work schedule.

There isn't anything we do that does not have some kind of downside to it. Whatever good we attempt to do might prevent us from doing something else. The person who takes hot soup to a sick friend has to neglect the weeding of his garden—it is impossible to be in more than one place at once. We live in an imperfect world, which usually means that we are forced to choose one thing over another.

When faced with difficult choices—What to do, where to be, which action to take—even the best of us can become frozen with indecision. But indecision is, itself, a choice. It's the choice of "not deciding." The person who fails to act because he cannot decide which action to take is making a choice of sorts. Perhaps no decision is better than any of the other available options; perhaps no action is preferable to all other possible actions. The point is that one must decide with his eyes wide open and then take a stand.

Commit to a position.

Upon graduation from a teacher's college in his native Italy, Luciano Pavarotti asked his father, "Shall I be a teacher or a singer?"

"Luciano," his father replied, "if you try to sit on two chairs, you will fall between them. In life, you must choose one chair." The tenor superstar chose one. After seven years of difficult study and frustration, he made his first professional appearance.

Whether it's developing a new product, creating better marketing methods—whatever we choose—we do our best when we give ourselves to it. Commitment is the key. Choose one chair.

Use ideals to guide your choices.

Suppose your company has just spent 39 months and $1.6 billion creating a new family of cars—a bold move that in all likelihood will determine whether your firm remains a major player in the hotly competitive auto industry. Then, an unforeseen problem arises shortly after you ship the first 4,000 vehicles: a washer on the suspension system of one car breaks during a test-drive training session. You know that quality and reputation are all important for these newly designed vehicles. What should be done?

That was the question Chrysler's chairman, Lee Iacocca, had to ponder. Should Chrysler fix the one car, hoping the broken washer was just an isolated incident? Should they check the remaining 3,950 cars that were not yet in buyers' hands, and quietly recall the 50 already sold? Or should they recall all 4,000 cars and loudly alert the public to the situation? A recall risked destroying consumer confidence in the new cab-forward cars. Iacocca chose the third option. Why? Because he was boldly committed to building a reputation for product quality.

Smart Solution 43

Margaret should be commended for recognizing that whatever she chose would have negative effects associated with it. It's a fact of life in our imperfect world. She was on the right track in creating the personnel listing, itemizing what she needed in order to arrive at the best decision. The biggest mistake Margaret could make would be to stall out and not decide at all. In proceeding with her decision, she should implement the following: identify her chief aims and list them in order of priority, emphasizing which goals or ends are most important to reach; list the consequences, good and bad, associated with each option; and select the option that best leads to the most desired end result.

It is incredibly easy to cause your engine to stall, to refuse to act because no option provides all the desired benefits without any of the drawbacks. Margaret needed to become realistic and see life as it really was, replete with all its imperfections. Otherwise she might become frozen with indecision, and stall out.

Dilemma 44

In your heart, you feel a particular action should be followed, but you cannot prove it will bring tangible benefits.

Gene was chief safety engineer for a Fortune 500 company. He believed that a solid safety effort involved far more than wall posters, slogans, and tabulating accident statistics. Gene thought the best way to advance safety practices was through behavior modification, with the emphasis on changing behavior, getting people to act in safer ways. Gene's secretary had a knack for writing stories gathered from within the company and retelling them in an interesting fashion. When she suggested the idea of sending a safety newsletter to her boss, Gene enthusiastically approved the idea.

The idea behind the newsletter, which went to production employees throughout the organization, was to encourage safe behavior by retelling accounts of people acting safely. The newsletter carried safety tips, news about company-sponsored safety seminars, ideas for supervisors to use to reinforce safe behavior, and anecdotes from the lives and work experiences of company personnel.

The newsletter received praise from readers, many of whom took it home for their spouses to read. It caused people to think and act more safely, but Gene was unable to provide statistics to back up such claims. He didn't have tangible evidence that his newsletter made a verifiable difference, evidence that the bottom line-oriented upper management demanded and turned to whenever they made a business decision.

Despite the newsletter's popularity, several cost-sensitive safety specialists within Gene's unit felt that the secretary should cease publishing it because its benefits couldn't be measured objectively.

There is a certain amount of comfort received from pursuing only those ventures and programs that guarantee a bottom line benefit. Although a complete disregard for bottom line considerations is foolish, obsession with only the bottom line can be equally harmful. Many things done within and by business organizations have to be done on the belief that they are right, and capable of making the organization a thriving entity which contributes positively to the world beyond the narrow scope of profit.

Merely thinking that you'll do well financially can never be enough to motivate you to carry a great venture on to its successful completion. To surmount the many difficulties that always arise, you must believe in what you do. The enterprise has to appeal to your finer side, beyond the ease and comfort of your bank account.

Efforts made in management development and training, safety newsletters, detailed quality inspection procedures, open corporate communication, and employee dialogue with the firm's leaders, are just a few of the things done by business people because they believe such policies are important. Even though proof does not exist that these efforts will produce bottom line benefits, they should be rigorously applied on the belief that they are the key to the entire process. and enthusiastically on the strength of the belief that they should be done.

See beyond the bottom line.

I know there are many people who firmly believe that a calculating approach to everything is just good business sense. They feel that every single decision in business must be justified economically. But this isn't how the most successful businesses operate. The profit-above-all-else approach too often neglects vital sources of goodwill, public acceptance, product quality, and development. AT&T's experience with the manufacture of telephones provides a good illustration of this idea.

AT&T came from a heritage of product leasing, specifically telephones. In their business environment, it was important economically to make telephones that didn't fall apart, as it was inherently costly to repair them. It's also inconvenient for people to own a product that goes dead on them in the middle of the night, especially if they live out in the country.

With deregulation and the break-up of AT&T, competition changed. A flood of cheap residential telephones came on the market that could be bought everywhere. AT&T faced a question: should it manufacture cheap telephones to compete at the low end of the market?

The president of Western Electric, the manufacturing arm of AT&T, acknowledged that they could make a cheap phone probably better than anybody else, and sell it for less. Ultimately, he decided against such an option—and maintaining such high standards didn't harm the company's sales or profits at all.

Today, AT&T is the dominant provider of residential telephones largely because they didn't make the cheapest ones. They chose to manufacture and compete at the quality end of the market, forcing their competitors to shift tactics towards the same end of the spectrum. As it turned out, AT&T was right: the American public had a very strong desire to own a reliable, high quality piece of equipment that continued to work year after year.

Here's an additional illustration. W. Atlee Burpee staked his firm's future and his reputation on the proposition that quality would sell. It was Burpee's stated opinion that "Quality is long remembered after price is forgotten."

Balance the bottom line with your own standards.

Another AT&T example serves this tip well. The company was marketing a personal computer made by Olivetti in Italy. Although the computer was UL approved, while experimenting with different methods of connection, one of AT&T's computer technicians found that the machine could be connected in such a way that the user might suffer an electrical shock. Underwriters Laboratories had already approved the computer's wiring and AT&T had 40,000 of them in their warehouse. What should be done about the possible problem?

AT&T stopped shipping. They immediately went back through each component, at their own expense, and fixed the problem on every one. Then, the company went out to every customer's location and made the necessary repairs, despite the fact that Underwriters Laboratories didn't believe such repairs were necessary. AT&T said, "We don't care. We are not going to put anybody who buys our product at any kind of risk." It was an expensive proposition at the time, but the company knew it was one they were compelled to do.

Act on your convictions.

In the 1950s, Ford was the first to introduce certain safety features in its automobiles: the collapsible wheel, door locks, padded visors, and seat belts. Under Robert S. McNamara's leadership, Ford employees looked to gather information on how to reduce fatalities. Their search led them to the Cornell Aeronautical Laboratories, which had been hired by the U.S. Army Air Corps in World War II. The aeronautical research unit found that more lives were being lost not from airplanes but from automobiles. After the war, this research effort was continued in North Carolina with the state police. Based upon their findings, Ford introduced several safety features. That decision was strongly opposed by both industry insiders and by some from within the Ford organization, who argued that it wasn't safety that sold automobiles, and also that it was a societal problem. McNamara disagreed with this thinking and moved boldly to do what he believed should be done.

Smart Solution 44

In insisting that the newsletter continue, Gene could have stressed the interest it generated in raising awareness regarding safety. This was an intangible benefit, difficult to measure, but one that was essential in getting people to change. He could argue that increased awareness for safety and the social pressures created from it are effective means of shaping behavior, the key reason why behavior-based safety management is so effective. Gene's engine could stall out if he insisted that every action taken, including his newsletter, be justified on economic grounds.

Of course, every expenditure and every action should produce value, but measuring all the benefits is never easy. Some benefits show up in ways we could never imagine possible; others creep in unnoticed. For this reason, it's necessary to expand our perceptive powers to see these other benefits. It is a matter of becoming aware of both tangibles and intangibles.

Dilemma 45

You begin each workday with high hopes of implementing at least one of your many ideas for improvement. But as the years pass by, none of your concepts ever turn into actions. You refuse to act because you can't get all the information you think you need, and you never feel any of your improvements are well-planned enough to achieve effective results.

Leslie was what many would call a natural born teacher. She had the ability to inspire young minds and her students loved her for it. Leslie developed an idea that she used with great success, one that she hopes will gain widespread acceptance in other classrooms throughout the country. Her idea was based on the proposition that people learned best when they had a need to know, when they saw they were able to achieve something utilizing certain knowledge. Leslie's innovative learning method replaced drills with hands-on exercises. She created situations in her classroom in which children achieved an observable result if they learned particular lessons they could apply. Leslie's technique created a "want to know in order to do something" motivation, which in today's schoolrooms is often overridden by a "want to know in order to win recognition and rewards" motivation.

Over the course of 16 years, Leslie created numerous learning exercises for the lessons her students needed to master state requirements. The problem Leslie had was that her method was largely untested, and she couldn't introduce it into the school's curriculum until it was. She had experimented with some of her ideas, but other teachers still had yet to try them. Leslie feared the other teachers wouldn't approve of her methods, which was why she had not presented them at teacher conferences. She feared her methods might be laughed at for being "too far out." Leslie knew she needed more information before she could present her theories to the other teachers.

Many ideas are hatched in people's heads, but few of them are ever brought to fruition. Laziness might be to blame, although most people seem to be easily diverted by fears that arise from within themselves. Leslie stalled out and didn't push ahead because she was not 100 percent certain that other teachers would react positively to her ideas. We can consider likely reasons for this attitude. One might be that Leslie feared failure so much that she was afraid to go beyond the thinking stage. By not acting, she protected herself from failure, from ridicule, and from feeling bad about herself. So she played it safe. But playing it safe is hardly an admirable quality.

Leslie might have employed another tactic to protect herself. It's called delay. By delaying, she avoids any possibility of failure, but to delay is to destroy. If Leslie delayed too long, she could destroy her ability to act, and, ultimately, her ideas and the good that might come from them.

TIP

Wager that your idea will work.

An entrepreneur was about to launch his new enterprise. He believed his product was well made and he thought it would find strong customer acceptance. The basic organization was in place to finance, produce, and market the new product. Marketing surveys had been conducted. Prototypes had been made and tested. The investors and creditors went over the business plan many times. Will it be successful?

Nobody can predict for certain. It takes a gamble, a trial, a great leap of faith that the venture will succeed. Were the owner to know all the problems, frustrations, setbacks and difficulties beforehand, the new enterprise might never begin. Worrisome difficulties are not the focus of a bold person's attention.

Once the venture is begun, the enterprise struggles and problems may arise. Disaster may lurk around any corner as financial obligations fall due. However, once started there is no turning back; without faith that the enterprise would work, it is impossible to withstand the troubles that always follow. Boldness is not simply risk taking, and it most certainly is not reckless, uninformed gambling on poorly conceived schemes. Boldness is the abiding commitment to face the future, no matter how terrible or tragic the problems therein may be.

Be bold. Act boldly.

How can you become a bold individual? You decide by an act of will that you will stand up for your high standards—you decide your actions must reflect your words. You commit yourself to what you believe, not because it gives you an immediate payoff, but because you believe it should be done, because you believe it is, in the long run, in the best interests of everyone concerned.

When you can act without hesitation, you do so without worrying what others might say or think about you. You act out of conviction, not expected rewards. And finally, you are bold in all areas, especially when mending a wrong or advancing a good cause. Effective leaders do this all the time.

Smart Solution 45

Leslie's progress shut down. Her stalled engine occurred because of her desire to delay, and she delayed because she wasn't 100 percent certain her ideas would work, or that others would accept them. It would be simple to tell Leslie to act, but informing her to do so would probably be futile at best. Leslie must honestly reason with herself and come to grips with what lay behind her inability to proceed ahead.

Leslie doesn't realize it, but she stalled out from her fear of failure. She imagined hundreds of reasons why her ideas might not work, and then used these reasons as "legitimate" excuses for not taking action. Leslie needed to face up to the fact that she concocted her own reasons for failing to act, and that the development of those reasons, if not grasped and eliminated, could lead to her being stymied further.

Leslie functions like many of those who never go forward with their ideas—the professor who never finishes writing his book, the artist who never paints the picture she dreams about and mentions to others, the business person who has a wonderful money-making scheme but never implements it. The fear of failure in these people extends beyond an inability to reach a level of success or a level of perfection. To these people—and Leslie might well be one of them—if their project isn't flawless, if it isn't of Nobel Prize quality, then, in their minds, it's a failure, and they will delay taking action because they cannot tolerate being imperfect.

Dilemma 46

You face a decision that you do not want to make, because no matter how you decide, someone will likely criticize you for it. It's easier to pass the decision on to your superiors.

Monica worked as a claims processing clerk for a large insurance company. Her department processed medical and hospitalization claims. Clerks had to maintain records of all claims submitted and follow prescribed procedures in making payments. They had to determine whether the person filing each claim exceeded the deductible threshold, whether the claim was covered by the insured's policy, and the amount that should be paid.

Sometimes, claims are filed more than once; the insurer will not pay for some procedures, and there are often limits on the amount the insurer will cover. Clerks were responsible for making the correct determinations and writing the insured persons form letters explaining actions taken when claimants made mistakes.

Sometimes a case was confusing. Most clerks handled these situations with occasional help from their supervisors, but Monica constantly needed assistance. Whenever she thought she might make an error because a case had some gray aspects to it, Monica went to her boss for help. Unfortunately, it's something she did far too frequently.

This is what is called passing the buck. Unable or unwilling to make a decision, a person passes it on for their higher-ups to take the responsibility. The reasons for buck-passing might be to avoid blame if a decision turns out badly, or to avoid the necessary process of considering all the aspects and their possible consequences. After all, thinking is hard work, and so is avoiding mistakes and decisions that are just too big or too difficult to handle.

Notice something about the statements: the word "avoid" shows up in each one. Buck-passers are "avoiders"; they are timid souls, afraid to stand up and take a stand. They run away from responsibility, from making themselves accountable for consequences, from the hard work needed when thinking through complex issues, from the possibility that others will think ill of them for making a mistake, and from the realities of life that challenge healthy individuals every day.

The chief source of most buck passing is an overpowering need for safety, which takes precedence above all else, dominating a person's every move. Mistakes, ridicule, criticism—these are what everyone fears most and tries to avoid by passing the buck and subsequently stalling out their engines. What Monica and other buck-passers have to realize is that by acting as they do—by avoiding decisions—they end up inert and create an indelible impression of themselves in the minds of others. It isn't an admirable impression.

Decide what to do on the basis of "what's right."

In 1982, police authorities attributed several deaths in Chicago to Johnson & Johnson's Tylenol, manufactured by its McNeil Laboratories. Someone had laced Tylenol capsules with cyanide. Johnson & Johnson received the report on a Thursday morning. McNeil management in Fort Washington just outside Philadelphia, acted immediately, recalling two suspected lots without lengthy discussion. As news media people descended on the McNeil Laboratories headquarters, its managers acted, setting up press conferences to keep the public informed. On their own, without going to Johnson & Johnson corporate headquarters in New Jersey for approval, the local management of McNeil handled the situation. They realized they had a severe crisis on their hands, and they followed their own judgment to do the right thing—remove Tylenol from store shelves immediately. Their first concern was for the public.

Smart Solution 46

The easiest way to overcome your unwillingness to risk making big mistakes is to build up your confidence by tackling small matters. Monica should recognize her fears for what they are, then surmount them by creating a plan for confidence building based on competence acquisition. By recognizing her record of success in handling smaller problems competently, and by doing well with decisions of lesser difficulty, Monica could learn to value her decision-making ability. Through experience, she would gain more confidence as she improved her decision-making abilities.

Chapter 8

The Cheap Suit

Stressing the best rather than the good

In every store and factory across the land, a constant weeding-out process goes on, separating those who accomplish meaningful results from those who merely keep up, going through the motions of acting busy. The world cries out for men and women who get things done, for people who act intelligently on their own initiative and see tasks through to their completion. These are people the world rewards and remembers, people who ignore trifling matters that waste time and talent, people who stick to big things, who produce more than they consume.

Too many people waste time with second-rate efforts instead of making first-rate contributions. It is as if they wore a cheap suit while their best one remained unused, hanging in their closet. So while they might look good, they would fail to look their best.

One of the mightiest forces known for getting yourself to complete the most important tasks is your own will. The trick lies in disciplining yourself to say "no" to little things, to the many pestering distractions that pull you away from doing what matters most. This chapter will show you how to improve your performance by concentrating your efforts on the things that matter.

Dilemma 47

You are new to an organization and want to do well. As you see it, getting ahead requires "networking." This means getting to know, and being known, by the right people, particularly those in power. So, you spend a good bit of your time and effort playing up to those you believe will serve as your sponsors.

Three months ago, Jane became a buyer in the housewares department at Longworth's, a chain of upper-end department stores. Prior to that, she spent over four years as a sales clerk in household goods for a much larger department store chain in another part of the country.

While employed there, Jane attended a seminar on how to move your career ahead and advance in corporate hierarchies. It was at this seminar that she learned the techniques of "networking," which involved making acquaintances with other professionals to improve one's advancement opportunities. Another idea Jane picked up at this seminar was "mentoring," whereby more experienced people helped less experienced people learn the ropes. Jane took this advice seriously.

Being new to the Longworth organization and having entirely different responsibilities than she had performed earlier, Jane decided she should find someone to be her mentor. Jane made a concerted effort to go out of her way to play up to whomever she could corner. She solicited their advice on anything from how to perform her work duties to who she should try to impress because of their level of power in the organization.

Imagine that you are new to an organization and want to move ahead. There's nothing wrong with pursuing the above aims, but let's consider how you might slip up while going about it. Using the concept of the cheap coat, we saw a mistake people might make when putting the good ahead of the best. The question is, which was preferable: concentrating your energies on performing well, or finding a mentor to help advance your career?

The former concern involves giving value. The latter concern involved trying to gain rewards for yourself. Of course, many people will say "Do both." This sounds reasonable but the means isn't all that simple. One desire or direction tends to become dominant, taking precedence over other considerations.

Jane had to look deep inside her heart, find her dominant desire, and then act on it if it really was the best thing to do. It becomes a matter of Jane using her will to select the best course of action. If a choice needed to be made between a person dominated by the desire to do a first-rate job, and a person dominated by the desire to move ahead, which one would you entrust with an important assignment?

Arrange your priorities in the right order.

One of the greatest lessons we can learn about achieving success involves how we inspire ourselves to make our finest efforts. Under certain conditions, people will do extraordinary things that they would not believe themselves capable of doing otherwise. Here's the secret to inspiring first-rate effort: serve something beyond yourself without reservation or hesitation.

People perform best when they are totally committed to some cause that's larger than themselves—something they believe in so much that no sacrifice is too great. J.C. Penney was thinking along those lines when he wrote, "To gain success, one must serve." Adventure comes by putting money second and the success of a great endeavor first—not the other way around. Concentrate on giving your very best and the rewards will follow.

Learn to serve something large by serving it. This skill can be learned in only one way—by one's actions.

How can you become a service-oriented person? First, put other things ahead of yourself. By an act of discipline, you have to stop looking at the world in terms of "what's in it for me?" Ask yourself, "How can I be of value to others?" Think of your work as a great cause—define what you do in noble language. As best as you can, try living for the great purposes that you can set for yourself. After a fashion, you'll actually be living this way without concern for yourself, or without being consumed with worry over how to get everything you can. When you do this, I guarantee something will happen to you that's never fully happened to you before—you are going to be happy, and successful.

Second, just go out and do it. Start serving a worthy cause. It does not have to be anything big. Any kind of service will move you forward. A person learns how to serve through doing, not from listening. Do not expect anything in return. If rewards come your way, fine; if not, say to yourself, "That's okay. The privilege of being able to serve is reward enough." Believe what you say. Your unselfish actions will inspire others to serve, too.

Obliterate yourself as your center of concern, and the extraordinary will follow.

The ideal attitude is to forget about the trivial aspects of your "self," by becoming fully engrossed in accomplishing a worthy end. This is how wise people escape the trap of self-centeredness and destructive consequences like greed, vanity, arrogance, and the like.

In hundreds of offices of AT&T managers and executives across the country stands a small bronze statue of Angus Macdonald, representing "The Spirit of Service" for AT&T. Macdonald was a member of a telephone plant crew that worked out of Boston. In the blizzard of 1888, when the lines going across the countryside were getting caked with ice and it looked as if they might go down, Macdonald and his co-workers kept telephone service alive.

On the night the blizzard struck, Macdonald and his crew put on snowshoes, went out into the drifts, and fought their way along the telegraph line looking for breaks. With their faces set against the bitter winds, they carried coils of wire, clearing snow from the cross-arms, finding breaks, and mending them. Sure, their fingers were numbed from the cold, but they worked for hours anyway—and the New York-Boston line did not fail.

Smart Solution 47

Jane could become a much more authentic and likable person if she concentrated her efforts on doing a first-rate job, rather than playing up to higher-ups and trying to impress those in power. It's okay to seek advice on how to become a better performer—inexperienced people can learn a great deal from their experienced elders—but Jane shouldn't try to stretch the mentoring relationship into anything else.

Jane will be seen by others as a valuable member of her organization, to the extent that she actually produced valuable results. Her overconcern with getting a mentor and promoting herself by words and attention-seeking maneuvers could easily backfire. Naturally, Jane needs to exhibit caution in her approach: her co-workers are not so stupid that they can't spot a self-centered upstart. Bluntly put, Jane's company pays her to perform, not to look good. She should live by the axiom that success follows performance, not flattery or schmoozing. By being service-oriented instead of self-success-oriented, Jane should become a better performer and earn a reputation worth having. If she follows this advice, advancements could surely follow.

Dilemma 48

You just completed an assignment which you performed quite well. Now you want to get higher-ups to notice your work so you can get the credit due you.

David had a flare for attracting people's attention. He instinctively knew how to cause others to notice something. This talent made him well-suited to advertising, a field in which he's been employed for five years. David joined his present employer, a small advertising agency, after graduating and gaining some experience through his school's internship program.

David's boss eventually promoted him to head up a new account. Although small, the new assignment promised to provide David with a wonderful opportunity to hone his skills and learn how to manage all aspects of an advertising campaign, from budgeting and research, to multi-media production and client relationships.

David learned that the advertising campaign he was putting together was producing better-than-expected results. The client company's sales were up substantially, and its management believed David's campaign was the reason why.

David was also very proud of the cleverness in what he created. His radio spots and print advertisements had the whole town talking. Area residents, joking with one another, frequently repeated the tagline from the advertisement. Understandably, David was pleased with himself, and was trying to think of the best way to get his boss to recognize his work so he'd get the credit he felt he deserved.

It seems to be a rule of life that we are often weakest after we've experienced episodes of strength, most vulnerable after being at our mightiest. For example, you might make a heroic effort to complete an important project, working tirelessly 12 to 14 hours a day, seven days a week, but once finished with the demanding task, you develop a head cold or catch the flu. The body remains strong throughout the ordeal, but once the job at hand is completed, the body weakens, tires easily and, all too frequently, deteriorates.

Similarly, a person may exhibit remarkable wisdom and sound judgment in handling a troubling, difficult situation and triumph because of it. Then, immediately following that success, this same individual will act unbelievably dumb on an altogether different matter, causing others to shake their heads in disbelief. Disaster seems to lurk in the shadows of triumph.

As soon as you complete one project quickly, become busy with something else so you won't be distracted by praise.

Every moment of our existence, we choose to do what we think is most important at the time. A woman playing golf, say, must believe that golfing is the most important thing she can be doing at that moment. This concept can help you realize what's really going on in your mind when you try to get attention for what you've accomplished, instead of working on something else. The issue becomes: which activity becomes more important?

Smart Solution 48

After climbing so high, David should take care—he could slip. In his eagerness to gain credit and receive praise from his boss, David could easily act incredibly dumb and thereby diminish his reputation. People too hungry for recognition tend to act in annoying ways; David might find himself inadvertently alienating his co-workers.

David could avoid doing something dumb immediately by wearing his "best suit." This meant focusing all his energies on another challenge instead of basking in the congratulations he receives for his past accomplishments.

Dilemma 49

You encounter a problem. You can either stop what you're doing now and fix it, which will involve considerable time, effort, and controversy, or you can let someone else remedy it.

Anne, an administrative assistant, went to her superior, Ross, to report an unusual and highly offensive series of events that took place in her work area. One of the managers with whom she worked was participating in an over-the-telephone "sex chat room." As a woman, and the wife of a minister, she was highly offended and upset with the situation. The person accused was a mild-mannered individual who performed highly technical functions for the company. Ross had difficulty believing Anne's tale. He also knew that the alleged perpetrator was highly skilled in areas the firm needed, and finding a suitable replacement would be difficult, if not impossible.

We all run into problems that we'd prefer not to deal with, problems that could be complicated and messy. The smart thing to do with these types of problems is to deal with them immediately and properly, to solve them so they stay solved. But doing the smart thing isn't always easy. Counter-reasons that tempt us to do nothing present themselves: The costs of solving a nasty problem appear too high, someone might get offended and become angry, we'll cause ourselves great inconvenience, it will take too much time. Ross faced one of these situations. He needed to act in order to stop it right away, but he knew that such action wouldn't be easy.

No matter how difficult, do not tolerate what is less-than-acceptable.

For many years, Zenith had been known for its quality products. Their motto, "Quality goes in before the name goes on," meant something important, something that emphasized the very best. Zenith's former chairman and CEO, John Nevin, once related an incident to me that involved a manufacturing problem at one of the company's plants. "We had a vice president of manufacturing named Jim Rooney, who was an engineering graduate. I remember having lunch with him one day when he told me that our St. Louis plant, which was our biggest color television plant, had been down for two days. The reason was that they had a major component failure in some of the parts they were installing. The television sets weren't meeting their quality expectations, so they just shut the plant down. That got my attention. I said, 'How do you feel about that?' Rooney replied, "I don't get upset when a part of the manufacturing process gets out of control, and you've got to shut down the plant in order to meet your standards. I don't get upset when components come into the plant that aren't worth a damn, and I find out they're failing, and I have to shut down the plant to get fresh parts. That's unavoidable in American business. When I really get upset is when I find some guy who will take his...mistakes, pack them in a box, and ship them to our customers. If they want to shut down the plant, that's all right with me.'"

Insist on high standards. Avoid what's cheap and easy.

Good reputations, our experiences tell us, are not built upon cutting corners; they're built on an adherence to high standards. James R. Eiszner, who headed CPC International, described a company practice his firm used to assure that high standards were met. "When a bottle breaks in our factory, the rule is if it breaks anywhere near the filling equipment, we take a hundred jars before and a hundred jars afterward and discard them—throw them in the dump. We recall products not so much because they represent a hazard, but because they represent a hazard to our high quality image. We will throw out eleven thousand cases of a product if it isn't what it should be, regardless of whether it is satisfactory to eat."

This is costly, but top-quality producing firms willingly pay the price that top-quality performance demands. In a talk before company employees, Eiszner once told his listeners, "We'll always have the best-quality products. That is a given in this company. It stems from the top and is repeated down through the organization. Everybody understands that if the image of quality could be compromised, you always err on the side of caution, eat the costs, and protect the quality."

Have high expectations for yourself and build a good reputation by living up to them.

The active pursuit of quality begins with high expectations for yourself and your organization. It rests on what you think about your ability to perform, and is frequently expressed by the weighty ideal that any performance failing to reach the highest standards of excellence is wholly unacceptable. Our experiences tell us that the reputation a business enjoys is earned largely by its ability to maintain quality standards in all that it does.

At Goodyear, for example, a simple slogan has guided decision making for some time: "Protect Our Good Name." Contained therein was a philosophy that encouraged all personnel to do the right thing. In one particular situation, it prompted Goodyear's chairman and CEO, Robert Mercer, to take immediate action in the quest for quality.

When visiting Goodyear's tire plant in New Delhi, India, Mercer noticed that the products being turned out were substandard in terms of appearance and performance. Goodyear had dropped from first place to sixth place in the India tire market, despite being there over 60 years. Quality leadership was not being maintained, but rather, an attitude of attempting to produce the most things for the least cost.

This wasn't what Mercer believed Goodyear should stand for. He asked what was happening. "They couldn't give me an answer. Pointing to the product, I said, 'That tire should not have the Goodyear name on it; it should never leave this factory because it's not up to our specifications.' The plant manager said, 'Well, that's the best we can do with the equipment we've got.'"

Mercer said, "If it's going to carry our good name, it's got to start with our quality and performance level....Shut down every piece of equipment you've got in this plant that is incapable of producing a product that meets our specifications." The plant manager stared at him for a moment, then said, "Do you realize I'll shut down 40 percent of the plant?" Mercer replied, "Let me tell you something, my friend. I'm trying to figure out whether we should shut down the entire plant, get rid of it and just pull out of India altogether. I want the operation to continue, so let's not challenge this. Just get it done." The plant manager had the entire plant shut down.

Mercer knew that they could get the job done if they had the right equipment, and $4 million was spent replacing faulty and worn out machines. Today, the plant is turning out good-quality products, and the spirit, attitude, and pride of the people there are all high.

Smart Solution 49

Managers aren't paid handsomely to handle easy challenges; they're expected to do the smart thing. Ross took the time he needed to investigate the problem Anne brought to him, and he learned it was true. The man she complained about was doing exactly what she said he was doing, and he later admitted it.

The act in question was certainly an offensive one, and possibly not immediately curable by counseling. Despite the man's unique technical ability, Ross terminated him.

Dilemma 50

You spend most of your time with routine matters, which you handle well. You do your work in much the same way you've always done it, but it isn't exciting. Still, you tell yourself, "Comfortable is good."

As Medical Records Director of a community hospital, Angie's department kept accurate, up-to-date patient records. She had worked in this area her entire career and had been director of medical records for the past 11 years. The hospital used a color-coded, two terminal digit system for storing and retrieving information. This system had worked in the past when the hospital was small, but Angie's unit currently handled 30 times the number of records it handled before, and the old system broke down frequently.

Angie understood why the color-coding system failed to serve the hospital's information needs as well as it once did. Problems existed in the system; people needing information couldn't find it quickly, records got lost, clerks wasted valuable time hunting through files manually. Angie blamed the new employees for her unit's sagging performance.

There's a world of difference between working for a paycheck and working for a worthy purpose. Angie had a good job and liked it. It was a comfortable routine, one that she followed day after day. Because Angie worked just for a paycheck, she saw her obligation in a narrow and unchanging light. The problem was, Angie's methods were out of date, inadequate for the demands of the times. Worse still, she refused to acknowledge her predicament. She was stagnating in a fast-changing world.

If we dig deeper into the situation we discover that, in her mind, Angie viewed herself as being responsible. After all, she did what she agreed to do, maintaining medical records. She performed her work in the same way year after year, giving her company eight hours of work every day for the agreed-upon amount of pay.

This is what happens whenever a person works for a paycheck instead of a purpose. People agree to the "bargain" and stick with it, doing exactly what they've always done. The overall purpose of their function never crosses their minds. Indeed, they cannot see the forest for the trees. Angie created other problems for herself because she lacked ambition, found her work uninspiring, and failed to tackle new challenges, to grow as a person.

See the larger purpose behind what you do.

I met with Gerald Greenwald once when he was chairman of Chrysler Motors, the operating arm of the Chrysler Corporation. Lee Iacocca picked Gerald Greenwald as his right hand man to help one of the greatest corporate turnarounds in our country's history. I asked him, "What motivated you to work so hard to try to save this company?" What he answered was most telling. I'm convinced it explains why he and his small circle of talented people worked so hard, and why they were successful in accomplishing a nearly impossible task—saving the giant automaker from bankruptcy.

In answering my question, he leaned forward, lowered his voice, and told me in an unmistakably sincere tone, "When I came to Chrysler in 1979, we had a mess on our hands. We needed to do the impossible, or 600,000 jobs had to go. The whole United States was in recession. We had to keep this company up and running. To me, all the work was worth it. The American people did give us a helping hand. I think our responsibility began with building the best quality, best value cars for the public, and in the process, be a role model for what a company could do."

"The dignity of self comes from jobs," Greenwald told me. "We were fighting to save 600,000 jobs. It goes back to a deep-felt feeling: I believe deeply in family, education, and the work ethic. If there is unemployment, there isn't going to be a very strong family structure or enough motivation for education."

Transform yourself to new heights by making your work an exciting adventure, not a routine of drudgery.

There are many examples that demonstrate how employees give their finest effort when they connect what they do with a great purpose. This happens because it transforms work into a grand adventure. William B. Walton, Sr., co-founder of Holiday Inn, understood the powerful force that lies latent in each of us. And he knew how to unleash it: the answer was by getting people to serve.

Walton said, "We saw ourselves—all of us, from the chairman of the board to cleaning people—as a company of people. We were in a crusade to bring to the American traveling public a highway haven, a home away from home to rest and refresh them."

Business leaders frequently conceive of a mission beyond profit through the goods and services they produce, inspiring themselves and their employees to unbelievable heights. When Steven Jobs, the co-founder of Apple Computer, put the project team together that first created the Macintosh, his vision was nothing less than the "user-friendly transformation of personal computing so that computer technology would be accessible to everyone." When Robert Mercer headed Goodyear, he said this of his firm: "Here's a company that's providing freedom and mobility to people in this country and around the world."

Other firms set high purposes for employees to reach for. Avon has a guiding motto that captures the underlying values of all they do. "Avon is a caring company that helps people around the world feel better about themselves." And at DeLuxe Check Printers, the commitment is, "To serve our customers as the best supplier of financial documents, and related products and services."

But such commitments are not simply the province of the captains of industry; they often belong to normal, everyday workers as well. A woman who applied nonreflective coatings to eyeglass lenses demonstrated such commitment when she explained the importance of her role in running the coating machine: "It's people's eyes we're talking about—if I don't do my job right, people might not be able to see very well!" I can just imagine this woman visualizing the people who later put on and saw through the lenses she coated. As she worked, she thought about how vital her job was, and how significant it made her feel.

Smart Solution 50

Angie will change and find her work more interesting as soon as she stops thinking about what she'll get and about how the old days were better because work demands were easier. She'd find joy in her job once she placed improved performance ahead of her own ease and comfort.

Angie's boss could help by enrolling her in training seminars to learn about better information retrieval methods, and by showing her the current demands for information. Once Angie started serving her organization's changing needs, she'd become enthusiastic and discover a satisfaction that far exceeded a regular paycheck.

Dilemma 51

You have many good ideas about how to improve things at work—product quality, cost reduction, employee relationships, customer satisfaction—but a steady stream of day to-day difficulties keeps you from implementing your improvements.

As head librarian for her community's public library, Sandra had many responsibilities and the demands on her time came unceasingly and arose unexpectedly. On her way to work, Sandra usually tuned her car radio to an easy-listening station as she began her drive. She enjoyed her mornings and used the time alone in her car to think of the changes she wanted to make. She thought about the fund raising drive that the library trustees suggested. She dreamed about a new addition, and about a badly needed branch at the outskirts of town where real estate development boomed. And she thought about introducing a combined reading and music program for children during the coming summer vacation months.

She heard her phone ringing as soon as she entered her office. Molly, head of audio-visual services, strolled behind her carrying a sheaf of papers and asking questions. This was only a foretaste of what her day was to hold, a day that constantly made demands on her time due to numerous meetings, interruptions, and emergencies.

Later, with the coffee in her cup growing cold, Sandra was once again in the midst of a stream of unexpected difficulties. She glanced at her watch and thought, "I'm already late for that meeting with the budget committee." The plans she contemplated during her morning drive to work would have to wait one more day.

Sandra failed to manage her time wisely. She wasted time by doing things of minimal consequence, instead of things that would make the most impact. Sandra tried to do everything, make every decision, and attend to too many details. She's trained her organization to be ineffective and inefficient. Sandra is her own bottleneck; every action needed her okay, so things stalled out and were poorly done because of it.

Know where your time goes.

You have only 24 hours a day, no more no less. Do you spend it wisely? Do you know how you spend it? Most people don't. At best, they have vague recollections of what they did during the day, but few people can accurately account for how much time they gave to each of the hundreds of activities that consumed their day. Like water in a leaky vessel, our time spills out in drips and drabs, much of it wasted on insignificant activities.

Producing an accurate accounting of where our time goes could be a powerful eye-opener. It could show us where we waste time on trivial matters that produce little value, perhaps show us that the most important things receive much less time than they deserve. Maintain a time log for a week. Do not rely on end-of-the day recollections, but record how you spend each minute throughout the day. After you have done this, study your log. Notice where you spent your time, and you'll be shocked at what you find. If time were money, and in a way it is, see if you are spending it wisely, getting the best possible value for what it costs you.

Distinguish the "vital few" from the "trivial many."

All the things we do are not equally productive or important. Some activities create more value than others; the 80-20 rule says that 80 percent of what we accomplish comes from 20 percent of our activities. The 20 percent used is known as the "vital few." Much of our time, we waste doing what is known as the "trivial many." These activities provide us with only 20 percent of what we accomplish.

The important thought to hold in your mind is that some activities yield greater benefit than others. Smart time management involves recognizing which activities are most important, giving adequate attention to them and less attention to those things which yield comparatively less value.

Discipline yourself to say yes to the important demands and no to lesser matters.

Time wasters—intrusions that eat up valuable time—are much like pestering telemarketing calls that come during the dinner hour. They interrupt us, and we have difficulty saying no to them because we want to be polite. Those who accomplish the most in life use their time wisely because they place prudence ahead of "politeness." They say no to intrusions, not due to any inherent nastiness, but because they believe accomplishing important results is more important than accommodating requests for their time. They shut the door to time wasters—the trivial many, the unessential 80 percent—by simply saying no to them.

What they do say yes to are the vital few, the essential things that produce the most results.

Spend your time doing what's most beneficial.

Ivy Lee was a well-known management consultant who advised industrial giants over a century ago. His clients included Rockefeller, Morgan, and the DuPonts, to name a few. During a visit to Charles Schwab, then president of Bethlehem Steel, Lee outlined his services. "With our services, you'll know better how to manage." Schwab, a man of action replied, "We don't need more knowing. What we need is more doing." He told Lee that if he could get himself and his people to do the things they already knew they should do, he would gladly listen and pay anything reasonable. Lee said that he could explain something to Schwab in about 25 minutes that would improve management efficiency by at least 50 percent. Realizing that he had only that much time before catching a train, Schwab told Lee to present his idea.

Lee produced an index card from his pocket, gave it to Schwab and said, "Write on this card the six most important things you have to do tomorrow." This took Schwab about three minutes to do. "Now," Lee said, "number these in order of importance." Schwab spent about five minutes doing this. "Now," said Lee, "put this card in your pocket and the first thing tomorrow morning look at item #1 and start working on it. Pull the card out of your pocket every 15 minutes and look at it until item 1 is finished. Then, tackle item 2 in the same way, then item 3. Do this until quitting time. Don't be concerned if you only finish two or three items or even if you only finish item 1. You'll be working on the most important ones. The others can wait. If you can't finish them by this method, you couldn't by any other method either.

"Spend the last five minutes every working day making out a "must list" for the next day. After you have convinced yourself of the worth of this system, have your people try it. Try out this method as long as you wish and send me a check for what you think it's worth." The whole interview lasted about 25 minutes.

In two weeks Schwab sent Lee a check for $25,000—about a thousand dollars a minute! Schwab added a short note saying Lee's lesson was the most profitable one he ever learned. Later, Schwab told skeptics that Lee's method was the most valuable investment Bethlehem Steel had made all that year because not only he, but his entire team, was getting the important things done.

Delegate. Delegate. Delegate!

Perfectionists—people who have to have things done just so, who does not trust the skills and judgment of others, who love doing more than managing—waste time doing things themselves because they cannot or will not delegate. Every decision has to get their approval, every action has to receive their touch. They feel they must know every detail of every move before it is made. These people create a bottleneck that clogs the flow of work. Productivity suffers. What's worse, their subordinates lose commitment, interest, initiative, the ability to act responsibly, and their enjoyment of performance.

Smart Solution 51

Sandra should've kept a time log so she could see where her time went, most of which was wasted "putting out fires." She should've faced up to the fact that she would never get to really important concerns because she wasted her time on unessential items that ate up her day and exhausted her. She should've picked out the few things she knew were the most important—the vital few that produced the best results—and gave adequate, uninterrupted time to them.

Sandra should've used Ivy Lee's $25,000 idea to keep herself focused on the most important topics. She should've said "no" to all the interruptions that intruded on her busy schedule, interruptions that took her attention away from the "essential few." Finally, Sandra needed to delegate. It harmed her organization and spoiled employee commitment when she tried to do everything herself.

Chapter 9

The Fat Cat

Getting better results by giving away more of yourself

Right from the start, society expects each of us to achieve for ourselves. From earning good marks in school to defeating competitors on playing fields, we're supposed to perform well and win. We learn to grasp what we want; the more we get, the more successful we feel. Is it any wonder that winning and acquiring become the goals of life and the way most people gauge their worth as individuals?

To some degree, this emphasis on individual performance—on getting and winning—benefits both the individual and society. But things are never as simple as they appear. A heavy emphasis on getting and winning causes most to believe that the best way to sate their desires and derive satisfaction from them is by aggressively procuring whatever they want and trouncing anyone who gets in their way.

Survey what's going on around you and you will discover that few things are more infected with error than the concept of success and how to reach it. What you will discover, I think, is that most beliefs about success are paradoxical—the harder people try to grasp those notions, the less likely they are to attain them and feel good about themselves. What's more, those who happen to become successful often become fixated on the outward signs of their accomplishments and quickly lose what it was that gave them so much satisfaction when they were consumed with struggling and hardship. Sadly, these dissatisfied people yearn for the "good old days" when life was alive, interesting, and challenging, and worth getting out of bed for each morning.

In this chapter, we'll look at what some of our country's most successful business leaders define as the reasons for their success. You will see how the best and brightest competitors escaped the "fat cat trap" of trying so hard to get something they rendered themselves ineffective. This chapter also shows how smart people rise above "what's in it for me?" thinking, which limits success, and how to obtain positive results by giving away more of themselves.

Dilemma 52

A headhunter calls and offers you a "once-in-a-lifetime opportunity" with a fabulous starting salary and terrific benefits. The problem is that you must make the move immediately, which would put your present employer in a difficult bind.

Arlene was a "driven lady." She set high standards and challenging goals for herself and worked like the devil to achieve them. She did well because she always gave her best effort and, after each achievement, she raised her sights to more challenging targets, going after opportunities that might better her financially.

Arlene was in her fifth job in four years, and with her current employer seven months. Each move brought her higher pay and a better title, two things that were important to her. She also enjoyed her reputation as someone who succeeds when given difficult assignments. Additionally, she was proud of her up-to-date knowledge. Many companies would love to have Arlene on their payroll because of what she could contribute to their bottom lines. As Arlene stated it, "Whoever wants me the most has to pay me the most."

A headhunter called Arlene one afternoon with a very attractive offer she had to decide about right away. Arlene already earned a fabulous salary; her company needed someone to head up a difficult project that would enable it to remain competitive, so they compensated her handsomely for her efforts. If she left now, the project would flounder badly, if not fail altogether. But the new opportunity carried a huge pay increase, and Arlene entertained thoughts about how she could use the money.

In analyzing this problem it's better to consider what Arlene's choice will do *to* her, not *for* her. When we consider what accepting or rejecting the offer will do *for* Arlene, we tend to focus exclusively on the tangible costs and benefits, and fail to see the long-term consequences, particularly for Arlene herself. When we consider what accepting or rejecting the offer will do *to* Arlene, we see something more important: the shaping of Arlene as a person. Each choice we make in life shapes us a little bit. Arlene shapes herself by her decisions, and you do too. This is why it makes sense to consider not so much what our choices do *for* us—what we might get—but, rather, what they do *to* us—how each choice shapes and defines us.

Each time Arlene chooses to "follow the money," the more she makes herself into a crude materialist. If she chooses to stay with her present employer to complete an important project, she makes herself more into a person who works for causes, not paychecks.

Work for a goal, not a paycheck.

The person who works for goals and not paychecks builds a self dedicated to commitments of adventure and accomplishment. Consider the case of John T. Dorrance from Bristol, Pennsylvania, who studied chemistry in college. After two years of graduate study, young Dorrance earned a doctorate. One foreign and three American universities offered him well-paying, secure teaching positions, but he turned them down. This made his father so angry he told his upstart son to consider himself dropped from the family.

But the 24 year old Dr. Dorrance had a larger purpose in mind for himself, and he knew that teaching chemistry would not lead him any nearer to it. He passed up the prestige and security of academic life and went to work for a Camden, New Jersey company that was packing 200 kinds of canned foods and losing $60,000 a year. His first week's pay envelope contained just $7.50, but the low pay didn't faze him in the least. He was working toward a goal, applying his knowledge of chemistry to a new idea—canning concentrated soups.

In time, John T. Dorrance reached that goal and made himself into a well-respected business leader. He started the Campbell Soup Company and revolutionized the nation's eating habits by adding canned soups to the American diet. The young chemist succeeded because he said no to a better paying position and yes to something he believed was more important. He passed the pocketbook test by opting to work toward a goal instead of a paycheck.

Smart Solution 52

Because she was capable and performed well, Arlene was able to get what she wanted. She received high pay and high-status positions, but that was all she got. By continually calculating where she could get the best for herself and changing jobs to get it, Arlene formed herself along certain lines. She made herself more calculating, more materialistic, more dependent on higher salaries and greater benefits for her satisfaction.

Were these the only human qualities worth developing and rewards worth getting, Arlene would be a much admired person. But the world admires other qualities: loyalty, dedication, unselfish service, concern for others, dependability, trustworthiness. The wholly materialistic person neglects these qualities and misses out on what they bring.

Arlene might never ascribe much worth to the aforementioned values, but an empty feeling could overtake her some day once she asked herself, "Is this all there is?" When she reached that point—and let's hope for her it comes sooner rather than later—she'd be ready to understand that the tangible, material world was exciting and alluring but vacant in relation to deeper, human terms.

Dilemma 53

You are a highly competitive person who works hard to achieve what you want, but your efforts are not paying off as well as you think they should. Others less competitive make more sales than you, covet promotions you'd like to get, and receive more recognition from higher-ups.

Long ago out on the West Coast, an ambitious young man whom we'll call Andrew got into business selling insurance. His first few months of selling produced little success. He knew, of course, that getting started would be difficult, so he stayed with it. He wasn't a quitter, and he knew better than to give up too soon. He worked hard studying his product, preparing lists of prospective buyers, and working on his selling techniques. But try as he might, few customers bought his policies. He redoubled his efforts, working longer hours, and calling on as many prospective customers as possible.

As the months rolled by, he realized he was getting nowhere; he earned barely enough to meet his living expenses. Selling insurance wasn't the work he imagined it would be. Discouraged, Andrew asked himself the question so many who struggle ask themselves: What am I doing in this business? Andrew was troubled by the thought that he might never become wealthy, something he wanted badly. He persisted, giving more effort to his sales techniques, but the more he tried, the less effective these additional efforts proved to be. Essentially, he was still getting nowhere.

One day, a very troubling question nagged at Andrew: "Could I be going about this all wrong?" Then, he saw the obvious, and it was so unpleasant he was embarrassed to admit that it was true.

Andrew began to look at himself and how he went about his work. He questioned his methods and came to a startling revelation. He really worried only about how he might convince customers to buy his insurance policies just so he could earn handsome commissions. If that were the way customers saw him, no wonder they wouldn't buy his policies.

Andrew had an idea. He would take a greater interest in his customers and try to see things from their point of view, putting them, and not himself, first. Andrew eventually gave up his "what's in it for me?" concern and, in doing so, discovered it began to make a difference, a big difference. Each day after that, just before he made a call, he'd give a simple prayer-like reminder to himself: "What can I provide my customers with right now that will make their lives a little more secure, a little better?"

Taking the other person's position was unnatural at first, and not easy to do. But the more Andrew tried, the easier it became. After a while, he hardly gave any thought to what he'd get from each sale and, instead, focused on the benefits the policies could provide his customers. By thinking about each sale from the customer's perspective, he changed the way he approached each potential sale.

Then Andrew was hit by another idea. The life insurance policies he sold provided an estate for ordinary people. It was the only product that did so. He told prospective buyers this, and they liked the idea. Because he respected and cared about his customers, they recognized his sincerity and bought policies from him. He honestly gave more of himself to others, and received far more in return than he would have imagined possible.

Before long, his work changed. What he earlier had seen as just a job became an exciting calling. His mission in life centered on seeing that everyone who wanted an instant estate could get one by buying life insurance. People who had been just customers a few years earlier became, in his mind and heart, friends whom he cared about and respected. Other people must have detected this change. They, too, wanted to buy insurance from him, and his business grew.

When he retired a wealthy man, after nearly 50 years in the industry, Andrew told his closest friends what he thought it was that made him so successful. It wasn't the product so much as the God-given privilege he had to be helpful to others. This was his outlook. Rather than focusing on "what's in it for me," he concentrated on providing real value for his customers. When he was able to do this naturally, his life changed. He actually became a very different person—and a mighty successful salesman.

Producing a profit is a paradox. The harder a person tries to grab for it, the more slippery it becomes. Yet, by forgetting the self and by concentrating on providing for the wants and needs of those whom the firm serves, success generally follows. I recall reading something the United Parcel Service Company's founder, Jim Casey, said along these lines, "Are we working for money alone?" Casey asked. "If so, there is no surer way not to get it." Profit, like happiness, is the by-product of purposeful living. To get it, forget it!

Focus on the doing, not the expected rewards.

Let me come out with it right here and in the simplest possible language: to achieve success, devote your attention and energies outwardly, not inwardly. Find a particularly worthy cause that captures your full loyalty and serve it faithfully. When you do, you'll start to be successful. You'll also rise above the pettiness that occupies most people, and you'll be free of the nagging cries for "more" that come from an unsatisfiable ego. This method is remarkably effective both in and outside the realm of business.

An extraordinary man named John Wooden once coached college athletics at a state university on the West Coast. He was quiet, deliberate, unassuming—an ordinary looking man. He approached his task in ways radically different from other coaches. He never tried to get his players "up" for a game emotionally. He would tell his players before games, "When it's over, I want your head up. And there's only one way your head can be up—that's for you, not me, to know you gave the best effort you're capable of giving." He was as concerned with his players' character as he was with their ability, because he wanted players who weren't preoccupied with getting the accolades. He emphasized constant improvement and steady performance, and often said, "The mark of a true champion is always performing near your level of competency."

Coach Wooden retired after 40 years of coaching, leaving a record unparalleled in American collegiate athletics. During the 27 years he coached basketball at UCLA, his teams never had a losing season. In his last 12 years there, they won 10 national championships, seven of those in succession. His teams in those years held the longest winning streak record in any major sport—88 games, spanning four seasons. But the amazing fact is, *he never talked about winning*. He once said, "I honestly, deeply believe that in not stressing winning as such, we won more than we would have if I'd actively stressed outscoring opponents." Coach Wooden's success can be traced to getting his players to devote their attention outwardly, not toward themselves.

Turn your work into acts of service.

A man named Joe Snavely wrote a book titled *Milton S. Hershey—Builder,* about the life and works of the man whose name is practically synonymous with chocolate in this country. One day, while Joe Snavely was in Hershey's chocolate factory, he noticed a sign above Mr. Hershey's desk: "Business Is a Matter of Human Service." This, the author wrote, was the sesame of Mr. Hershey's creed and success.

Henry Ford, founder of the giant automobile enterprise that bears his name, boldly lived by the creed that any business that first thought of earning a fixed dividend was bound to fail. Either profits would come from doing a job well, he believed, or they would not come at all. Ford, over a half-century earlier, ably captured the essence of what is being illustrated here when he remarked, "A business absolutely devoted to service will have only one worry about profits. They will be embarrassingly large."

Build on a bedrock foundation of serving.

The firm McKinsey & Co. entered the consulting business in the early 1930s. The firm's purpose was to provide advice about effective management practices to top-level executives. The foundations of its culture go back to the beliefs its founding father, Marvin Bower, held about what a McKinsey consultant should do.

Bower held that the beliefs that were most important were: put the interests of the client ahead of increasing the company's revenues; remain silent about the client's business operations; be truthful and do not fear challenging a client's opinion; and perform only work believed to be in the client's best interests.

Smart Solution 53

Let's take a look at the idea behind Andrew's success, which was to ignore the inner voice which asked him, "What's in it for me?" The callousness of Andrew's maxim can easily receive agreement from armchair observers, but it is deceptively difficult for anyone to apply consistently. The heart of that challenge lies in learning how to aim your efforts outward, and those efforts must prove authentic, or otherwise they will not work.

Considerable practice is required to perfect any skill, and sometimes established habits that push you in the opposite direction must first be overcome. This is true whether the skill is golf or the ability to be more empathic towards another's needs.

Dilemma 54

You feel that your company owes you more than you are getting paid. It is tempting to run errands during working hours, use the telephone for personal calls, take time off for personal reasons, and pad your expense account.

Ron worked as a production scheduler at a plant on the eastern edge of the Rockies that manufactured exterior steel doors. Door sales came largely from the eastern part of the country, where the majority of the country's population resided.

Because of the time difference, Ron found that his days went better if he got to work an hour or two ahead of the 8 a.m. starting time. By coming in early, Ron took urgent messages from buyers in the east when they were available.

Ron felt overworked because he had to attend late afternoon meetings at his plant and handle last-minute emergencies with production personnel, which occurred at any time. Ron also felt underpaid for the workload he carried. This was why he felt it was okay to take an extra hour at lunch to run errands, do shopping, or just relax and talk to friends.

Ron may be perfectly justified in what he does but that doesn't make it a smart thing for him to do. His obtaining of the "extras" he feels he has coming to him to compensate his efforts and inconvenience is certainly detrimental both to him and his employer. Ron had what may be called an "exchange mentality." This involves seeing everything in terms of "I'll do this to get that." People who operate this way tend to overvalue what they give and undervalue what they get.

Just imagine the burden this way of thinking places on everyone—all that calculating you do to figure out what you give up and how much you need to get back in compensation wastes enormous emotional and moral time. Do this long enough and such questionable moves crowd out dealing with important concerns such as your customer's needs, the development of ways to improve service, generating ideas for new products, and implementing operation improvements.

This is a sure-fire way to stagnate and invite ruin from your more proficient competitors. Over-concern with self is perhaps the greatest poison known, and Ron poured more of this "poison" into himself every time he calculated and grabbed back that little something extra.

Resist temptations to take for yourself.

From his days at Ford, Robert S. McNamara was highly regarded because of his reputation for propriety. His personal actions measured as high ethically as his business decisions did in terms of thoroughness and logic. One Christmas, an advertising agency sent gifts to many of Ford's top executives. The other executives were pleased to accept their gifts, but not McNamara. He returned it with a note—it wasn't proper for him to accept.

When he was controller at Ford, McNamara billed out more than $2 million to corporate executives who had made use of Ford facilities without compensating the company for them. He told me that he billed people for their misuse of company resources not to penalize them for their misbehavior but to set a standard for expected behavior.

When McNamara was planning a skiing vacation to Aspen, he decided he'd need a car with a rack. A colleague told him that he could use a company car in Denver; they'd be happy to put a rack on it and he could pick it up at the airport. Ford loaned out hundreds of courtesy cars to VIPs weekly. McNamara wouldn't hear of it. He arranged to rent a car from Hertz, which would also bill him extra for the ski rack.

I think we would do well to recognize the fact that it is the accumulation of many things that makes us who we are. It is the unthinking, habit-formed decisions we make daily that form our selves and form our strength of character to respond correctly when temptations come our way.

Give away more of yourself and success will find you.

One of the most helpful concepts we know is this: success is achieved not by serving in ways valuables to yourself, but by serving others in valuable ways. The amazing thing about success and the genuine fulfillment people derive from it is that it's not something they find directly. Instead, *it finds them.*

Consider the experience of a highly successful business leader who applied this powerful idea every day. His name is Jack Reichert and he once headed the Brunswick Corporation. It's important to mention something he told me that says much about his approach to life: "I'm a tither to my church and have been for about 25 years. And the more I give, the more that comes back to me. The more I'm willing to serve, the luckier I become. My management philosophy is that one leads by serving." The person who turns from living for himself, primarily, to serving something worthwhile, makes not a little change but a radical one. His interests and abilities broaden. He becomes a deeper person.

Smart Solution 54

Ron made himself smaller and more miserable with each attempt to get back what he thought he was due. If he didn't stop it, he'd enfeeble his ability to produce his best. Mark McGwire didn't hit home runs by keeping his eyes on the scoreboard; he focused on connecting his bat dead center with speeding baseballs.

Ron needed to forget about getting, concentrating his attention more on giving. In doing so, he'd have more enthusiasm, more energy, would perform better, and would derive greater satisfaction from what he accomplished. He'd also set a standard for others in his organization to follow, and not poison them with the same debilitating mental framework that held him back from becoming a productive employee.

Dilemma 55

Your last raise was far less than you expected it would be. Now you are angry with your boss, because you believe others might have gotten more than you did.

Amber processed service requests for a specialty steel supplier. As part of the customer relations department, Amber's unit worked to assure the highest levels of customer service possible. In her role, Amber received calls and letters describing problems customers were having and notified the appropriate technical expert to handle the specific difficulty. This work required a fairly good technical understanding of the business, and delicate inter-personal skills in responding to disgruntled customers.

Amber's knowledge of specialty metals was extraordinary. She used the jargon of the business as well as anyone else, and she could discuss the metallurgy of her firm's product intelligently. But Amber had a tendency to receive information in a way that made customers feel she was unconcerned about their problems and requests for solutions. As a result of this shortcoming, Amber didn't receive as high a performance evaluation as she expected, and her yearly pay increase was less than she thought she deserved. She was furious with her boss because of the poor rating she received, and she thought it unfair that a person as knowledgeable as she would be given such a pitifully small pay raise.

Being knowledgeable is never enough to bring success. Attitudes and relationships count for much in determining how well you do. Amber's performance fell short because she approached her job with the wrong attitude. It is plain that a problem like Amber's is not easy to overcome because of its source—Amber herself. Most of the problems we deal with on a daily basis spring from within our own selves, and this is why a change of heart must come first if any improvement is to occur. Otherwise, the problem persists—as Amber's attitude worsens, her performance will further decline.

Do "right" by how you serve and success will come.

The practice of looking at business situations from the other person's perspective is one of the best ways to succeed. It's not only a safeguard against greed, but an excellent way to improve relationships. This is not an idealistic theory, but a practical maxim that works.

Let me tell you the story of Cyrus H. McCormick, who was fundamentally an inventor, not a businessman. Yet, his concerns first and foremost were for his customers. He wanted the farmers who bought his reapers to be successful. This approach proved to be the pivotal cause of his success. McCormick's early attempts to license the manufacturing of his reapers were disastrous. The few that were built did not perform well because of poor workmanship. It nearly ruined him. In 1847, McCormick went to Chicago and met William Butler Ogden. With Ogden's financial backing, McCormick got a new start. He insisted on a particular manner in which his customers were to be treated, and a specific method to conduct his business.

Every machine he produced would be sold, without haggling, at a fixed price of $120. For $30 down and the promise to pay the balance within six months, a farmer could have one of McCormick's machines. McCormick refrained from the common practice of hiring lawyers to collect from slow-paying farmers whose crop yields were poor, or who were down on their luck. Manufacturers used scare tactics and whatever fear-inducing methods they might concoct to force payment. McCormick wouldn't.

His competitors thought he was foolish for not squeezing slow-paying farmers—"He'll get caught holding the bag," they said. The critics were dead wrong. McCormick's formula proved to be a strong inducement for farmers to buy his product. Demand for McCormick's reapers grew faster than he could build them, and he mowed down his competitors as his business expanded.

Demonstrate concern for your customers.

Many years ago, before checks were personalized with your name and identification, people used bank checks. Banks bought these checks in large quantities, perhaps a half a year's supply at one time. A newly hired salesman for Deluxe Check Printers in St. Paul, Minnesota, eager to do well, took an order from a West Coast bank for 5 million checks. He was so elated with his huge order that he telephoned his company's president, George McSweeny, to tell of his windfall.

Stunned by the news, McSweeny asked the salesman, "Five million checks? What is the size of the bank?" The salesman told him. "Well, that will be more checks than they'll need for several years. You go back and tell him he should cut that order back to less than a million. And give him the reasons why." The salesman did as he was told. The bank president was flabbergasted. The next time this bank needed checks, who do you suppose they bought them from?

Smart Solution 55

Whether Amber can recognize her own faults, including her bad attitude problem, depended on her. Amber needed a dose of reality, a slap in the face to get her attention. She needed help in seeing herself as the source of her problem. Perhaps a friend or a caring boss might have the courage and good sense to tell her the truth. All too often, people do not level with others because they fear it will hurt the other person's feelings, or that the other person will become mad or defensive. Regardless, Amber could use the help of someone who wouldn't shrink from revealing painful truths about her personality.

Chapter 10

The Leaky Boat

Plugging holes that destroy trust

A reputation for being trustworthy is one of the choicest assets you can have. With it, you will enjoy the full confidence of others. When you give your word, people look to believe in you and look to trust you.

Sensible people would no more willingly deal with an untrustworthy individual than they would set out in a leaky boat to cross a treacherous body of water. Yet, many of us unintentionally act in ways that create leaks in our reputations, making ourselves less trustworthy, less believable, and less desirable as friends and associates.

This chapter shows how smart people handle everyday situations in ways that earn them the full confidence of others. It explains how you can "plug the holes" that can cause trust to leak out.

Dilemma 56

You already made a commitment to something, but then a better opportunity comes along.

Tom, who owned and operated his own business, said he'd take on a job for a customer, a small outfit that used his services infrequently.

But before beginning the job, Tom received a huge order from a new customer, one whose business he'd wanted for a long time. The small outfit, which placed the first order, badly needed the work done right away, otherwise they would be in a serious bind.

The second opportunity came from a much larger customer whose business was expanding rapidly. Tom had to decide to fulfill his original commitment and say "no" to a firm whose business he'd like to have, or let down the small company. Tom's competitors also wanted to do business with the large, growing company, and Tom knew it.

Imagine that you've made a promise to be somewhere on a particular date. You've agreed to it well in advance and it's marked on your calendar. But before that date arrives, something else comes up, something you'd really prefer to do. This poses a conflict. You cannot be in two places at the same time, so you have to choose. I think we all face this kind of situation at one time or another.

You can either choose to honor commitments, or make ongoing calculations and jump at the best opportunities whenever they present themselves, regardless of what's been promised. Bargains mean something to people who live by their commitments. Those who deal with these people learn that what they commit to they'll do, and these people make themselves trustworthy because of it. The opportunist who lives by choosing the best thing that comes along, even at the last moment, can only be counted on for just trying to get whatever he wants. The problem with this approach is that fewer and fewer opportunities tend to come to this person because of the development of an inconsistent, erratic reputation.

Live by your commitments, not calculations.

A woman named Gertrude Boyle once faced a situation that tested her trustworthiness. In 1970, Gertrude was the chairman of Columbia Sportswear Company, the largest manufacturer of outerwear in the United States. At that time, her company grew from $600,000 in revenues to more than $250 million, at a rate of 30 to 40 percent annually over 10 years.

These are extraordinary accomplishments—it was little wonder that the president of the United States invited her to the White House for a dinner honoring outstanding entrepreneurs. There was just one complication: Gertrude had already made a commitment to the American Diabetes Association.

I can imagine what would be going on in the minds of others who found themselves in a similar situation. Those wanting to accept the president's invitation would likely say to themselves, "How can I think of a respectable excuse why my earlier commitment cannot be honored? After all, it isn't every day one is invited to the White House." It would have been easy for Gertrude Boyle to tell the Association, "Sorry, something better has come up. I'll do something for you next year." Instead, she told the president's staff that she had given her word to the Diabetes Association and couldn't go to Washington.

Go out of your way to live by your word.

At Miami University in Oxford, Ohio, where I teach, we have something called an Executive-in-Residence Program. It involves a top-level business leader who visits the campus for two days a semester. The visiting executive attends selected classes in the business school, gives lectures, and meets with students and faculty to discuss current issues. Naturally, our students are keenly interested to hear "how it really is" in the business world from these captains of industry. They are, indeed, impressive individuals.

I recall one such visit. Students were asking Dick Heckert, who was chairman and CEO of DuPont, general questions about how to succeed in business. "What advice would you have for those of us about to enter business?" one student asked.

Mr. Heckert didn't hesitate a moment before answering. "My advice is fairly simple," he said. "Do what you say you are going to do; keep your promises, especially if it's inconvenient for you. Go out of your way to act responsibly. If you do that, if you make good on every obligation, others will see it. They will come to realize you are dependable. People will know you can be trusted to keep your word."

Smart Solution 56

Faithfulness to one's commitments builds trust and leads others to want to continue dealing with you. If you want other people to shun you, if you want them to tell others not to trust you, here is the recipe: stick to your promises only if it's convenient to do so. Otherwise, if something better comes along, or if you will be inconvenienced by doing what you promised, or if you find you will benefit more by doing something other than what you agreed to, vanquish those impulses and honor your commitments.

Dilemma 57

After cutting a deal, you realize it was based on faulty information. If you follow through as promised, it will cost you dearly.

Eager to win her boss's approval, Julie volunteered to take on a special assignment that required collecting and analyzing information using a sophisticated software package on her computer. Julie thought this job would require about four to five hours to complete. Realizing that she had several hours of free time on Wednesday and Thursday evenings to do it, Julie promised she would complete the report by the following Monday morning, when her boss needed it for an important meeting.

But as Julie got more involved with the data collection phase, she realized that the special assignment was turning out to be much more complicated than she had first imagined. When Friday morning arrived, Julie realized that she had collected only about three-fourths of the data she needed. It would take her the better part of Friday to collect the remainder. The computer analysis and report writing, which she planned to do on Friday, would have to be done later, but that would cut into her weekend and she had already made plans with friends. She could either tell her boss that the assignment was too daunting and ask for an extension on her deadline, or she could give up her plans with her friends and spend her weekend completing the assignment.

What people are most concerned about becomes clear by examining the patterns of what they choose to do. Their habits tattle on their hearts. Each of us is continually writing a story of our trustworthiness in the minds of others by how we choose to follow through with our agreements and commitments.

Keep commitments regardless of cost.

One of the most inspiring illustrations of the power of being faithful to an agreement comes out of the history of the Timken Roller Bearing Company in Canton, Ohio. Again, we must go back in time, over many decades ago, to understand this illustration. Timken was a small, struggling company, its product line consisting mostly of roller bearings, but they were beginning to branch out into a new line: axles.

Timken had not yet manufactured axles on a large-scale basis, but a contract they eventually signed with the Ford Motor Company, an important first step in Timken's expansion, would soon change all that. Timken planned to grow by supplying major manufacturers with reliable high quality parts. Their owners knew that success depended on quality and reliability, particularly when it came to delivery promises and standing behind their products.

Production finally commenced on Timken's Ford contract. Some of the axles were already shipped, and it looked as though a satisfying and profitable deal was going well. Then, Timken's accountants reported that the actual costs of production were running much higher than they had anticipated—unforeseen expenses showed up. All totaled, Timken underbid the Ford contract by 40%. Inexperienced in these procedures at the time, it turned out that Timken bid poorly and terribly underestimated what its costs would be.

Timken faced a problem. It could go back to Ford and say, "We mistakenly underbid and want to be paid 40 percent more, now that we have your business." Or, they could resolve themselves to the fact that a deal was a deal, and do the only honorable thing: take it out of their own pockets.

There comes a time when you have to grit your teeth, follow through with your proposal, and cut your losses. That's what Timken's leaders did. Despite the fact it was just a small firm, struggling with cash flow problems of its own, they held up their end of the bargain.

When you think about it, a substantial price increase would have upset Ford's budget. That would not have been fair. It wouldn't have been fair to Timken's competitors either, who bid somewhat higher for

Ford's business. And too, there were long-range considerations to be concerned about, such as establishing a reputation as a company that operated by its agreements. Making good on their commitment would be a feather in their cap, one that would help them win future contracts with Ford and other large-scale manufacturers.

That's how Timken chose to deal with the problem. Ford later learned how the company had resolved its crisis, and word spread. More business came to Timken from Ford. Other manufacturers wanted to do business with Timken, now known as a company with a solid reputation for living by its agreements. Ultimately, they grew and prospered.

Smart Solution 57

Julie should see her problem not in terms of what's convenient, but in light of her commitment. Doing exactly what she promised enabled her to purchase a trustworthy reputation for herself. The price wouldn't be cheap; she'd have to forego having fun with her friends.

But she needed to ask herself what was more valuable and what would be longer-lasting: a trustworthy reputation or a weekend of fun? The weekend of fun would be pleasurable temporarily, but the earning of a solid reputation provided benefits such as self respect, feelings of accomplishment, and being able to remain in the good stead of her co-workers and supervisors alike.

Dilemma 58

You face a situation in which it will be costly to do well by someone who is no longer in a position to do you any good.

Lisa graduated from college and began working for a rapidly growing chain of retail stores that sold young women's casual attire. Having no practical experience in the retail field, Lisa turned to more seasoned co-workers for advice. One of these people was Helen, a woman 15 years Lisa's senior. Helen gladly helped Lisa learn the ropes. Being bright and hard-working, Lisa did well; she advanced, becoming a buyer in only three years, and a senior buyer four years after that. Helen, who also advanced ahead of Lisa, continued showing her more about the business. Had it not been for Helen's help and support, it would have taken top management longer to recognize Lisa's talents and ambition.

A larger retail establishment ended up buying the chain Lisa worked for, and placed its own personnel in key management positions. Having strong opinions about how merchandise should be displayed and sold, the new managers made several changes that departed from previous methods the former management followed. Lisa wasn't convinced that these new methods would work, but she kept her opinions to herself. Helen, on the other hand, voiced her disapproval diplomatically and it caused the new managers to categorize her as being "out of touch with today's shoppers." As with many other corporate takeovers, a "we" versus "them" climate emerged, causing a split between those who embraced the "old store's" methods and those who thought the "new store's" methods were better.

Because she worked hard, performed well, and went along with the changes, the new management came to think of Lisa as one of their own, and she advanced further in the organization because of this. Lisa now occupied a position on the same level as Helen.

One of the members of the "new management" team got into a sharp exchange of words with Helen over the accuracy of certain figures in a report. It turned out that Helen was right, but the other manager refused to admit it and began spreading untrue rumors about Helen. Other members of the "new management" clique heard these rumors and began looking for evidence of other shortcomings she had about which they could spread gossip.

Lisa can stick up for Helen by discrediting the negative remarks others made about her and by not adding further gossip about Helen to the rumor mill, which thrust Lisa back into the "old management" clique. Or, she can remain silent and stay out of the mess, thereby maintaining a favorable image with those in power, which will surely help her chances for advancement.

It appeared that Lisa was in a situation in which she must declare loyalty to Helen, who helped her career at the beginning, or to the new management, which could determine the future course of her career with the chain. If Lisa chose to stand up for Helen out of loyalty, she'd damage the new management's trust in her. If she stood up for new management and opposed Helen, presumably to advance her own career, she'd destroy Helen's trust in her.

This was not an easy choice for Lisa, since she needed to consider the broader aspects of the situation, and its possible ramifications, before she acted. She certainly needed to consider how her actions would affect the level of trust between both members of management and her co-workers.

Stand by those who stood by you.

An acquaintance of mine named Phil Hampton, who was vice chairman of Bankers Trust of New York for many years, once told me about a situation that caused the firm to stand up and meet what they considered an implied obligation to their employees.

Bankers Trust had put a small part of its business on the market, and they received several bids for the bank branches they wanted to sell. Naturally, Phil was most interested in the best offer, so he proceeded to enter into negotiations on the final terms of the sale. Bankers Trust stipulated that it was not just selling an asset, it was selling a business complete with loyal employees.

Phil made it clear from the start that Bankers Trust expected the purchaser to guarantee their employees the pensions they had earned. Bankers Trust also stipulated that the sale was contingent on the buyer's agreement to keep all current employees on the payroll for at least one year.

When the top bidder's proposal came in, Phil's team examined it. They found it was worded very vaguely in regard to the stipulations they specified. Phil expressed his concern, and the prospective buyer agreed to come back with another offer, one that addressed the employee issues. They told Phil, "We may have to offer you less for this business." Phil said, "Fine. The deal is negotiable."

But the second proposal was still vague. After thinking it over, Phil and his team came to the conclusion that this prospective buyer really had no intention of treating the Bankers Trust employees fairly. Phil broke off the negotiations. Eventually, Bankers Trust sold the branches to another buyer, accepting $5 million less than what they were previously offered.

Phil told me later, "We put profit maximization behind the welfare of the people who had been long-time, loyal employees." That seemed to me to be a supreme example of following through with commitment, even though the only thing to be gained from it was the knowledge that the honorable thing had been done.

Earn trust by showing genuine concern.

On U.S. Highway 2 just west of East Glacier Park in Montana stands a statue of John Stevens, the railroad construction engineer who built the Great Northern Railway line through the west. This feat brought Stevens to the attention of President Theodore Roosevelt. Roosevelt had a problem and Stevens was his man. The Panama Canal needed building. The French had tried, but gave up in defeat in 1889, leaving only a third of the canal dug. Natural challenges and construction costs had left their investors in ruin, and after a year of trying, the Americans had done little better. Roosevelt turned to Stevens.

Panama was described as a death trap. Malaria, typhoid fever, yellow fever, intestinal diseases and pneumonia were rampant. Few who went to work on the canal survived. Stevens arrived in Panama to find a demoralized workforce. Their living conditions were despicable. Sanitation was practically nonexistent; rancid odors and filth were everywhere. Men who had gone there to work were trapped in a jungle over 2,000 miles from home.

Stevens talked to the men, and they found they could talk to him. He listened to what they had to say. They liked him immediately. Sagging morale turned upward. Canal construction would go forward, but first, Stevens ordered an all out war against pestilence of every sort, especially the dreaded yellow fever. It lasted for two years before digging resumed. "The digging is the least important thing of all," Stevens said.

Stevens ordered his men to fumigate cities, oil cisterns, and cesspools weekly, clear brush, drain swamps, and lay pipes that brought in clean drinking water. They paved streets and sidewalks, built mess halls, barracks, houses, schools, churches, reservoirs, and laundries. Stevens restored hope and a sense of purpose. He earned the workers' respect because he put them ahead of the work.

Smart Solution 58

Lisa should plug the holes that destroyed the trust between the people in her organization, as well the trust in herself. She should not engage in gossip, which means not listening, spreading, or adding to it. If she heard either side in the battle saying bad things about the other, she should inform that person that their comments were harmful to the organization, and then just walk away.

Lisa could promote better relationships by acting to build trust between people in her organization. She could prevent herself from getting involved in petty squabbles.

If asked about Helen, Lisa could tell the truth: that she thought well of Helen, that new management was treating her badly. Lisa should have stood up for the truth and challenged any false statements, rebutting unsubstantiated charges made against Helen. Likewise, she should have held to the same standard regarding any comments made by old management advocates against new management. By standing up for the truth, Lisa promoted trust.

Dilemma 59

A manager in another department is thinking about promoting someone who once worked alongside you, and asks for your input on the matter. You don't particularly like this other person and believe you are better qualified for the position.

Greg, a senior partner in a temporary agency, approached Gail for her input, wanting to know what she thought about Debbie, a person who Gail worked alongside for several years. Greg needed someone to take over a new operation, and he was considering Debbie for the position. This put Gail in a difficult situation because she didn't particularly care for Debbie and would've liked the new position herself. She thought she was better qualified.

The kind of situation that confronted Gail befuddles most of us. She could either do whatever it took to get what she wanted, or she could put her self-interests aside and act according to principle. Ambitious people generally know what they want and tend to have elevated opinions of their abilities. They have little hesitancy about making their wishes and opinions known, but is it best for them and their organizations to always do that? This is what Gail needed to ask herself.

No doubt Greg considered Gail for the position. After all, he isn't stupid. There had to have been some reason why he chose to ask her about Debbie. Perhaps he needed Gail in her present role, or was considering both Debbie and Gail and wanted to find out what each was made of. Perhaps Greg simply wanted someone else to give an objective view about Debbie; hence, he expected Gail to tell him the truth. Despite all of this, what indeed would have been the smartest way for Gail to respond?

Pursue principles rather than your immediate wants.

Whenever we can trust someone to pursue only what he or she wants, we can find it difficult to trust that person at all. Conversely, the person who demonstrates a commitment to high principles above all else is thoroughly trustworthy and, because of it, an asset to their organization. Indeed, organizations depend on most of their members to act on principle most of the time, otherwise they could not function. Without individual member self control, organizations would disintegrate. Policing is just too costly and stifling. These realities lead to an important reality: individuals have an obligation to subordinate their immediate wants to ideals such as honesty, cooperation, and fair play. To do well, people working in organizations must be free to act and that freedom requires everyone to choose right over wrong.

Tell the truth consistently and people will rely on you and what you say.

Integrity often comprises setting higher standards above your own. In business, it's also an excellent way to set a tone of honesty. I learned about one company's experience with this great idea a few years back when I visited Charles Lazarus, one of the most energetic men I've ever met. He started Toys "R" Us and, since its founding, has turned it into the largest toy store chain in the country.

Charles told me about his company's "load and count" policy, something that developed out of a mistake made by one of their suppliers. In the early days, when manufacturers would ship entire railroad cars of merchandise to Toys "R" Us, the railroad insisted that the receiver accept the shipper's "load and count." Whatever the shipper said was loaded and counted, that's what the buyer had to pay. One day the receiving department at the Toys "R" Us warehouse received a large order of bicycles. After they were unloaded and counted, someone noticed that there were three more bicycles in the carload than the shipper billed them for.

Now, if you or I got shortchanged, we'd squawk about it. But if we got more than was coming to us, that thing called temptation might very well raise its ugly head. It would be so inviting to just shut up and accept the order. Charles immediately decided to say no to the temptation, and he ordered his purchasing department to pay the manufacturer for whatever was sent.

Did this have an effect on the company? Absolutely. His employees loved the decision. They learned that their boss was going to honor the same rules of honesty that they were expected to work by. There were no exceptions or excuses made for anyone. Years later, because of this practice, suppliers now take Toys "R" Us at their word. The huge toy merchandiser is trusted because of its reputation for honesty.

Smart Solution 59

Gail should do the smart thing, provided she maintains high principles. She should be honest in telling Greg what she knew about Debbie's abilities and work habits. If Debbie worked hard and competently, Gail should say so. She should make her reasons clear to Greg along with any evidence she had to support her claims. Finally, Gail should express the fact about her own interest in the position. If Greg was a sensible person, he'd appreciate Gail's honesty, but in the same breath, Gail also should say that if Debbie got the job, she was willing to cooperate with Debbie and work together harmoniously and productively for the good of the organization.

Dilemma 60

You find that a job you performed isn't up to standard, but it's highly unlikely anyone will ever know about this situation if you remain silent.

Justin worked as a mechanic at an automobile repair shop. He diagnosed problems customers had with their automobiles and made the necessary repairs. Most jobs involved replacing defective parts. The workload varied from day to day; some days were extremely difficult, as customers insisted on getting their vehicles back quickly.

Justin realized that he might have charged a customer for a new belt the previous day. In his rush to get the job finished, Justin thought he might unintentionally have left the badly worn, but still serviceable, belt in place. When he arrived at the shop, sure enough, there was the new belt sitting on his bench, still in its box. The customer didn't get what he paid for.

Justin can go in either one of two directions: the path of least resistance, or the path of difficulty, something that living up to high principles often required. Let's consider the first path. By remaining silent, Justin probably will not be found out—few people know what they are seeing when they look under the hood of their automobile. Justin does not have to face the embarrassment of admitting an honest oversight. He need not go through the bother of trying to contact the person whom he inadvertently shortchanged.

The other path involves putting principles ahead of ease and feelings of embarrassment. It involves fixing a mistake. This action takes a stand for something greater than Justin's comfort and sends a message about who Justin is and about the business that employs him.

Do as you would do if the whole world were watching you.

In Akron, Ohio, former Goodyear chairman and CEO Robert Mercer learned that a tank at one of the company plants in the area contained methylocyanate. This was the same chemical that caused the deaths of thousands in Bhopal, India. Mercer's reaction was swift and firm. "Get rid of it!"

"But," came the response from the plant, "we need it to make the accelerator for one of our most profitable products." Mercer stood firm, "It's gone. Shut it down. Bail that stuff out of there and get rid of it." Plant personnel insisted, "If that happens, we'll have to close the plant."

Mercer would not retreat. "Close it! There's no appeal to it. We're not going to have that stuff in the middle of a residential area."

The power of public outcries tends to prevent companies from being bad neighbors. I think that if the public had learned of the dangerous chemical in Akron, many members of the community would have been alarmed, and rightly so. Robert Mercer knew this, and his example illustrates how someone who did what he believed to be the "right thing" did so without having to be forced to. As a consequence, he avoided the threat of a public outcry.

When a problem arises, act in a forthright fashion to understand it and solve it.

Here's a superb example of honesty and forthrightness. When he headed Zenith Corporation, John J. Nevin chose to deal with a television failure openly and immediately. The failure was a major problem for Zenith, costing them a considerable amount of money to fix. The senior engineering executive walked into Nevin's office one day, closed the door, and said, "John, this failure is much more serious than we thought. There's reason to believe that we might have a radiation problem." He explained the problem to Nevin.

Twenty-four hours later, John Nevin was on a plane to Washington. He and the senior engineering executives met with people from the U.S. Bureau of Radiological Health. The men from Zenith told them what they had discovered in their latest tests. Zenith had a good reputation as a reliable television manufacturer, and its leaders knew that nothing would strike terror in a mother more than the suggestion that the television her child was sitting in front of was a radiation hazard. The regulatory bodies in Washington, D.C., have a procedure that, by law, they must follow in establishing that a manufacturer is in conformity with radiation standards. If the regulatory agency reached a conclusion that radiation standards were not being met, the manufacturer had an opportunity to protest. If the protest failed, there was a formal investigation to see whether or not a health hazard existed. These steps took time, and both the regulators and the Zenith executives knew it. They agreed that they were going to waive all the procedures.

The regulatory agency issued a press release: "Zenith has found some of its receivers...to not be in conformity with radiation standards.

The Bureau is now beginning an investigation to determine if there are any possible adverse health effects." Within three months, enough testing had been done that the Bureau issued a bulletin saying that the worst impact on the consumer would be a radiation dose equal to that from a dental x-ray. The company moved quickly to eliminate further health hazards.

Smart Solution 60

If Justin located the owner of the car he fixed, as difficult as that might be, he could then either send a check to cover the cost of the belt that wasn't installed or have the owner return to the shop at a later time, and install the belt then. By taking such a step and maintaining high standards through his simple action, Justin would help to establish foundations of trust that would last through the years. This might lead his co-workers to learn by his example, perhaps initiating their own similarly positive actions.

Dilemma 61

You made a bad decision that's not paying off and there's little hope for it. You dread losing face and wonder how to get out of it.

Melissa headed the coatings department of a mid-sized manufacturing company. Occasional customer complaints about product durability prompted Melissa to introduce a new process. She thought her action would also be a good way to impress higher-ups with her technical knowledge. After considerable arm twisting and promises that greater sales would come if better quality coating were produced, top management went ahead and ordered the expensive new equipment.

Technical personnel from the company supplying the new equipment got the process up and running, but it did not perform flawlessly when operated by Melissa's underlings. After six months of using the new equipment, sales didn't improve as Melissa predicted. Her people didn't have the technical experience and skills needed to operate the equipment, and product quality was marginal because of it. The cost of hiring more people to operate the equipment outweighed the estimated benefits from additional sales.

Melissa's desire to be recognized by top management clouded her judgment, causing her to advocate a new process that was beyond her department's abilities. She badly miscalculated the economic benefits of the new process. It wasn't working and probably wouldn't work. She found herself between a rock and a hard place, and she desperately wanted to avoid losing face but couldn't figure out how not to.

If not careful, her company could get itself into a trap of pouring good money after bad. All too frequently, people and organizations get themselves into hopeless situations and instead of getting out, they go deeper. Melissa and her company's top management, who stood to look bad too if the new process flopped, will be tempted to invest additional time and money to make it work, even though the prospects of earning an adequate return on their investment are nil.

Don't allow expectations for much-wanted recognition to blind you to reality.

Every little boy secretly imagines himself hitting a home run, running for a touchdown, or sinking a three-pointer to win a game in the final second of play, and then basking in the hero's spotlight afterward. Dreams are wonderful. They inspire and challenge us to perform our best. But dreams can also cloud one's judgment, causing you to underestimate the costs and difficulties that reality presents. The desire for recognition can be dangerous to one's credibility whenever it conceals the realities of delivering what you promise.

In business, saving face is trivial compared to saving money.

No one likes to admit failure. We want to succeed and look good because of it. And too, it's a mark of courage and determination to stick with a difficult challenge and overcome the obstacles blocking success. But there are also many situations that are hopeless, situations where sound judgment dictates getting out of them—and the earlier the exit, the better. You stand to lose some trust whenever your pursuits fail, but you stand to lose far more trust if they persist, throwing good money after bad. People too consumed with saving face are really more interested in themselves than they are with the well-being of their organization's success, not only causing considerable financial damage, but damage to their own credibility.

Smart Solution 61

Melissa would gain more trust and arrive at a better decision regarding the new process if she put the interests of her company ahead of her desire for recognition. Throwing good money down a hole, which was a likely possibility, could produce only waste and diminish her reputation accordingly.

Were she to admit her miscalculation and the resulting mistake right away and then figure the best way to salvage the situation, management could be relieved from the burden of trying to make an unworkable process work. Melissa would gain more trust by doing this than she would if she were to persist in vain.

Dilemma 62

Your boss, a person you don't particularly like, asks you to tackle an extra assignment. You have plenty of work to do as it is, and you don't feel like getting involved in anything more than your comfortable routine.

Lindsey worked in the purchasing department of a company that made labeling equipment. Her duties included preparing specifications for competitive bids and coordinating the purchase of items from vendors with the manufacturing department's production schedules. Lindsey had to keep on top of many things, as she worked with others to meet her obligations. In her line of work, there were no extra busy times and no especially slow times during the year—every month was busy because her company was growing rapidly.

Her boss was relatively new to the organization, and Lindsey believed he was a poor choice for the job. She saw her boss as being less experienced and less knowledgeable about the purchasing function than she was. Since becoming her boss, he made what Lindsey thought were poor decisions, such as re-establishing ties with vendors that weren't reliable, and neglecting to insist on performance features that engineers specified in purchase requests.

Lindsey's boss asked her if she'd be willing to serve on a committee to study quality improvement measures, part of a TQM (total quality management) effort that top management wanted implemented throughout the organization. Lindsey would just as soon not take on this extra responsibility, and didn't know how she should respond to the request.

Lindsey can either act big-mindedly or small-mindedly. She can either set aside her dislike of her boss and accept the assignment, or she can decline and stick with her usual routine.

Earn your trust by placing the good of your organization ahead of yourself.

When we examine the actions and ponder the inner drives and motivations of those we most trust, we find that deep inside these people dwells an authentic commitment to something beyond themselves. They genuinely care more for a great cause or a high ideal or others they'd gladly serve than they care about their own comfort and well-being. Whenever we see that what they honor most is good, we are attracted to them and trust them.

Among the most useful pieces of advice any member of an organization can offer is this: give all you can to help your company flourish. Be supportive of those to whom you report, and make sure they succeed. Gladly accept assignments and work enthusiastically on carrying them out.

Put the good of your organization and those who work alongside of you ahead of your immediate desires.

Thirteen machinists and assembly technicians from ATS, Inc., in Westerville, Ohio, pooled their money to buy Powerball tickets, hoping to win a $295.7 million jackpot recently. They had visions of becoming wealthy, buying whatever they wanted and doing the things they dreamed of doing. Luck visited them. The ticket they bought in Richmond, Indiana, 100 miles west of their Columbus, Ohio suburb, earned them the coveted prize. The winners chose to take the $161.5 million lump sum, which worked out to $6.8 million apiece after taxes.

But these 13 workers, who had dreamed of being rich, chose not to merely take their money and run. Shortly after winning the jackpot, they released a statement that they would "not leave the company until there are qualified people trained to fill our positions." Out of loyalty to their employer and to their friends and co-workers, the 13 winners didn't think it was right to burden those who worked alongside them with extra work.

Smart Solution 62

Lindsey's biggest problem lay within herself. It was her negative attitude, her dislike of her boss. This caused her to do very dumb things, things that could result in a bad reputation for herself. If Lindsey enthusiastically accepted the additional assignment and worked hard to do a good job, her boss would see her as a helpful employee, one to be trusted. Lindsey stood to gain far more by acting big-mindedly than by letting her petty dislikes rule her actions.

Chapter 11

The Derailed Train

Connecting with people to produce results

In today's world, no one goes it alone. Teamwork, organized effort, and cooperation are the methods with which work is carried out, and how organizations succeed. The more effectively we function with and alongside others, the better we produce. This is why smart performers pay particular attention to establishing and maintaining productive, satisfying relationships.

Our working relationships connect us with others, much like cars on a train. No great harm comes if just a few wheels jump off the track momentarily, but if too many people are careless—if too many wheels get off track for too long—the train might derail and the individual cars disconnect. The same thing happens in work relationships. If too many people act in ways that diminish the quality of relationships, organizations become derailed and everyone in them becomes disconnected, unable to work together effectively.

As they direct more and more of their efforts at earning a living and moving ahead, many people tend to act in ways that weaken good relationships, making them less productive, less satisfying. This chapter shows how smart performers keep everyone on track and moving forward by creating and maintaining effective working relationships.

Dilemma 63

Your plan for a major change is logical and thorough. It includes engineering details, budget considerations, cash flows, logistics, information needs, work schedules, and the like. However, others resist these changes.

When Beverly realized that customer preferences for clothing styles changed much more rapidly than they did in the past, she tackled the difficulty immediately. Previously, the purchasing and production personnel in her organization developed designs jointly. Beverly changed this procedure by hiring an outside consultant to design the clothing her company produced and marketed. "We live in a time of specialization," Beverly remarked. "People should spend their time doing what they're trained to do. Generalists are a thing of the past."

Logically, Beverly's change in procedures made perfect sense. In her company, it seemed more efficient to have trained specialists do what had earlier been done by those with less experience. But problems soon followed. Beverly's critics, people in production and purchasing, insisted that the new designs were difficult to make, and the materials specified in the design too hard to find in suitable quantities. Worse, those in the production and personnel departments didn't coordinate their efforts quite as well as they did prior to the change. Production and purchasing employees blamed each other for delays, mistakes, and numerous screw-ups.

Many a change fails because those charged with carrying it out resist. They usually resist because the change diminishes their importance or destroys their well-established relationships with others. Even minor alterations in established routines can cause those affected to become resistant and hostile. Any time you consider how to better organize improving established procedures, it makes good sense to consider the people affected directly by the change. Smart people treat others like human beings, not as worthless objects. Before initiating change, smart people ask themselves who will be glad and who will be mad. Knowing this, they arrange matters in adjusting to strong feelings.

Cooperation, teamwork, and commitment are the products of good relationships. These desirable conditions cannot be purchased—they must be earned. How can management earn these qualities? Popular prescriptions now include things like employee involvement and empowerment. The idea is for management to include all employees as part of the team. Instead of an "us" vs."them" (a management vs. labor) atmosphere, the idea is to create a "we" organization, where everyone from the bottom to the top is part of the same team. Everyone works for the good of the organization, treats them as whole human beings with minds and feelings, not objects that appear in the cost section of an income statement.

Don't treat people as "things to be used."

Employee commitment is rarely secured in the workplace. Why is this? Perhaps the answer lies in management's failure to be authentic.

I had once spotted a cartoon someone had taped to the wall of the building in which I work. The first frame showed a manager shaking hands with an employee and saying, "You are part of the team now. We are going to involve you in what goes on here. You are empowered to act freely." The next frame had the same manager telling the employee, "We have to down size now. We don't need you anymore. You're fired."

If you believe that you can have more by being friendly, for instance, then you'll be friendly. It's all very calculating. We do whatever is needed, within reason, to get what we want. In doing so, we "get off track," so to speak, destroying the quality of human relationships. We treat people in ways they do not like being treated and they resent us for it.

People see through phony schemes; just like the person who posted the cartoon, they can spot hypocrites, and they don't trust them. Effective relationships are built on authenticity, on treating the other person properly and without calculating how one might best manipulate another to gain something.

Do not consider others as merely another expense.

Many years ago in Chicago, a man named Paul Galvin had an idea. Being aware of two growing products—automobiles and radios—he began to envision how to use them jointly. What if you could make a radio that could operate in automobiles? It was more than a wild dream. Paul Galvin went to work on his idea and made it happen, and his company, Motorola, prospered because of it. But there is another fascinating dimension to Paul Galvin.

Paul also had very definite ideas on how those who built his products should be treated. One day while Paul was visiting one of his plants, he noticed a group of women working on the production line. That wasn't so unusual, but these women were bundled up in overcoats trying to keep warm. Paul asked the shop foreman why. The foreman said that because they were running production on a single line, and the remainder of the shop was idle, costs were cut by conserving fuel and heat.

Paul Galvin reacted sternly. "I don't care if there is 1, 10, or 100 women working. You treat them all alike and don't save money by abusing anyone." Paul was the kind of human being who treated everyone with great respect.

Care about how those below you will react to your plan.

Dave Kimball, who once ran General Signal, once told me about a useful idea he picked up that could prove invaluable to those of you made up of highly competitive natures. Dave attended a dinner that was followed by an inspirational speech. The speaker's discussion was about earning the respect of people below you in job title and not worrying so much about gaining the admiration of those higher up, which so many of us are prone to do. The speaker boiled his point down to two words: "Look below."

Dave thought this was good advice. He wrote the two words "look below" on a 3 x 5 index card and put the card in his top desk drawer. He has kept it there ever since, taking it out and looking at it when he faces a really tough decision that affects his employees. Indeed, it has proven to be an invaluable guide to Dave in the years that followed.

The idea behind "look below" is that no matter how brilliant a plan may appear from above, if the actions called for aren't tolerable to others, especially those who have little say in the matter, it probably isn't a good direction to take. It might even be unfair or distasteful to those who have to implement the plan. And if they felt negatively about it, it's fairly certain they won't do an effective job of implementing it. Such a plan would certainly not enjoy the wholehearted support of those who were expected to carry it out.

Smart Solution 63

We can't say for sure whether the problems Beverly's company faced came from difficult-to-make designs or from people whose jobs were made difficult by a poorly conceived change. Her employees were bothered by the change, which was reason enough for their displeasure. Beverly's people were left out of the decision and pushed aside from having any input about what their company's products would be. Unknowingly and unthinkingly, Beverly enacted a change that diminished her employees' status and altered their relationships.

Legendary Buck Brannaman of Sheridan, Wyoming, known as the Horse Whisperer, once said, "It's easy to understand why a horse wouldn't be interested in a person crawling up on top of him like some would-be mountain lion, and clamping down his feet!" Buck knew how to train horses so well because he saw things from the horse's point of view. And this is exactly what Beverly needed to do.

Beverly could go a long way to reconnecting with her derailed employees by sitting down with them and listening to their concerns. She should not argue or lecture them on the logic of her decision; she should just listen and understand.

Beverly could also have her employees suggest methods for overcoming the difficulties they encountered with the new designer. Perhaps they could've advised the designer about their sewing capabilities and the limitations of fabric availability. Many possibilities existed but, regardless of which was chosen, the basic approach needed to involve employees in the operational processes, and to allow them to take an active role in the changes.

Dilemma 64

Your work unit decides to move in a direction that you think is inadvisable. You are tempted to put down others by being sarcastic.

Brad prided himself on his intellect and preparedness. If he attended a meeting, he was fully informed on all the issues. As an engineer, Brad placed the most importance on evidence that backed up his opinions.

A problem arose in his firm regarding product features. The question was which new features the company should develop to improve the marketability of existing products. The marketing people conducted a study to get a feel for what customers perceived to be important, so naturally they argued for those particular features. Brad thought those were merely minor, cosmetic changes to what the products could already do. He thought the firm should neglect pretty much what the market research people advised and invest heavily in new technology. Brad's position was that the market would follow superior technology, and that market research was of limited value because customers were unable to imagine what never-before-used products could do.

But Brad and the few who agreed with him were in the minority. He was annoyed with the majority who seemed to go along with whatever got presented by smooth-talking sales people using colorful media presentations. Brad was tempted to put down the glib presenters and their computer-generated visuals.

Everyone believes his or her opinion is "the correct" one. The more strongly people feel about issues, the more vigorously they tend to speak out in support of their positions. These truths suggest a major difficulty with smooth-functioning relationships in team settings. Effective teamwork demands that everyone act in ways that hold the work group together while, at the same time, getting everyone to voice their thoughts about the issues at hand. In the heat of fierce debate, it's easy for your emotions to take the upper hand, leading you to say things that make you feel better momentarily, but might harm your relationships.

As you make your way through life, it's tempting to undervalue the ideas of others and overvalue your own point of view. But this tendency is detrimental in the establishment of effective relationships; it usually gets people off track.

Display sincere concern for the thoughts of others.

The board chairman of a major paper company once told me that he believed any problem was important to him if it was important to just one person in his company. He ran his organization on the principle of keeping his directors sensitive to issues that bothered their employees.

This approach worked. Things that ordinarily would not have received top management's attention came out in the open and were dealt with positively. Because of it, employee dedication and performance were extraordinary.

The chairman and his board of directors worked hard and with sincerity to uncover what bothered employees. What they learned was eye opening. By taking this level of interest, the chairman and his board of directors learned much more about what was on the minds of their employees than they could have possibly imagined. It was through dealing with these matters above board that they came to earn employee respect and loyalty.

At brown bag lunches held every other month, employees and one or more of the company's directors discussed concerns. At one of these meetings, a woman who worked in a clerical capacity started to speak, but hesitated. "This is dumb," she said. The directors insisted she say what she wished to say. What bothered her was the location of a file cabinet. She wanted it moved, but never felt she should ask. It may have appeared to be a little thing to the directors perhaps, but consider how important the matter was to the woman. What do you suppose that woman thought about those directors every time she looked at that file cabinet sitting in a different spot?

At a paper mill in Michigan, employees revealed another irritation during one of the lunch meetings. A bridge connected the main parking lot to the plant. Next to the plant were just a few parking spaces where the managers parked. Employees had to park in the main lot and walk over the bridge to the plant, yet the managers could drive right up to the building. They told the management, "Look, you drive, we walk. Yet we get here a lot earlier than you do." Managers never realized this had been bothering employees. They changed the parking situation immediately, putting it on a first-come basis.

Others might be right. Listen to them.

It is widely understood that a receptive management ear listens, provided employees feel comfortable voicing their feelings. The trick lies in how to develop that level of comfort. The solution is to create confidence. This requires two things: sincerity and action. Act with sincerity and do something about what you hear. Sincere listening is one thing—strong action demonstrates deeper evidence of genuine concern for employees.

Lewis Lehr, who was CEO of 3M, once told me that if he didn't understand what employees thought was right, then perhaps he didn't know what was right himself. In other words, employees just might see something that he was missing—they might be seeing something not right in their minds that he didn't sense was wrong in his. Therefore, he tried to be more open-minded in understanding their point of view. Talk about humility! And, he paid attention to what his employees had to say. It worked.

This leader was an excellent listener, because he heard more than just his employees' words. He saw directly into their hearts and understood how they felt. His example demonstrates an important standard for effective understanding: listen to more than just the words and try to get a sense of how your people feel inside.

This leader paid attention to the organization chart; he was mindful of the chain of command. He didn't want to undermine anyone's authority. Nonetheless, he had many discussions with people who held positions lower down in the organization. He had what's known as an open door policy and it was effective in getting to deep-seated problems.

Here's an illustration of what this policy brought out into the open. One morning, Mr. Lehr received a telephone call at home from a group of employees. The factory workers were very unhappy with what was happening at the plant. Lewis was a welcoming listener. "Fine," he said. "Do you want to meet me at a restaurant, or do you want to come to my office?" They wanted to come to his office. There, five factory employees told him what they thought was wrong where they worked. Lehr got into it and learned more about the matter. The reason the employees felt they could come to the CEO was because he had earlier befriended an employee in their factory—an elevator operator who had a health problem. Someone was trying to put her back in a line operation she couldn't handle. Lewis made a few suggestions about the situation and the woman stayed on as an elevator operator.

Word of this passed among the employees. Trust developed. If employees thought they had a problem, they knew they could talk to him about it. Lehr corrected a situation that could have festered and caused all manner of unpleasant results. Labor-management relationships strengthened because both parties dealt with the problem up front and directly.

Smart Solution 64

Two bits of advice could help Brad. First, he needed to display a sincere interest in what others said, listening to their ideas carefully without challenging them, trying to determine what positive elements their ideas might contain. Even if the ideas did not contain credible points, it wouldn't have hurt to restate them in a "modified" form. Second, Brad should take an attitude of "you might be right." Perhaps what the other person said had merit. He should recognize, with an open mind, that the best people do a magnificent job of building enthusiasm by treating what others have to say with respect and not contempt. This does not mean agreeing with dumb ideas, but rather that you listen to people courteously and, if necessary, that you disagree respectfully.

Dilemma 65

One of your associates needs your help, but you are too busy with your own responsibilities. Besides, it's highly unlikely that this person will ever be in a position to reciprocate the favor.

Warren knew more about computer software than anyone else in his organization. He spent most of his spare moments reading software manuals and "playing" with his computer, teaching himself. He gladly answered simple questions co-workers had about using software. A co-worker who Warren had an on-going difference of opinion with was in a difficult bind. He needed to complete an important project that was behind schedule but he was totally stumped about how to use his computer to perform the necessary operation. Warren learned about his co-worker's plight but felt he was too busy and he knew that it might take a couple of hours to help his co-worker out. Besides that, Warren felt that he really didn't "owe" this other person anything, especially in light of him causing Warren so much grief from past verbal disputes.

Among the great tragedies of life stands something that is not caused by nature but caused by man. It is the unrepressed desire to "get even." Too many people destroy themselves and others by trying to even the score. The list is long and sad: battles between the Hatfields and the

McCoys, the Protestant Irish and the Catholic Irish, the Jews and the Palestinians. In the end, no one wins. Each party destroys itself as it tries to get even, and in the process suffers more casualties and misery itself.

Some people never commit this mistake, yet they frequently omit the opposite from their daily routines—they fail to help when cries for help come to them. Perhaps the greater tragedy in our world is this act of omission: having deaf ears, blind eyes, and a hardened heart when calls for help come in. Open warfare destroys good relationships, but this is of minor consequence in comparison to the loss of meaningful relationships which arise from not responding affirmatively when calls for help are heard.

Answer calls from help, regardless if the person asking will not be able to help you in return.

Not causing people harm and resolving sources of irritation are one thing; actually helping them out whenever possible is something else. My favorite anecdote about William K. Kellogg, of Kellogg's cereal fame, involved this principle. It goes back to an earlier time when travel across the country by automobile was difficult. In those days, anyone who motored across the country had to be willing to bear the annoyance and discomfort of sinking into mud, choking on dust, running out of gasoline, or getting lost. Roads were poor, signs to mark the way were sparse, and there were many miles between filling stations. In 1915, Kellogg, together with his chauffeur Henry Johnson, set out from the east and headed to San Francisco.

West of Omaha, Nebraska, Kellogg's Franklin roadster became stuck in thick mud. Seeing their plight, a farm boy tried to assist, but it was more than his team of horses could handle. A little while later, the boy's father came along, and with a second team they pulled the car to safety.

Grateful to his rescuers, Kellogg asked the farmer, "What do I owe you?" The farmer just looked at him. A bit puzzled by the silence, Kellogg turned to the boy. "Doesn't your father hear well?" he asked.

"Oh, I hear all right," the farmer spoke, "but what I am trying to do is recall where I've seen you before. About 25 years ago, my wife was very ill and our local doctor advised me to take her to the Battle Creek sanatorium. She was there quite a while, and I began to run out of money. In desperation, I went up to your office, and you assured me that my wife would not lack for treatment simply because I had run out of money. That's why, Mr. Kellogg of Battle Creek, you don't owe me a penny."

TIP

Look for little things you can do for others and start doing them.

The repeated act of serving shapes us into more than just productive workers. It leads us to become wonderful people who truly care about others. George Schaefer, who ran Caterpillar Tractor, told me about the first boss he had at that company. This was when George was just starting out in their accounting department. His boss was a Swedish fellow who was the general auditor of the company, and he was tough and thorough—some even thought he was mean, so gruff was his exterior. However, this was a man of high principles, with a heart equally as big.

Schaefer had been sent out to Caterpillar's California plant to work. He was called back to Peoria, Illinois, for a meeting one April. And, of course, it was already warm and sunny out in California. But when he arrived in Peoria, a cold snap came sweeping down from the north, bringing temperatures down to 25 degrees. When he walked into the office the next morning without a coat, the general auditor asked where it was. George said that he didn't think to bring one; he thought the weather would be warmer. His boss went home and brought one of his coats back for George to wear. It was only a small thing, but it showed something large—an attitude of helpfulness and kindness.

Smart Solution 65

If Warren chose not to raise a finger to help someone who needed assistance, he'd probably remain the same person and his organization wouldn't grow to operate more effectively. The relationship between Warren and his co-worker would also remain exactly as it stood: poor, unattractive, and counter-productive.

But suppose Warren decided to help this person he disliked? Then what? We can identify several obvious consequences, all of which are desirable. Warren and this person would likely ease their hostilities as they softened their mutual dislike. The organization would perform better. The other person would be grateful to Warren and, out of gratitude, less likely to do things that irritated him. Warren might discover that being helpful to an "enemy" removed the burden of disliking him, resulting in a more professional, far more preferable, and ultimately more productive, work environment.

Dilemma 66

Your subordinates made you look good through their extraordinary effort on a recent project. You want to use this accomplishment to boost your career opportunities.

Dick headed a team of industrial sales people. Some of his unit's tasks involved developing leads, cultivating relationships with buyers, obtaining technical information that customers wanted before buying, contract preparation and coordination with his firm's legal department, and coordinating delivery promises with the production department. Everyone depended on the cooperation of the team's members to accomplish their mission, which was sales.

Dick's role involved organizing his unit, coordinating its efforts, and representing his firm in signing sales contracts. Dick was the person customers wanted to talk to because of his high-level position in the organization. It might look like Dick did the selling but that wasn't exactly true. He relied heavily on the ground work and research his staff performed. His last year's sales were exceptional; Dick's unit sold 35 percent more than it did the previous year. Dick wanted to use this accomplishment to move his career ahead.

Without carefully controlling the desire to make yourself look good in the eyes of higher-ups, it's easy to make yourself look bad in the eyes of those below. While there's nothing wrong with being concerned about your reputation, there's something terribly deflating about taking credit for 'bolstering' the images of your superiors. This might work to your benefit once or twice, but over the long haul, those below would probably rebel against it.

Several years ago, Dick Heckert, who was chairman and CEO of DuPont at the time, told a group of students at Miami University, "We have a way of identifying people where I work. We call it the 'flower theory.' If you look at a flower from above, it appears beautiful. But if you look at it from below, it isn't so pretty. When we look at managers, we always wonder, 'How do those looking up, from below, see them?' A boss looks at a subordinate and that subordinate appears to be doing a good job. And that's good. But how do the subordinates, looking up from below, see that manager?"

Recognize people for their abilities and their contributions.

Most people crave recognition. We all want to feel needed and useful. We want to know that what we do counts for something significant. Yet, many a life is rarely touched by the uplifting influence of recognition. As a result, many fine men and women never fully blossom into what they might otherwise become. It cannot be urged too forcefully that people should recognize each other, and that managers in particular should recognize their employees.

There are two important aspects of recognition to keep in mind. The first is to recognize people for their abilities by putting them to work on challenging assignments. The second is to recognize people for their accomplishments, for the good things they have done.

People have a need to be needed. The first way we can show recognition is by putting people to work. I recall reading about a man who was a high-powered, successful business executive. He ran, almost single-handedly, an important operation for his company that nobody else fully understood. When this man reached the age of 64, top management decided they had to get someone ready to assume his job when he retired. They brought in a bright young man who apprenticed under the executive, learning the complexities of his function. On the executive's 65th birthday and against his objections, the company retired him. He didn't want to leave, and in fact protested, but the company had rules, and they forced him out.

A few months after his retirement, a dramatic change overcame the man. He felt useless and began to withdraw from his family. He seemed to be losing his zest for living, and losing it fast. In less than a year after his retirement, this once lively, productive businessman was hospitalized. Friends and family tried their best to support him and help, but he didn't respond. His condition worsened. After a while, those who knew him gave up trying to lift him out of his state of decline. They stopped visiting him. He had become a vegetable.

Within a couple of years, the young man who had taken over the older man's job died tragically. Now, the company faced a problem—no one was able to perform this important function. What were they to do? A decision was made to try to approach the old man and see if he could pull himself together and come back to his old job. Several of his former co-workers went to the hospital to talk to him. The idea of returning to his old job began to sink in and he responded with new life. Within a few days, this man who had become little more than a vegetable was back at work, functioning as he had before retirement.

Again, a young man was brought in as his understudy. And within a few years after that, the older man was retired for the second time. Within a year, he re-entered the hospital, this time never to leave.

Thank people when they do a good job. Do it frequently.

There is a second way we show recognition that people love. It is by the simple act of saying "thank you" for a job well done. This shows that your work matters, that it is valued. Many years ago, when I worked for the Anaconda Company, I taught this important idea to our mining foreman, Claude Huber, who took this lesson to heart and used it the first chance he got. Claude worked in one of Anaconda's underground copper mines in Butte, Montana.

At quitting time one day, Claude noticed the especially fine job of timbering one of his men had done, shoring up a newly cut underground shaft in the mine. Claude took the time to inspect it, commenting favorably about what he observed. The old man who had spent all day doing this job appeared pleased at first. But then something strange and unexpected happened. He began to get emotional, and said to Claude, "That's the first time anyone has ever told me that. Nobody even cared before."

What a horrible thing it must be to feel that what you do doesn't matter. But what an incredibly wonderful feeling it must be to realize that it does matter and especially that others notice. I know that this experience taught Claude an important lesson. I also know it did a great deal to uplift the spirits and motivation of the man in the mine shaft. And I'm sure he performed many jobs in the same excellent fashion from that day forward.

How often should we thank people and recognize their efforts? This is an excellent question, a question I'll answer with another: how often do you need to take in a breath of fresh air? The answer to both questions is exactly the same: regularly. Human beings need recognition frequently. Like breathing, recognition sustains us to keep going. It's worth mentioning that recognition can come from any level and we all can add to the betterment of organizational relationships by giving it to those above, to those alongside and, of course, to those below us.

Share rewards with those who made them possible.

Many years ago, a young man working for an insurance firm had an outstanding year. Around Christmastime, he was informed by one of the firm's managers that he would receive a nice bonus for his very productive performance.

Most young men would have immediately begun to visualize how such a windfall might be used, especially those with a young family at Christmastime. But this man didn't do that. Instead, he told the manager that he didn't feel he could accept the bonus because, although he had some success, it was largely due to his team, who provided him with the backup necessary, and that the only way he could accept the bonus would be on the basis that it would be shared with the group. And that's what was done. How do you suppose the people working for this young man felt about him?

As the years rolled by, this man's unselfishness rubbed off into other areas of his life. He was active in community affairs. He was a leader in social circles. Everybody who knew him saw what a fine man he was and wanted to be his friend. Customers wanted to buy from him. In time, his superiors recognized his outstanding performance. They saw how much business he was bringing into the firm, and he was promoted. The pattern continued. It was an unbroken story of service and success and his promotions continued, concurrent with the firm's sales and earnings growth. When Dickinson C. Ross retired, he was chairman of the board of Johnson & Higgins in Los Angeles.

One more example of this idea comes from the realm of literature. In 1962, author John Steinbeck, writing to his literary agent, Elizabeth Otis, mentioned all the things he was doing to polish his reception speech for the Nobel prize, which he had won and would soon be presented with in Stockholm. Steinbeck wrote: "I hadn't thought of the Nobel loot as a commission. We started this thing together and we're going to finish it that way. If along the way you had limited yourself to being an agent, you would not have done the hundreds of things you have done. You have shared the bad times with me and they have been long and many, and if you could do that, you are damned well going to share the good ones. You are as responsible for this prize as I am. So, let us not argue and be concerned. Not only do you share in the honor but in the money as well."

Smart Solution 66

If Dick wanted to increase his subordinates' commitment to their jobs and spark their performance to even greater heights, he'd see to it that each one got their fair share of the recognition and the rewards.

Chapter 12

The Proud Peacock

Trimming the feathers of out-of-control egos

Our minds enable us to be constantly aware of ourselves as independent beings. We realize that we have freedom to think and do as we choose. We constantly evaluate ourselves and our situations. We make it our business to know whether we get what we want, to determine how well we stack up against our own standards and to evaluate how well we compare to others.

But our self-awareness, which enables independent thought and free will, also challenges us to be fully honest about our abilities and accomplishments and to act in ways that do not irritate others.

Even the best of us, at one time or another, blunders when it comes to being fully honest. We want so much to think we have worth that we tend to exaggerate our abilities and accomplishments. Just as a small animal does what it can to frighten away predators when guarding its territory and protecting its young, we too pretend to be bigger, stronger, and better than we actually are.

The ego can become difficult to master. Like proud peacocks who spread open their feathers to show, we fool ourselves and waste time strutting about instead of scratching out an existence. This chapter shows how smart people win everyday battles against their egos by "trimming their feathers" and making themselves more likable because of it.

Dilemma 67

You want others, especially your superiors, to notice your strengths and accomplishments. You reason that getting ahead begins with getting noticed.

Annette loved to be the center of attention. If all eyes and ears were not trained on her, she did whatever it took to call attention to herself. While this helped her gain support from her superiors, who saw her as competent and aggressive and eager to do well, it had a negative effect on those who worked with her. In meetings, Annette usually had the first and last word. She expressed her thoughts forcefully, arguing that they were the "best" while sharply criticizing opposing views. In small group settings, she insisted on having the final word; it was either her way or an unpleasant scene followed. Annette's methods led to a minor promotion. Management placed her in charge of a newly formed unit of inexperienced, recently employed people. Soon they began to gossip disparagingly about Annette.

People focus their attention on preparing themselves for the future during the formative years of life. In mainstream society, they generally develop optimistic expectations for bright, happy, prosperous times ahead. They learn to visualize the job they'll hold, the material possessions they'll have, and the lifestyles they'll enjoy. In so doing, these people begin to develop images of who they are; they identify self with position, wealth, and prestige—all the things they want and equate with success and self worth. But what they do not think about, what they fail to see, is the potential destructiveness of over-concern for self.

See the destructiveness of an out-of-control ego.

Look around and you will see many people who want you to think that they are a good bit more important, wealthier, and smarter than they actually are. What is it that causes them to be this way?

Most of us have a tendency to want others to think well of us, and so we try to get their approval, their respect, and their admiration in any manner of ways. The truth is, these attempts rarely work. In fact, most of them do not work at all; they produce quite the opposite effect.

I think a great many of life's tumbles are caused by tripping up over our own egos. I once discussed this important idea with Mike Wright, former chairman and CEO of Super Value Stores. What he told me was not only true, but provided some excellent, practical advice everyone could use. He said, "As you get higher in the organization, you worry about whether people are really telling you the truth. I think you change by being at the top and you won't know it, and other people won't be telling you. They are scared to. So, you've always got to keep saying to yourself, what am I doing to be a jerk around here? "

Deliberately act in ways that demonstrate humility.

Practically everyone wants to be somebody special, to feel important, to enjoy prestige. Practically everyone wants to have nice things, the money to buy whatever they want. And, practically everyone wants recognition, to be looked up to with admiration. Pride tricks us into thinking that by acting in ways that make us feel important, we will make others believe we are important.

Pride deceives us into believing that having material possessions and getting recognition really are all there is. What's worse, it leads us into thinking that the more we get, the more satisfied we'll become with ourselves. And so, many pretend that they are important and grasp for material possessions, believing that doing so will bring the happiness and contentment they desire. These actions fail to secure what people hope to get.

What can you do if you have an ego that's out of control? Just recognizing it—even faintly suspecting the possibility—is a positive first step. There is the cost of an out of control ego to consider also. Think of what egotism does to you. One excellent way to overcome a tendency to act self-important is to ask yourself, "do I want that to happen to me?" Isn't humility far more attractive?

Consider this incident. Indiana's Evan Bahy was the nation's youngest governor at 34. His youth sometimes led to humorous situations. Already in office two years when the Democratic National Committee met in 1989 in Indianapolis, Bahy held a reception at the governor's mansion. It soon became obvious that he wasn't well known in national circles.

The governor greeted guests at the door with, "Welcome to Indiana." Dignitaries, thinking he was a young staff member, handed him their coats and walked on to the reception. Bahy hung up the coats. Later, with amusement, he startled the guests when he delivered the official welcoming address.

Smart Solution 67

Annette needed to realize that upper management saw more than what she thought she projected with her behavior. She could learn that we all have blind spots. Her blind spot is how she abrades others with her attention-grabbing actions and criticism of her co-workers. One thing Annette could do is seek out someone who could tell her how others felt about her actions. She needed to get "a reality check" from someone who would tell her the truth—and she needed to listen.

Another thing that would help Annette mend her broken relationships with co-workers would be to allow them time to speak up in meetings. She needed to learn that by holding her tongue, she'd be able to hold on to her friends, maintaining productive relationships with her co-workers, and win support with her good ideas.

Dilemma 68

You've made a bad decision that's not panning out and there's little hope for it, yet you do not want to lose face.

City Microwave Company was once the undisputed market leader in the design, manufacture, and sales of radar detectors motorists used in their automobiles. Throughout the emergence and growth stages of the product life cycle, City Microwave led the way with its innovations, performance, quality, and customer satisfaction. As the product entered the mature stage of its life-cycle, management failed to reduce bloated overhead expenses and profit margins shriveled. Where before, performance and product features determined sales and profits, now price became the key to success, and rival products were just as good. City

Microwave could no longer freely set its prices; it had to better the low-cost prices of its competitors if it were to remain in business.

Continued losses led the firm's board of directors to bring in a turnaround specialist from the outside, Mr. Jacques. The new CEO had a vision: City Microwave would exit the "dying, useless, and unwanted radar detector business" and provide the public with "the next great consumer electronics offering, cordless telephones." This CEO's dream was to move the company out of the "trivial" detector market and into the "respectable" business of designing and manufacturing cordless phones.

To accomplish his plan, Mr. Jacques centered all company resources on developing and supporting cordless telephones, something with which the company's technical and marketing people had no experience. Many throughout the company expressed grave concerns. City Microwave would have to compete with much larger rivals who had been turning out telephones for years, including high-tech firms like Motorola. At first, the new CEO merely ignored his critics, but he later avenged his dissenters through the immediate dismissal of any subordinate who voiced a contrary opinion.

The outcome was disastrous. New detector offerings in the hyper-competitive electronics market became outdated and surpassed City Microwave's products in features and innovations, since there was no longer any serious ongoing development in the firm. City Microwave's R&D teams, who knew everything about detectors but very little about anything else, worked diligently, trying to learn about phones. But they couldn't learn fast enough to be competitive. City Microwave fell further behind the already established cordless phone giants. With the cash cow let out to pasture and R&D costs mounting in the phone business, Mr. Jacques and his dream moved City Microwave to the brink of bankruptcy.

Long-time employees tried to persuade Mr. Jacques to return the company to the business it knew best, radar detectors. Repeatedly, they showed him business and market information, hoping to convince him of his error. They showed him hard information that would have allowed him to save face and return the company to profitability. Even the stockholders got involved, bringing in several consulting groups to help the company correct its course. They handed Mr. Jacques the simple and the obvious conclusions several times, and in unmistakable terms. He'd have none of it; his ego simply wouldn't allow it. In the end, it cost

Mr. Jacques his position and the stockholders everything they held in the company, which went bankrupt.

It can be extremely difficult to distinguish between visionary ideas that initially appear unworkable but are possible when combined with extraordinary effort, and unworkable aims that pop out of ill-informed minds. The closer people are to a situation, it seems, the more difficult it is for them to spot the difference between the two. We are all aware of the naysayers, those who tell us things such as, "It cannot be done. We tried that once and it didn't work. That may be okay for another organization, but it's not appropriate for us."

But all ideas are not on-target solutions. Some ideas are just plain dumb. A strong-willed ego supporting the former can be a good thing. A strong-willed ego committed to the latter inevitably proves destructive. The basic impediment to determining between visionary and unworkable ideas is an out-of-control ego that cannot abide dissent, an ego so rigid it does not tolerate honest questions and never allows for the possibility of error.

Admit your mistakes and limitations.

How can you learn to humble yourself to receive useful suggestions from others rather than remaining blind to your shortcomings? There are several practical things anyone with courage can use to get this information from others. One way is to ask for other's ideas, first by admitting that you had probably not yet seen all the sides of an issue yourself.

The founder of Motorola, Paul Galvin, was reported to have developed this capacity. In the course of running his business, Paul managed to convince his associates that he did not consider himself infallible. They soon learned that they could go to him and say, "Paul, your decision yesterday was wrong." If the facts they supplied stood the test of his scrutiny, he would accept their analysis. He pursued good, clear thinking and did not stand on his position or office, because he was not too arrogant or proud to accept other ideas. Results were what he was after. Paul often said, "Follow the right decisions regardless of when, or how, or by whom these decisions were arrived at." Here was a man who was particularly impatient with those who could not admit their own mistakes. Sounds like strange advice in our competitive world. What happens to people who do follow such advice? It might surprise you.

When a mistake occurs, do something about it immediately.

A General Motors advertisement appearing on the inside of the back page of an issue of *Smithsonian* briefly told of a courageous decision made by one of the corporation's division managers. The ad's headline read "We blew a deadline, ticked everyone off, cost the company a bundle, and we did the right thing." This was the story:

> What if you ran a division of General Motors and were due to debut an important flagship model...and it wasn't ready? Nothing drastic you understand, just a few glitches that meant not every car coming off the line was right. What if you'd sworn to your bosses you'd be ready? What if you had a lot of potential customers waiting to get a first look? What do you do? Here's what Chevrolet's Jim Perkins and his team did: They pulled the plug on the introduction and said, "When we know we've got it right, we'll bring out the car." That night, Jim Perkins did what people who do the right thing always do. He got a good night's sleep.

Smart Solution 68

Mr. Jacques was simply overwhelmed by his ego, and he let it block him from admitting that his idea was not working. Is it possible for people such as Jacques to change? Perhaps. This is why each of us would do well to develop the capacity to entertain opposing ideas with hospitality.

"You might be right" is an important expression to add to your vernacular. Great minds tend to have the capacity to entertain opposing thoughts; it is proof that they are open and alive. Great minds are strong because they rise above egos that make people rigid, that shut out dissent and honest questions.

Mr. Jacques could have saved himself and his organization from failure by doing the following:

- Analyzing the position the company sits in, in regard to the market, the competition, sources for gaining and sustaining competitive advantage.
- Involving key employees who are knowledgeable of the above areas in open, honest, forthright debates and discussions.
- Admitting that he does not have all the answers, but also arguing for those ideas he believes are valid and workable.
- Pushing his ego aside by acting in ways that implicitly say to others, "you might be right."

Dilemma 69

You have a strong opinion of yourself and believe your abilities are extraordinary. But your boss criticizes your work performance and you resent it. As you see things, your boss tries to intimidate you and make you feel stupid.

Wes considered himself to be a good bit smarter and far more able than his counterparts. When his boss sharply criticized how he was performing, pointing out its flaws, Wes was stunned. Shortly afterward, Wes grew angry and began telling others about the awful things his boss did in the past, trying to "even the score." Wes told co-workers that his boss liked to intimidate people and make them feel stupid.

Faced with news that conflicts with their self-image, many people become defensive, then hostile, and later, they twist the truth and try to get even. Many people cannot handle hearing unflattering things about their performance. They have such a strong need to feel good about themselves that they are often incapable of handling anything else.

Although Wes wanted everyone to believe his boss was a terrible person—and he probably would succeed in convincing like-minded friends and associates of what he claimed—the truth is that he had a dual problem. The first and smaller aspect of the problem was his inadequate performance, something that can likely be corrected rather easily. The second and the larger and more troubling part of Wes's problem is his inability to receive truthful information about his performance. He simply couldn't welcome constructive criticism.

Learn to profit from honest criticism.

"The most important criteria for any teacher is honesty," said Jean-Pierre Rampal, the great flutist. "It's necessary to say what you believe is true about the way a student plays. For some people, this is a bitter pill to swallow."

One day, a young American girl played for him. He stopped her after she had played only a few measures. He tried to explain that she played the music badly; she needed to work harder. "My dear, the sound isn't good, the technique is faulty, and what you played sounded bad," he told her.

With tears in her eyes, the flustered girl protested: "No one has ever spoken to me like that before." Her response carried the implication, "How dare you!"

Rampal told her that he didn't want to hurt her feelings, but he wasn't about to lie to her. "What good would it be to say *'bravo, c'est magnifique!'* when the whole class can hear that you play badly?" he said. By the time she dried her eyes, the girl had begun to understand that her teacher wanted to help. She resigned herself to accepting his honest criticism and to work harder. The maestro spoke only the truth to his students, and if they wanted to learn, then hearing that truth was the price they'd have to pay.

Some people are only hurt by criticism; they are incapable of turning it into a source of encouragement. They have such confidence in their skill, their wisdom, their judgment, that it never occurs to them that they are not fallible.

We all know people like this. As long as others compliment them, they are pleased. But let someone dare criticize or even question whether there could be an improvement, and they are offended. They regard as an enemy anyone who intimates the slightest measure of disapproval, or hints, however delicately, that they could do better. Anyone who resents and rejects criticisms cuts off their best means of growth and improvement. Such a person is no longer teachable, no longer a learner; they glean no benefit from the opinions of others.

Replace pride with efforts to improve.

Pride is a powerful emotion that prevents us from knowing the truth about ourselves and eliminates any possibility for improvement. What happens is that when pride gets the better of us, we cannot bear to humble ourselves to maintain our standards, particularly those that have not been reached.

What happens is that we are unable to say, "I have failed. I am not as good as I think I am." Pride makes us want to think so highly of ourselves, that any time we fail to achieve a high standard, we immediately disparage that standard or we assert that the standard is faulty. We become trapped by our pride, unable to improve until we give it up.

We can choose to respond to the truth about ourselves in essentially one of two ways. We can see it as an offensive "put down," or we can see it as a source for help. Little of significance comes when we choose the first approach. But when we open our lives and see ourselves as we are—when we are honest with ourselves—then we are open to revision, to change, to beneficial improvement. The key is getting the upper hand on our pride.

When I was a boy scout, I wanted to earn the pioneering merit badge. To earn that badge you had to either construct a bridge in the woods or build a scale model bridge having the correctly engineered superstructure. It was evident to the merit badge counselor that I was far more interested in earning the pioneering merit badge than I was in the subject itself. And my model bridge reflected that fact. It was a flimsy, hastily pieced together bundle of sticks with little thought behind it.

The counselor wasn't impressed with it. He explained that before he'd pass me on the badge, I'd have to learn quite a bit more about bridge construction—how superstructures worked, how they held up loads, that some members of the structure were under tension and others under compression. He told me that I needed to understand how these forces canceled each other out at any point.

Like most youngsters facing a situation of failure, I was disappointed. For a short while, I felt he was too harsh on me; I even thought about finding another merit badge counselor who would be more "reasonable." I wanted to forget about that merit badge: who needed it, anyway? Luckily, these thoughts and feelings left me. My dad produced one of his college textbooks on structures and had me read a section that explained how trusses worked. Then it became clear why my bridge model was woefully inadequate.

I resolved to try again. I applied the knowledge I had gained—my bridge would have a Warren truss, shaped in the form of an inverted "W." I carefully drew a full-size bridge truss plan on a large sheet of paper and cut small sections of wood in the correct lengths. Then I lashed them together as the manual indicated.

I ended up with a model bridge I was proud of. It had a properly designed truss; the knots were up to scout standards, and I knew the physics behind the bridge structure. When I confidently returned to the merit badge counselor several weeks later with my model, he grilled me on what I had done and, assured that I had met the requirements, approved me for the pioneering badge.

After signing the merit badge form, he told me that others had called him the "tough old Scoutmaster from Pittsburgh." He took pride in knowing that whenever he passed a scout on a merit badge, that scout knew the subject. He said, "I didn't know if you'd ever be back. I knew that if you didn't come back, you'd probably never learn about bridge construction. But if you did your homework, you'd not only pass the requirements, but you'd feel that you learned something worthwhile."

The important thing to analyze here is how we can move from the worst kind of failure to the finest kind of success. The answer lies in overcoming our pride; it lies in first humbling ourselves to time-honored standards that civilization has come to realize are worth having.

By humbling ourselves to high standards, by admitting the truth when our performance falls short, we see what improvement is needed. Then our wanting to reach these standards can take over and lead us to make whatever effort is required to reach them. It is a paradox of sorts—to become great, you must first admit to your inadequacies and humble yourself before higher standards.

Of course, this is never easy, because pride is omnipresent and must first be conquered. Learn to conquer pride and improvement becomes possible.

Smart Solution 69

Wes improved his performance when he learned to accept criticism. His ego made him super sensitive. As a first step, he could call a "time out" for himself, putting aside any hostility he felt toward his boss. He would do well to think about matters from his boss's perspective, seeking to understand how she judged his performance. The best thing Wes could do to overcome his self-imposed rigidity to change would be immediately doing what his boss wanted, in the manner in which she wanted it done and forget about his bruised ego, which prevented him from giving his best and winning his supervisor's approval.

Dilemma 70

Wanting to impress others with your abilities, you find yourself interjecting comments into conversations that you subtly hope will earn you admiration. You even put people "on the spot" to demonstrate that you know something that they do not; however, this strategy could easily backfire.

Steve's work took him all over, and sometimes, out of the country. He was a professional fund raiser who worked for a highly-regarded organization that specialized in helping colleges and universities build their endowments. His organization charged a flat fee of 5 percent of the amount raised, which client organizations willingly paid because the professional fund-raisers were so effective.

Steve met with well-to-do college alumni and prominent public figures. His work involved giving speeches, attending luncheons and banquets, and golfing at exclusive country clubs. Within the span of a year, he had sat next to former Vice President Dan Quayle, attended the Preakness at the invitation of the governor of Maryland, and played golf at an exclusive club in Scotland, which made him an honorary member.

Steve liked his work because he met interesting people, enjoyed giving speeches and traveling in the company of wealthy individuals. Indeed, Steve likened himself to being "one of them." He lauded this over friends and associates by name dropping things such as, "I had lunch with Dan Quayle last week," or "The governor of Maryland invited me to the Preakness." He thought others would be impressed with his importance when he told them he was a member of a golf club in Scotland that charged a $150,000 membership fee."

One of the most trouble-causing consequences of self-awareness is that we use it to set ourselves above others. We'd all secretly like to think we're being somewhat better than the next person, at least in some small way. You enter a room filled with strangers and immediately your thoughts turn to what it is that makes you better than the others there.

Thinking well of yourself, wanting to feel significant, is fairly typical, but acting out those feelings creates serious problems. No one likes an egotist.

Fasten your attention on others, and learn something about those you meet.

Egos tend to cause us to wonder, "How am I better than those around me?" It's a useless concern, one that creates far more harm than good, and it's a concern that leads many to answer the question in the worst possible fashion.

Consider the alternative. What would happen if, instead of tooting your own horn to accentuate yourself, you found something interesting, valuable, or praiseworthy in someone else? Suppose you took the time to learn something interesting about the other person and discussed their attributes instead of your own? How different might conversations become? How much nicer might they be to engage in? How much more satisfying would they feel? And how much better would people get along and enjoy being with others?

Pat the backs of others, not your own.

Pride can hold back otherwise able people from becoming effective team members and leaders. This is because those infected with pride are intolerant. They regard others as being unworthy of dignity and respect. But when one controls his or her pride, practically anything is possible.

Harry B. Cunningham, the man credited with being the father of the K-mart operation, was a person who had a special touch with people. He controlled his pride, patted others on the back, and gave them a boost. His subordinates said that he was one of the most gracious men they ever had the pleasure of working for. We all know that there are people in business who cannot seem to compliment their people. Harry Cunningham was just the opposite. He would compliment employees even when, perhaps, they didn't fully deserve it. And his employees would go out and break their necks to make sure they deserved it the next time he came around. He was that type of person; he built people up and they stretched to become the kinds of employees he inspired them to be. That's leadership, giving credit where credit was due, building up those who do the building.

Smart Solution 70

Steve could not begin to change until he saw what a fool he made of himself every time he tooted his own horn. While this reality might not penetrate the thoughts of all people, there are many who would stop to reflect on their own behavior. A tiny glimmer of reality could trickle through their egos and register in their minds. "Should I act so smugly?" they might ask themselves. "Maybe I shouldn't try to show others how important I think I am by dropping names and bragging about what I've done." Emotionally healthy people think about such things as they reflect on themselves and how they act. Hopefully, Steve would do so as well.

An excellent way to change yourself involves three elements: committing yourself to the change publicly, monitoring your actions, and altering your habits. Announcing your intentions does two important things: it admits a flaw, and it puts others on notice to regularly judge your progress.

Steve also had to monitor his own actions. This meant consistently taking stock of what he said and did. Doing this several times each day would be necessary to yield better results than simply doing it weekly, or monthly, but altering habits requires cleverness. Steve could think about what he might discuss with others without repeating his pattern of self-centered comments. He could create five or six standard questions that focused on what others experienced, which would steer the conversation away from himself. Perhaps he might ask a successful acquaintance, "What do you know now about your work that you wished you knew when you got started?" or "What's the most difficult part of your job?" These questions could get others to think and discuss more relevant and interesting topics.

Dilemma 71

You work for a person who doesn't treat you with the respect and courtesy you deserve. When this person asks you to do things, it sounds like an order and, when you do what you're asked, you don't receive adequate recognition.

Cheryl was a systems analyst for a food processing company, a job she'd held for more than two years. Her responsibilities involved writing operating programs for other departments in her organization. Her boss, Marta, was considerably older than Cheryl, and tended to treat her as a mother might treat a young daughter—always checking up on her, being critical of her mistakes, and not allowing her much independence in handling her work. Cheryl resented her boss's methods, particularly because she treated her differently than others.

Cheryl felt like telling her boss off when Marta criticized the way she handled an assignment. Cheryl's work had a few flaws and glitches, which she ironed out with the help of the user department, but her boss found out about the mistakes and lambasted her in front of two other people. Cheryl wanted to strike back but didn't know how, or whether it was a wise thing to do.

You can usually think of a valid reason to justify a desired action. Indeed, much of the time people do just what they feel like doing and then, only afterward, concoct a rationale to justify their actions. Clearly, Marta made a huge error in judgment when she reprimanded Cheryl in front of others. It demeaned Cheryl and made her angry. She wanted to even the score and soothe her injured ego.

A hurt ego is about as nasty and treacherous as an injured animal. Terribly frightened and in deep pain, an injured animal will snap at anything to protect itself. This described Cheryl's mental state as well, not a good state to be in because the accompanying out-of-control emotions could lead her to further harm. Vicious, out-of-control animals are usually dealt with severely, and the same thing could happen to Cheryl if she went on the attack.

Rise above your desire for revenge.

Francis Bacon wrote an essay, *Of Revenge*, in which he laid out some very useful advice which happens to apply here. Bacon called revenge a kind of "wild justice." He said that although the first wrong offends the law, "revenge putteth the law out of office," meaning that civilized society breaks down any time a person acts out of anger and beyond what civilized behavior demands. "Why should I be angry with a man for loving himself better than me?" Bacon asked in his essay. Sure, someone might offend or harm you because they love themselves more than they love you. But, as Bacon tells us, that's no reason to hate someone just because they're exhibiting a very human failing.

If you want to add to the level of civility, if you want to be bigger than that which harmed you, Bacon advises doing one thing: "pardon your offender, for it is a prince's part to pardon." Act the part of the prince and pardon your offenders; do not diminish yourself and society by taking revenge.

Smart Solution 71

Cheryl should spend her time and energy doing what's far more productive and civilized—working at her job, perfecting her abilities, and acting in a more civilized manner. She should exert some effort to gain control over her emotions. She would do herself a big favor by not dwelling on her hurt feelings, because doing so would create more hostility within herself than civil sensibility. By paying attention more to what Bacon advised in his essay instead of what her emotions might lead her to do, Cheryl could rise above her hostility and move on.

Dilemma 72

You made a stupid mistake and your boss wants to talk to you about the matter. You wonder how you should handle yourself.

Devon worked in the human resources department for a mid-sized grocery chain. His daily duties involved preparing job descriptions and evaluating their relative worth for pay purposes. He spent much of his time interacting with others, gathering information from them and creating job descriptions from the information obtained.

Under pressure to prepare descriptions for an entire unit, Devon irritated several busy managers in the finance department by failing to set up meeting times with each of them beforehand. He showed up in their offices, expecting them to drop what they were doing to provide him with the information he needed. They told Devon's boss that he wasn't respectful of their time because he insisted on arriving at their offices unannounced. Word got back to his boss, who called Devon in to discuss the matter, presumably to dress him down for creating ill will with the finance department. While waiting outside her office, Devon wondered to himself what he should say and how he should act.

Devon made a stupid mistake which made his boss angry. As she saw things, Devon harmed his relationship with the finance department. This was a problem because human resources was a staff function; it did not have line authority. The role human resources played in the organization and the influence those in the HR department had with others depended on good relationships. Devon damaged those relationships and his boss was understandably upset about it.

As Devon saw things, he had a job to do and he was doing it. He wouldn't admit that he had made any error because that would suggest he was less than capable, and few want to admit to such a thing. To protect himself, Devon felt inclined to defend his actions.

Learn how to take a chewing out.

One of the most useful talents one can acquire is the fine art of taking a good chewing out by the boss. At one time or another, everyone slips up and deserves a reprimand of some kind. The wrong way to acknowledge a reprimand is to give excuses, to argue back, to defend your actions. The right way is to lower your head, accept the tongue lashing, apologize, and promise not to make the mistake again. Most supervisors would rather not chew out their employees if they don't have to.

Smart bosses respect and tend to forget the mistakes of contrite employees faster that those of argumentative ones. In most cases, bosses remember the arguments that follow their reprimands with subordinates far longer than what it was that led them to have a discussion with the employee in the first place.

Smart Solution 72

Advice to Devon: Go into your boss's office and admit your mistake. Take the chewing out. Keep your mouth shut. Accept the blame. Promise that you'll not make the mistake again. Be contrite. Forget about your hurt feelings.

Chapter 13

The Dead Battery

Energizing self-improvement by learning from experience

Let me tell you about an incredible idea that will lead to enormous personal improvement and self satisfaction. If you are disciplined enough to apply this technique regularly and can practice it effectively, I guarantee that you will experience amazing results.

Here is the technique. Treat everything you do as a learning experience and then act on what you've learned. Turn everything you do into a lesson. Think of every act, every decision, and every thought as an experience from which you learn something, and then put that new knowledge into practice. It will produce amazing, ongoing improvement. Do not be deceived by its apparent simplicity. It's not nearly as easy to do as it might seem at first. This technique may well be one of the most difficult things you ever try. It may also be the most beneficial and among the most satisfying.

I must caution you, up front, that your improvements will be barely perceptible at first. This is because early changes are usually small. But don't become discouraged as you first start out. After all, you are just learning how to use this idea. Have realistic expectations. Don't discard the technique before you can apply it effectively. Remember, perseverance pays off. Wilson Greatbatch, inventor of the implantable cardiac pacemaker, was once asked what accounted for his success? "Sticktuitiveness," he responded. This is a dominant characteristic of all successful people, from inventors to entrepreneurs. It's what you'll need if you are ever to master this technique. Give it time and an honest chance so it can work for you. It takes a fair amount of experience and practice on your part before the small improvements that it leads to are numerous enough or large enough to make a noticeable difference. If, however, you faithfully apply this technique over time, expect astounding change in what you do and in yourself as a person.

From this chapter, you will learn how smart people turn experiences into lessons, lessons that will keep your own battery charged and performance level high.

Dilemma 73

You've grown comfortable with the status quo. It's easier to just get by in your established groove than to try something different. Privately, you admit to yourself that this is not good for your career. Still, "comfortable" feels better than tackling risks outside your specialty.

Bob was in his late 30s and, already, he was viewed as "going nowhere." At a fairly young age, Bob found a subject in school that interested him and he pursued it. His jobs have always been centered in a specific area of interest. It shouldn't be any wonder that Bob defined himself in terms of his work specialty. It's something he was pretty good at, but boredom finally set in. His daily work routine was filled with sameness. It was a comfortable existence but not very interesting or fulfilling. Bob found it increasingly difficult to be enthusiastic about his work. He gave his best effort but found his greatest enjoyment was off the job with his family, service organizations, church, and hobbies. He lived just for his weekends.

Like apples, some people ripen as they grow older, while others turn soft and rot in spots. The sad thing about Bob's situation isn't so much Bob—and there are many like him in the workplace—but the acceptable and widespread acceptance of his state of affairs. Let's face it: someone who busies himself trying to venture beyond his area of specialty is unusual. But that's the thing Bob must do to break himself free of the chains that hold him, void of interesting challenge and the possibilities for growth. If Bob follows the path he's on, his soft spots will turn to rot.

Activate your curiosity.

Samuel Johnson (1709-1784), the great English scholar and philosopher, once said that curiosity is characteristic of a vigorous intellect. Curiosity prods us to find what we admit we don't understand, and helps us to replace our ignorance with new knowledge.

This is what Douglas Danforth, former chairman and CEO of Westinghouse, suggested young men and women do: become curious. "Have a curiosity about what's around you," he told them. "In the business world, if you start out in engineering, have a curiosity about marketing, about manufacturing, about finance.

"Don't let yourself stay just within your own envelope or your own discipline. Because people are very willing to share their knowledge and experience, the most flattering thing you can do is to ask them, 'Tell me a little about what you do in marketing. I don't understand anything about it. Would you mind having lunch with me, or if I stopped by after work, would you chat with me? Could I come with you when you call on a customer?'"

This is exactly what Danforth did as a young man starting out in his career. Because he was curious, he asked questions, lots of questions. Douglas began his career in manufacturing, but he thirsted to know more about other areas of the business. He learned an incredible amount just by demonstrating a bit of curiosity and it served him well.

Develop a habit of asking questions.

I asked my graduate students to write about their experiences learning on the job. One of them, Christy Veits, works for Batesville Casket

Manufacturing in Indiana, summed up her findings with the following suggestions:

- You should ask a lot of questions about what you see going on around you.
- You should be prepared to alter the form of the question or even the nature of the question.
- You should never assume that the first answer you receive is the right one or that there ever will be a "right" answer.
- There are no standard procedures for complex processes, only knowledgeable and intuitive people.

Smart Solution 73

One of life's great tragedies is when a person's mind hardens and stops growing. The person physically lives, but mentally dies. As we get comfortable doing the same things each day—the same schedule, the same friends, the same entertainment, and so on—we glide along a groove of mindless habit.

Through avoiding the unknown, the untried, the seemingly difficult, obsolescence sets in. We become stagnant in our thinking, our attitudes, our ability to adapt to change. Before long, we get trapped by our own lethargy; we do just enough to get through each day. We procrastinate, rely on time-tested methods, and neglect opportunities. We stop learning, assuring ourselves with the familiar statement, "I already know enough to get by." This is mental stagnation, the beginning of decline. How can you escape the onset of obsolescence, with its inherent stagnation?

The answer is by implementing a self-renewal process of mental regeneration through seeking and developing—new hobbies, travel, friends, and continuing education. Whatever the method, the aim remains the same: avoiding mental and emotional paralysis via ongoing learning and novel experiences. This will enable anyone to live a richer, more productive, and more rewarding lifestyle.

In Bob's case, he must act. For starters, he could spend an evening at a bookstore and browse through whatever captured his interest. Bob should purchase a few interesting books and set aside thirty minutes each night to read them. He might also take notice of the music sections in the larger bookstores. He'd also do well to look through his local newspaper and find a lecture, concert, or other cultural event. The idea is for Bob to stimulate his mind with novel experiences, and to unwedge himself from comfortable routines.

Each of us would do well to get out of the country and visit a distant place where different cultures, foods, and sights can be experienced. If you are becoming a bit stagnant, then say *yes* to the next challenge that comes your way. Don't let fear of failure cripple your confidence and destroy your self-respect.

Dilemma 74

Your organization tends to make the same kinds of mistakes, over and over.

Ed's organization performed near the "bottom of the heap." This result wasn't due to lack of effort, but rather to so many stupid mistakes. Everyone relied on following the routine that worked well in the past, and no one was willing to try other approaches for fear of being criticized. One person summed it up with the remark, "It's one step forward by our efforts and two steps back by our mistakes."

Ed's organization was not merely plagued by costly mistakes; it was also plagued by people who wanted so much to "look good" in the eyes of others that they refused to admit their own shortcomings. Understandably, nobody in the organization wanted to look bad, so everyone tacitly agreed to look away. Each employee sought to watch each other's backs, all the while protecting themselves. Instead of fixing the procedures, mending their methods, or identifying incorrect assumptions, Ed's organization covered up, looking the other way and finding outside culprits to blame.

Make ongoing learning a regular part of your organization's day-to-day procedures.

CIGNA, the insurance giant, has a process that's become standard operating procedure. Any time senior management at corporate headquarters makes a major decision, they come to meet months later and do a "post mortem" on those decisions once they've been cut loose and implemented.

At these reviews, managers ask themselves, "What lessons did we learn from this?" How the decision turned out wasn't the issue. The important thing CIGNA managers ask themselves is: "What can be learned from the experience?" This is, indeed, an effective method for identifying ways to improve.

Create a culture of honest introspection. Make ongoing improvement more important than "looking good."

Human nature, it would seem, is such that we are inclined to report only on the things we've done well. We all like to feel that we're pretty good at what we do. This fact, I think, explains why many people never fully realize the potential improvements that their life's lessons could bring. Maybe this same inclination is holding you back from honest introspection and improvement.

It is true that our desire for approval is often far stronger than our desire for improvement. What hope is there for us? While we might not be able to choose how we feel, we can choose what we do. The fact is that those who choose improvement above personal comfort are the ones who improve. The profound question for each of us is this, what do I prefer for myself, comfort or improvement?

Turn your critics into useful allies. Their criticisms frequently mean that they care. Deputize your critics to work for the good of the organization—don't shut them out so their hostility might work against you.

Sometimes a slap in the face is better than a kiss on the lips. A criticism may be unpleasant, but such a criticism can awaken us to worthwhile improvements. From whom can we obtain reliable information about ourselves? Friends are often quite tender and, hence, unwilling to provide painful information. They are afraid to offend, and also, having much the same likes and dispositions as we do, are not likely to notice our faults. In truth, they may see more of our virtues than our shortcomings.

An adversary, however, is much more likely to serve as a faithful monitor. Propelled by dislike, he is sure to ferret out the slightest slip-ups and defects, and to make them known in such large and alarming ways that even we cannot miss them. A person who is willing to give due consideration to distasteful challenges is, indeed, an open-minded individual. Nathan Ancell, the man who founded Ethan Allen Furniture, developed enormous respect for a man named Bill Morrissey, who wasn't afraid to say what he thought. And Nathan listened to what Bill had to say, because Nathan was wise enough to know that truth can come from anyone.

Bill was the plant manager of a small furniture factory that Ethan Allen had acquired early in its history. In spite of the fact that he reported to Nathan Ancell, Morrissey wrote to him in longhand. In multi-page letters, Bill questioned everything his boss was doing. Bill told Nathan that he was worried the company was going to take advantage of his factory and take advantage of the people who worked there. He challenged Nathan strongly and questioned his moves.

Bill Morrissey didn't know Nathan Ancell that well and he didn't know whether his boss's motives were imaginary or genuine. Bill challenged Nathan like no employee would ever challenge a boss. He had guts, and he wasn't afraid. Because Bill challenged his boss honestly and straightforwardly, Nathan's respect for him grew by leaps and bounds. Nathan valued Bill's letters. He must have, because he's kept Bill's letters in his vault as a reminder of an honest man. Indeed, it is a big-minded person who can hear the truth and respond to it honestly.

Imagine what Bill thought about Nathan when he responded to his letters. Ideas to improve the plant came out of Bill as a consequence of all this. Nathan's company reaped the benefit of Bill's ideas and built loyalty throughout.

Smart Solution 74

To fix his "sick" organization, Ed needed to take the lead and set a standard of honest reflection. In doing so, he must emphasize the idea of "improvement" over "approval." He can do this by holding discussions and admitting to those mistakes he'd made, which, in turn, would encourage others to make similar admissions.

Executing such a decision would be vitally important, as Ed needed to reward expressions of honesty and underscore any improvements that came from it. He could change his organization's reward structure, basing pay increases in part on honest self-assessment.

Dilemma 75

Your performance has slipped lately, and in a recent performance appraisal session, your boss identified several shortcomings that needed attention. You are hurt, angry and frustrated about what to do.

Ellen had always prided herself on her work performance; she worked hard to do well and earned above-average pay increases because of it. But during the last few years, Ellen got into a rut about her duties. Her perceptions of her performance were based more on what happened long ago than what happened recently, which, when compared to her co-workers, was below the norm. There was a feeling that Ellen's performance had slipped, but she didn't see it that way.

Ellen's boss reviewed her accomplishments of the past year and found them to be lacking. Her annual performance appraisal session turned out to be a "real shocker." It was the first time she was rated "below average," and she was upset.

As alluded to earlier, a sense of self-importance, fed and nurtured by self-flattery, is a source of great mischief. It deadens a pursuit of the truth and declares the slightest criticisms one may receive to be "false and unfair." It stops dead the processes of self-improvement. This is largely because pride keeps us from knowing the truth about ourselves. But pride doesn't just stop there. It can even trick us into thinking our faults go unnoticed.

To begin with, you might try listening to what others think about you. Make no mistake about it, this can be rough, especially if you've rejected little hints that have been coming to you over a long time. It's hard to bear the painful sting of criticism, but ask yourself this question: can I tolerate the fruits of my shortcomings? As you listen to what others say about you, remember that we all change for the better the more we eliminate our prideful attitudes and actions.

Create a step-by-step plan for improvement and get busy following it.

Someone I know who had always done well at work received the worst performance appraisal he had ever gotten. It was tough and, at least in his boss's mind, true. Rather than getting angry, this person got busy. Reasoning that it would be easier to go make specific improvements than to try to change his boss' opinion—something that was not likely to happen—this person immediately set down on paper specific changes that would remedy his failure points. With specific goals and plans in place, this person began to feel better, particularly because taking positive steps is a much better tonic for a bruised ego than expressions of negativity.

This person has tremendous ability; previous high-quality accomplishments proved that. So, self-confidence was not an issue, but working the plan was. Again, it's worth emphasizing that this person put all his energies on improving and none on getting angry at his boss, which really would have only made the boss defensive and created hostility—neither of which would have done either any good. Improvements materialized in a short while, and just as fast as the poor performance was noticed by the boss earlier, the recent improvements were recognized as well.

Smart Solution 75

Ellen could "turn things around" for herself by applying the following guidelines:

- Fix the problem, don't fight. Go to work on changing yourself instead of going to war with the person who gave you the poor performance rating.
- Don't try to live off past accomplishments. Remember, in a hotly competitive world, the past really does not matter as much as the present and, more importantly, the future.
- Set goals. Develop a plan of action.

- Work the plan. Don't get bogged down in worry. Maintain a positive attitude and get on with doing positive things. Produce results that your boss will recognize.

Dilemma 76

You want to look good in the eyes of others, and believe yourself to be a strong performer. You feel the same about your organization, but the truth is, others perform better than you. It is difficult to admit this because you are a proud person.

Not long ago, the Case company, manufacturers of construction and farm equipment (tractors, backhoes, and loaders), faced financial difficulties to the tune of nearly $900 million, because their competitors were doing a better job of supplying customers with what they wanted. It was a difficult pill for proud Case employees to accept. Regardless, sales were off, costs up, and losses mounted as customers turned to their rival's products.

Without humility, the admission of ignorance, it is impossible to be curious and find solutions to vexing problems. Socrates expressed his humility toward learning when he said, "I neither know nor think that I know." The important lesson to be grasped is that humility allows you to escape the bonds which prevent admitting your ignorance. But once made, your mind opens up to learning; and from that, to improvement.

The capacity to wonder is at the heart of curiosity. It involves looking at things and asking, what makes it work, and could I make it better? But there needs to be action—you have to correct what's wrong and emphasize what works well.

Invite customers into your inner circle, ask for their opinions, and learn from what they tell you.

Tim Boyle, CEO of Columbia Sportswear in Portland, Oregon, probes customers' minds. He is keenly interested in knowing what they like about the rugged outerwear his company makes, and he's eager to modify the products his customers do not like. Several times each year, Tim invites buyers from stores around the country to accompany him into the great outdoors. They go to rugged places such as Montana where his guests hunt or fish. Tim calls these outings "cast-and-blast" outdoor adventures, but they are, in fact, his laboratory for testing what people think about Columbia's products.

From his cast-and-blast outings, Tim returns with fresh ideas for new products or modifications to existing ones. The trick lies in his ability to listen and his keen eye for sensing something that isn't quite right. On one adventure, Tim supplied his guests with fishing vests. They mentioned they'd like it if the pockets were larger to hold their fly boxes, so he redesigned slightly larger pockets. On a duck hunting trip, Tim noticed that his guests, wearing Columbia hunting jackets, were shivering from the cold. There was a strong wind and everyone got chilled on the back of the neck. Tim is not one to sit still; he improvised an improvement on the spot. A detachable collar was removed from another Columbia jacket and wedged into the hunting jacket.

The important quality to be gleaned from Tim's method is his relentless pursuit of improvement. It is easy to think you have it made once armed with a record of success. But the pursuit of perfection says no to the easy things and yes to the great challenges. I'm reminded of something General Charles DeGaulle once said: "Difficulty attracts the man of character because it is in embracing it that he realizes himself."

Smart Solution 76

To their credit, a new team of managers at Case got on with fixing their problem, putting performance improvement ahead of ego protection. After a decade of having ignored their customers' wants and needs, Case took a new direction: designing and manufacturing products to please their customers. The new chief executive told Case employees, "We need to be asking what the farmer and contractor really need."

Case involved their customers in the process. Company engineers asked longtime customer Larry Willingham to fly to Case's facilities in Burlington, Iowa, to test the company's new loader backhoe. Willingham thought this was going to be just another factory tour, but on arriving there discovered differently. Case personnel put Larry behind the controls of their new loader backhoe. For three 11-hour days, Willingham loaded trucks, dug ditches, and leveled dirt. He rated Case's equipment against rival machinery from Caterpillar and Deere. In the evenings,

Case engineers drilled Larry with questions to learn more—what he liked, disliked, wanted, and preferred.

Willingham liked everything he saw except for the loader backhoe's weight, which was nearly 16,000 pounds, much too heavy for the truck he owned to haul. He told Case engineers that he intended to stick with the lighter weight Deere model he had. A year later, Case unveiled the new model, a 12,900 pound unit. They paid attention to everything Larry Willingham had told them. "I definitely felt they listened to me," he said. And for Case, the results were favorable too. In the years that followed, sales and profits rebounded into the black and continue to rise.

Dilemma 77

You stuck your neck out to push a new idea that you believed in, but the idea turned out to be a flop. Now you are discouraged, so much so that you are inclined to avoid risks in the future.

Bill advanced rapidly in his first eight years with the Richmond Baking Company to become Director of Operations. Richmond Baking's sales came from products that relied on two different types of production. The first type was fairly simple, well established over many decades. The second type was highly automated, high volume, and exact in nature. Outside consultants engineered and set up the second type of production process, which was written out in a procedure manual and followed closely. Running these established lines gave Bill the false belief that his firm could produce anything with relative ease and the company would prosper even more.

Bill decided to bring out a new retail cracker product, believing his firm could make it without difficulty. It was a colossal failure. The cracker was very thin, difficult to handle, and required packaging in a way that was different from their other products. Months of unprofitability followed, with low production volumes, low yields, mediocre quality, and frequent equipment breakdowns.

Every experienced fisherman knows what it's like when the fish are not biting. The fishermen try their luck in one spot and then another, hoping to find hungry fish. But as the hours pass by without even a nibble, they begin to wonder if they should try a different spot or pack it up for the day. When failure stares us in the face, it's difficult to choose between quitting, or gambling that success will eventually come.

Those who continue learn from their experience. Smart people realize that, although every risk taken may not work out as hoped for, each one offers valuable lessons from which they can learn and build on. The key thing to keep in mind is that smart people turn their experiences, successful or unsuccessful, into lessons. They do not retreat from trying new and different approaches because they failed. Instead, they examine and learn from their experiences, which won't occur if you're so self-absorbed you avoid taking risks.

Accept your setbacks as opportunities to improve.

The Russians have a proverb: "The hammer shatters glass but forges steel." If you are like steel, you can accept the setbacks life hurls your way and, using your imagination and perseverance, let them amend you for the better. This seems to be a common trait of successful men and women. I recall reading about the great Russian composer Igor Stravinsky, who revolutionized the music of his time. As early as 1913, Claude Debussy was praising him for having "enlarged the boundaries of the permissible" in music. American composer Aaron Copeland said that Stravinsky's work had influenced three generations of American composers; later, Copeland revised his estimate to four generations, and added European composers as well.

Stravinsky's parents sent him to the University of St. Petersburg to study law, but his real passion was music. One of his classmates there was the son of the great Russian composer, Rimsky-Korsakov. In 1902, Stravinsky visited the great man, gave him some of his piano pieces for him to critique, and asked if he could become his pupil. Rimsky-Korsakov studied them and told the 20-year-old Stravinsky that he'd need more technical preparation before he could accept him as a student.

Shattered by this at first, Stravinsky decided to take it as encouragement. He went to work as Rimsky-Korsakov said he should, and a year later he applied again to the master and was accepted. It was under Rimsky-Korsakov's supervision that Stravinsky composed his first orchestral works.

Exercise your imagination. Try to see failure points as possible advantage points.

One Sunday afternoon in San Francisco, the Cincinnati Bengals took the field in a late season football game against the 49ers. San Francisco was touted as among the top NFL clubs at the time, having scored an average of more than 30 points per game. The Bengals were near the bottom of the league with 1 win and 10 losses for the season. They had scored an average of only 11 points per game.

Cincinnati's team looked terrible during the first few minutes of the game. The 49ers took the opening kickoff and drove the ball down the field in four plays to score a touchdown. It looked like the three touchdown-plus point spread the bookies gave was an accurate assessment of what might unfold. But the Bengals had a defensive ploy that was designed to disarm the 49ers of perhaps their most potent offensive strength, wide receiver Jerry Rice, who at that point was nearing the top spot for the most touchdowns scored by any professional player.

The 49ers' second possession went entirely differently than their first; they couldn't move the football at all. In fact, the Bengal players pushed the 49ers backward, scoring a safety. The game stood at 7-2. Throughout the remainder of the first and second quarters of play, the 49er offense was ineffective; the Bengals scored two field goals and led at halftime, 8-7.

What took away much of the 49ers offensive punch was the Bengal defense against Jerry Rice. The Bengals' defensive player would block Rice just as he got off the line of scrimmage. It disrupted his timing and rendered his patterns out of synch with quarterback Steve Young. San Francisco's coaching staff saw clearly what was happening, but didn't quite know what to do about it.

That was about to change. They soon realized, and correctly so, that what was previously thought of as a negative could be turned into a positive. The idea was simple. The man who was blocking Rice was taking himself out of the play. Seen in this light, the most effective offensive ploy became clear to San Francisco—send a runner through the spot where the defender was tying up Rice.

The change in viewpoint and its resulting tactical alteration of the game plan worked to the 49ers' advantage. After the half, their offense came roaring to life, scoring two more touchdowns, as San Francisco went on to win 21-8.

Smart Solution 77

Bill was a fighter, not a quick-to-be-discouraged quitter. With failure knocking at Richmond Baking's door, Bill immediately turned to his best people for help. His team committed itself to making the new product successful. They addressed the production problems one by one, learning as they went along. Slowly, the team, working round the clock and monitoring every aspect of the process, got the line up and running. Everyone contributed; challenged minds identified problems, which were solved after numerous suggestions, discussions, and trial and error attempts to find what would work. Learning resulted, because Bill's team worked intelligently, implementing what eventually worked.

Dilemma 78

You are fairly new to your organization and don't have much experience. Your boss gives you assignments but does not tell you exactly how to carry them out. You ask for help, expecting your boss to explain exactly how to perform the assigned tasks, but he isn't helpful; in fact, your boss gets irritated at you for asking for guidance all the time.

Krista graduated with honors from a fine university, where she majored in accounting. Once she obtained employment with a well-respected accounting firm, her boss expected her to tackle difficult assignments on her own. She didn't remember from her accounting courses exactly how to treat the odd circumstances she encountered at work. So, needing answers for how to proceed each step of the way, she frequently went to her boss for those answers. However, her boss told her to figure it out for herself. This offended Krista, who now believed her boss was tactless and rude.

While it's probably true that Krista learned through experience that she should be told how to do everything expected of her, it's time for her to grow up and start thinking for herself. If she continually turned to her boss, just as she probably turned to her teachers for "the correct answers" while in school, two things could happen. She won't learn how to be strong and independent, solve problems, or size up situations to determine the best course of action, and she'll irritate her superiors by taking up too much of their time with her childish pleas for direction.

Learn to think for yourself.

This is what Mike Abrams of Cincinnati Financial did. Mike's boss selected him from a pool of in-house applicants. Even though he had a degree in finance, Mike wasn't prepared for the job responsibilities he encountered—the workplace didn't fit into the well-defined and simple-to-follow textbook examples he learned in school. His boss, the Chief Investment Officer, heaped many responsibilities on Mike and expected him to perform them on his own.

At first, Mike turned to his boss, the vice president, for guidance. But the precise answers of how to do things, what Mike wanted and expected, didn't come. Instead, Mike's boss assisted him by providing only general guidance. Mike didn't understand the reason for this, but later realized that his boss was so demanding because he wanted Mike to develop his own critical thinking techniques.

Later on, his boss told Mike that he heaped a lot of work on him to determine his breaking point. In Mike's words, "I just worked through the tasks and did not break. I didn't realize it at first, but I came to understand that this was what successful mentoring involved. It accelerated my advancement."

Exercise your imagination.

A good rule to follow when it appears that you are beaten by an insurmountable obstacle is to consider every possible way around it. Let your imagination soar. Too often, men and women remain mired in frustration and fail as a consequence, not because there is no way out but because they are unable to see a way out. The trick to finding an answer in the face of the impossible is to switch mental gears, switch your thinking to a different plane, consider possible solutions outside of the conventional approaches. Ask yourself if there is any other way the challenge could be met.

World-renowned wood finisher George Frank has authored several technical volumes on the subject. He began his apprenticeship in the trade shortly after World War I, but finding employment at home was impossible. His native Hungary was near economic collapse then, and the best work he could get was in a pigsty.

In 1924, George Frank was a full-fledged cabinet maker and a master of stains and coloring when he arrived in Paris looking for employment. The first good job George found was with Ferdinand Schnitzspan. No one could pronounce his name, so his customers simply called him Fernan. His employees addressed him as "Patron." He ran a fair-sized wood-finishing shop and his men liked him. George looked upon Fernan as a father figure.

France was rebuilding after World War I, so there was plenty of work. Fernan's best customer was the Banque de France. His shop had the contract to finish the oak woodwork for the bank's newly opening branches. In June, Fernan's men shipped out all the woodwork for a branch in Lisieux, which was scheduled to open on July 16th. Midway through the second week of July, bad news came. Fernan had made an error: The woodwork was stained too light, and the bank's architect refused to accept it. Fernan and his employees would have to go to Lisieux to darken the branch before the opening date. All other work would have to wait.

Fernan and six of his best men squeezed into a car, along with the materials they needed, and set out for Lisieux. Upon entering the bank, they noticed the error was obvious, but the enormity of the rework job was even more discouraging. Even if they worked 24 hours a day, the job would take between ten and fifteen days to complete. Every possibility Fernan contemplated ended with the same conclusion: the restaining could not be completed in the time remaining.

Being the youngest and least experienced, George did not open his mouth, but his mind worked furiously. What could he draw on from all his schooling that would solve this problem? As failure gripped the group of workmen, George got an idea. He touched Fernan's sleeve and timidly said, "Patron, I think I can do the job by tomorrow night."

All the men, especially Fernan, looked at him in disbelief. This was not a time to be funny. George held his own and explained his solution. Obviously, the job could not be done by hand work, but what about creating a gas? If they made a strong enough concentration of ammonia gas, there was a good chance it would go through the finish and react with the tannic acid in the oak to darken it.

The men sealed off all the doors and windows and made 30 simple alcohol burners. Each burner consisted of a ten-inch-square board with three nails driven in it. At the center of the nails they set a dish containing a half pint of alcohol. Then they placed a bucket of liquid ammonia on the nails.

They men scurried around with wet towels over their faces as they lighted the alcohol burners and exited the bank, leaving the lights on so they could see what was happening from the outside. All the ammonia had evaporated by the time the alcohol burned out. It created a heavy concentration of ammonia gas. That evening, there was nothing more for them to do but wait. Suspense ran high; no one could sleep. They played cards, drank apple brandy, and waited. From time to time, they checked to see if their experiment was working, but due to the gas, it wasn't possible to tell.

The next afternoon, the architect arrived and peeked through a window. Everyone looked at him and waited for his reaction. He smiled and nodded his head in approval. The ammonia gas had done the trick and the bank opened as scheduled.

Smart Solution 78

Krista should give up her childish notion that her boss must tell her how to do every aspect of her work. She could dig out some of her textbooks from school and digest materials that she obviously never fully mastered. She should learn to spend her spare moments thinking about the questions she had and developing her own solutions. Most importantly, Krista needed to start experimenting. Many people fear failure so much that they refuse to try, thereby crippling their ability to learn from trial and error. This is precisely what Krista must do—try one approach and then another until she found what worked. She needed to learn from her experiences and cease being so preoccupied with failure.

Conclusion

I prefer to think of this final section of the book as a beginning, not an ending. This is because all that I said in the previous pages isn't nearly as important as what you will record in the pages of human history by what you do and how you do it.

You might ask yourself this question: "When my actions speak, what kind of story will they tell?" I hope they will tell stories that dignify your existence. To help you do just that, I'd like to leave you with two important ideas.

The first idea is to use the gems of wisdom I discussed in the introduction as reliable guides in all you do. As you have read here, this is how smart people handle the difficulties they face and become exceptional achievers because of it.

Be aware of this: you can either put your principles first or your appetites first. Smart people live according to the former approach and derive lasting satisfaction because of it. Those who follow the latter path may get what their appetites cry out for, but often little else of value and nothing of lasting significance. I think it is far more important to work at creating lasting value than to worry about grabbing valuables for yourself.

The second idea involves your ongoing improvement. This is something smart people do amazingly well. If you worked as hard at improving yourself as you did trying to grab things for yourself, you'd become a superb producer, a highly valued contributor to any organization.

I'd like very much to hear from you and learn about the difficulties you face in your workplace. Please write to me by post or e-mail at the address below and tell me about the struggles you encounter at work and how you tried to respond to them in the smartest possible way. I want to hear about your failures as well as your successes, and what you think you've learned from your actions.

Charles E. Watson
Professor of Management
Richard T. Farmer School of Business
Miami University
Oxford, OH 45056
E-mail: watsonce@muohio.edu

Index